Praise for *Business Analysis*

"James and Suzanne have brought their deep and wide experience in business and systems analysis to bear on the importance of good analysis in agile domains. They cut through the hype and tackle the misconceptions that are rife around agile analysis by providing concrete advice and useful tools for anyone undertaking the vital analysis activities in agile development."

—Shane Hastie, Director of Agile Learning Programs – ICAgile; Lead Editor – Culture & Methods, InfoQ.com

"What is a user story but a requirement? But is it the right requirement? The user said it was, but how does the user know? And how can you discover it?

"Two words: Step back.

"If you step back—and this book shows you how to do that—you can discover the real requirement. Why do you do this? It's the only way to deliver real value to your customer.

"And what could be more agile than that?"

—Stephen J. Mellor, Signatory to the Agile Manifesto

"This new book is a must-have for business analysts looking to bridge the gap between agile and other development approaches. It combines the best of both, into clear and simple guidance, presented in a delightful and light style."

—Neil Maiden, Professor of Digital Creativity, Cass Business School, City, University of London

"*Business Analysis Agility* provides the express on-ramp that business process change projects have sorely needed."

—Stephen McMenamin, Ex CIO & VP of Hawaiian Electric

"The Robertsons share a plethora of tools and techniques that help you infuse agility in your business analysis. The book includes multiple examples and lively scenarios that engage and invite smart problem and solution exploration."

—Ellen Gottesdiener, Agile Product Coach, Founder EBG Consulting

Business Analysis Agility

Business Analysis Agility

Solve the Real Problem, Deliver Real Value

James Robertson
Suzanne Robertson

♦♦ Addison-Wesley

Boston ● Columbus ● New York ● San Francisco ● Amsterdam

Cape Town ● Dubai ● London ● Madrid ● Milan ● Munich ● Paris

Montreal ● Toronto ● Delhi ● Mexico City ● São Paulo ● Sydney

Hong Kong ● Seoul ● Singapore ● Taipei ● Tokyo

Many of the designations used by manufacturers and sellers to distinguish their products are claimed as trademarks. Where those designations appear in this book, and the publisher was aware of a trademark claim, the designations have been printed with initial capital letters or in all capitals.

Cover Photograph: JonathanC Photography/Shutterstock

Credits for movie posters in Figure 5.7: (a) CASABLANCA -1942 POSTER, Moviestore collection Ltd/Alamy Stock Photo; (b) FILM STILLS OF 'CITIZEN KANE' WITH 1941, ORSON WELLES IN 1941, SNAP/Shutterstock; (c) 1930s USA Gone With The Wind Film Poster, The Advertising Archives/Alamy Stock Photo; (d) FILM STILLS OF 'BREAKFAST AT TIFFANY'S' WITH 1961, BLAKE EDWARDS, AUDREY HEPBURN, POSTER ART, ELEGANT, SOPHISTICATED, SMOKING, CIGARETTE HOLDER, SNAP/Shutterstock.

The authors and publisher have taken care in the preparation of this book, but make no expressed or implied warranty of any kind and assume no responsibility for errors or omissions. No liability is assumed for incidental or consequential damages in connection with or arising out of the use of the information or programs contained herein.

For information about buying this title in bulk quantities, or for special sales opportunities (which may include electronic versions; custom cover designs; and content particular to your business, training goals, marketing focus, or branding interests), please contact our corporate sales department at corpsales@pearsoned.com or (800) 382-3419.

For government sales inquiries, please contact governmentsales@pearsoned.com.

For questions about sales outside the U.S., please contact intlcs@pearson.com.

Visit us on the Web: informit.com/aw

Library of Congress Control Number: 2018953964

Copyright © 2019 Pearson Education, Inc.

ISBN-13: 978-0-13-484706-1
ISBN-10: 0-13-484706-7

1 18

Executive Editor
Chris Guzikowski

Development Editor
Kiran Kumar Panigrahi

Managing Editor
Sandra Schroeder

Senior Project Editor
Lori Lyons

Copy Editor
Gill Editorial Services

Indexer
Ken Johnson

Proofreader
Christopher Morris

Cover Designer
Chuti Prasertsith

Project Manager
Suganya Karuppasamy

Compositor
codemantra

Contents at a Glance

Contents

Foreword

Those of you who have been part of a project team building large software systems, or who have installed major software products for use in a corporate setting, will probably know that your project was misunderstood by your organization's leadership. Too often, such efforts are thought of as "software projects" because they almost always involve the development or configuration of large amounts of software. As a result of seeing them as software projects, most organizations emphasize the importance of staffing the project with the best information technology talent available to ensure its success. Any business analysts assigned to the project are mistakenly viewed as little more than a messenger to unburden the techies from having to talk to business people.

But experience tells us that these are more than merely software projects. They are in actuality *business process change projects*. And as such, the business analyst is not a peripheral character, but central to the role of understanding the business, both current and future versions. Competency in business analysis becomes a critical success factor for your project. *Business Analysis Agility* is a ground-breaking resource that can help you ensure that you get business analysis right on your next project.

During these projects, the organization decides on changes it wants to make to how it does business, and it implements these changes by modifying its business processes. While it is true that many of these business process changes involve the deployment of new software systems—either to carry out new or improved business processes, or to streamline existing business processes through greater levels of automation—the effect of the changes goes well beyond the boundaries of the organization's software systems. Employees need to be trained to interact differently with each other and with external parties; decisions are made differently; new products and services are offered; and so on.

Getting business process change right requires leadership from the business itself. Your information technology team and your external system integration consultants can help you in many ways, but they are not the right people to tell you how you want to run your business. For that, you need people who understand your business both as it is today, and how it should evolve to meet new and future challenges and opportunities. Much of this work falls to the business analysts.

The role of business analyst has been around for decades. Unfortunately, the process by which business analysts are identified, selected, recruited, and developed has been haphazard and inefficient at best. At the beginning of a business process change project, personnel from the sponsoring organization are selected to join—or at least to work with—the project team. Training for and orientation to the work they are expected to do on the project is typically minimal, informal, and just in time.

The project's leadership is then on the lookout for those business folks who show an aptitude for business analysis work. This usually amounts to a small minority of the business personnel on the project. Of these, only some find that they like the work enough to want to do it again. Some promising candidates want nothing more than to run for the hills once the project is completed.

The few business analysts who shine on their first project, and who want to do more work of this kind, are quickly snapped up for assignment to the next large business process change effort facing the company. After two or three projects, they will have become journeyman business analysts who can operate on their own in the project environment.

The main problem with the way we cultivate business analysis talent today is that it makes it harder for us to achieve all the important objectives for our projects. Those objectives are to bring about the most advantageous business process changes as inexpensively and quickly as possible. The two keys to achieving these objectives are (1) making correct and durable decisions about the desired business policies and processes as quickly as possible; and (2) verifying as quickly as possible that the business process changes to be implemented work as intended. Achieving these objectives hinges on effective business analysis.

To see why this is true, consider the factors that cause a business process change project to fall short of its objectives. We know there are four primary failure modes for such projects: (1) costing too much; (2) taking too long; (3) delivering an inadequate set of business process changes; or (4) delivering them to an organization that is unprepared to carry them out successfully. All four of these failure modes can be caused by failures of the business analysis roles on the project.

Let's look at the four failure modes more closely. A significant fraction of all large-scale business process change projects never implement any process changes at all; they are cancelled before they deliver. One very common cause of project cancellation—as well as less-complete project failures—is spending more on the project than the chartering organization is willing to allow. Cost overruns always raise project risk, and in extreme cases can trigger project failure.

While it may seem simplistic, it is sadly true that the principal cause of project cost overruns is nothing more complicated than taking too long. For most projects of this kind, calendar duration drives cost more so than does any other factor. So anything that causes the project to take longer drives it toward two of the cited failure modes: cost overrun and schedule overrun.

To deliver an appropriate set of business process changes, the project team needs to do two key things: (1) identify the right set of process changes, and (2) verify that the proposed solution to be implemented carries out the desired changes correctly. The first of these objectives requires effective requirements identification, and effective communication of the requirements to those constructing the solution. The second requires effective (and efficient) testing of the solution to ensure that it works as intended.

As you know if you are familiar with large business process change projects, requirements definition and system testing are two of the most voracious consumers of calendar time on the project. Doing these two activities as well and as quickly as possible goes a long way toward ensuring the project's success. And the lion's share of the work toward both these goals falls to the business analysts and business sponsors on the project. The same is true for our fourth failure mode. Business sponsors and business analysts lead the preparation of the business organization to use the new solution.

Given its pivotal role in avoiding these failures, we can safely say that no single capability is more crucial to successful business process change projects than effective business analysis.

In *Business Analysis Agility*, James and Suzanne Robertson have provided a structured, effective, and efficient way to guide new business analysts from their first projects to full mastery of this critical skill set. There is no longer any need, nor good reason, to continue the "trial by fire" approach to business analyst development. *Business Analysis Agility* provides the express on-ramp that business process change projects have sorely needed.

—**Steve McMenamin**
Former CIO and Senior Vice-President,
Hawaiian Electric Company

Preface

• Why did we write this book? • Who is it for?
• Why you should read it • What it will do for you

What This Book Will Do for You

We kept hearing from product owners and agile team members who told us more or less the same story. They worked closely with their customers and kept delivering what the customers asked for. Then, once the product was delivered, the customer came back with, "I know you gave us what we asked for, but it turns out to be not what we need." We hear the same complaint from traditional teams.

Sometimes agile team members told us that there was an early presumption of the solution, and they were halfway through delivery when it became apparent to everyone that the solution was not what was required. Traditional teams have been grappling with this problem for many years.

We also heard from product owners who said they felt pressured to deliver a solution even when they knew that solution was not the right one.

Our clients asked if there was some way to avoid these kinds of mishaps. *Yes, there is, and that is what this book is about.*

Delivering a solution—software, consumer product, service—does not mean that you are delivering value. If the solution fails to solve the customer's real problem, to meet the customer's needs, then there is no point building it.

This book is about finding the real problem, understanding the real needs, and then deriving the best solution—the one that most accurately fulfills those needs.

Part of the problem we set out to address is to dispel the notion that "anything upfront" is bad. Without *some* upfront analysis, projects have no scope and are simply shooting in the dark. The trick is to make anything upfront as short and effective as possible. We can show you how to do that.

We also heard from many business analysts who asked us how they should work with agile teams. These were business analysts who were often working in a business group and not considered part of the agile development effort. These business analysts wanted to either be part of the agile team or have a much closer—and more effective—relationship with the team. We also talked to business analysts who felt that the traditional way of producing a requirements specification was heavy-handed; they wanted something more iterative, more reactive, more agile.

This book is about an agile approach to business analysis—one that integrates with agile development methods and frameworks and takes advantage of agile thinking. It's an approach that leads you to better ways of discovering the real business problem. It's also an approach that leads you to delivering a better, more valuable solution.

Who Is This Book For?

This book is for you if you are involved in some way with delivering solutions. You might think of yourself as a business analyst, a product owner, an agile team member, or a business stakeholder. Perhaps you don't care about your job title; you just want to deliver the best results you can. Perhaps your job is some combination of the above or some other role involved in improving your client's business by delivering exemplary solutions, products, or services.

Business Analysts Working on Agile Projects

The business analyst role is not prescribed in Scrum or in most other agile methods. However, many organizations are coming to realize that business analysis skills and ways of thinking are needed on agile projects. Whether you are called a business analyst or not is irrelevant; analysis and systems thinking is one of the prime ingredients for achieving the right outcome.

We show you how to do business analysis as part of an agile team. For business analysts operating independently, we show you how to interact with an agile team.

We show you how to define customer segments, identify what is valuable to each of them, and find solutions that will bring about that value. Further, we show you how to use safe-to-fail probes to find the optimal business solution and how to investigate and understand it to ensure that the solution—software, product, service—you develop will deliver the right outcome.

Business Analysts Working on Traditional Projects

Traditional projects are those that produce a complete requirements specification before starting to construct the solution. In many cases this is necessary, such as for outsourcing, medical applications, and military projects. If you are working this way, we show you how you can use agile practices to be more effective when producing your specification.

The activities we describe in this book are equally applicable to traditional projects. To be more effective, you must identify the right customers, solve the right problem, find the optimal solution, and produce a lean specification containing only those things that you have determined to be necessary.

This book will help anyone who has a stake in delivering real value by delivering the right solution to the right problem.

Product Owners

The product owner role is a complex one. This is acknowledged by most authors, industry pundits, and product owners themselves. The product owner is charged with maximizing the value of the product, and as we shall say many times, the product's maximum value comes when it solves the customer's real problem and satisfies the customer's real needs. Discovering the real problem to solve, and finding the best solution to that problem, is what this book is about.

We aim to show how effective business analysis can help you bring about the right result. You'll learn how business analysis thinking ensures that you write better stories, and that the stories in your backlog are those that bring about the best possible solution.

If you as a product owner intend to be hands-on discovering the customers' needs, this book has techniques for you. If you intend to work closely with a business analyst in your team, this book explains what business analysis is, what value it has, and why you should make your business analyst an invaluable friend.

Agile Team Members

A multifunctional team is one in which the members collectively possess the skills necessary to deliver the right solution. One of these skills is business analysis. Business analysis is not about writing requirements, but about uncovering real problems and real needs. Your solution must solve the right business problem. There is no other way to deliver value.

Among other things, agile team members participate in a conversation with business stakeholders and the product owner about the detailed requirements for the product. It is here that analytical thinking makes a powerful contribution. By stepping back and seeing the larger picture, by understanding the importance of well-designed information and convenience, by properly understanding the values of the customer, team members make better decisions and produces better solutions.

Business Stakeholders

Every business is (or should be) in a constant state of change and improvement. In this book, we discuss business analysis and how it is used to study and analyze your business problems (or your business opportunity or required change). Analytical thinking reveals the real problem to solve and goes on to find the optimal solution for it.

Most improvements involve to some extent computerized automation. Business analysts are traditionally the bridge between the business and IT, so we will show you the business analysis activities, and by knowing this, how you as a business stakeholder can most effectively participate with your agile team.

In short, this book is for you if you want to deliver better solutions that provide value by solving the real problem. It's for those who want to discover how being an agile analyst—meaning nimble, reactive, quick—can speed up the discovery part of development and produce more accurate results. It's for those who want to understand the significance of customer values, the importance of correct scoping, the advantages of good solution design, and the advantage of effective story management.

Regardless of your role, its name, and its responsibility, there is no doubt that good business analysis skills can enhance it.

We hope you find our book about business analysis useful.

Note

Register your copy of *Business Analysis Agility* on the InformIT site for convenient access to updates and/or corrections as they become available. To start the registration process, go to informit. com/register and log in or create an account. Enter the product ISBN 9780134847061 and click Submit. Look on the Registered Products tab for an Access Bonus Content link next to this product, and follow that link to access any available bonus materials. If you would like to be notified of exclusive offers on new editions and updates, please check the box to receive email from us.

Acknowledgments

It would be hard indeed to think of any socio-technical subject where an entire book could be written by an author working entirely alone. In the case of this book, there were two of us writing as co-authors. Even then, we needed (and received) help. We are very grateful for the comments, suggestions, and corrections from the following people:

James Archer, Peter Doomen, Ellen Gottesdiener, Shane Hastie, Peter Hruschka, Andrew Kendall, Katarzyna Kot, Tim Lister, Mark McCarthy, Neil Maiden, Chris Matts, Adrian Reed

A special thank you goes to Steve McMenamin. Steve's insights and experience, not to say the time he invested, were incredibly helpful. Thank you, Steve.

We must also give credit to the team at Pearson: Christopher Guzikowski, Kiran Kumar Panigrahi, Lori Lyons, Karen Davis, and Suganya Karuppasamy all worked their particular magic to bring this into reality.

Thank you everybody.

About the Authors

James Robertson is a business analyst, problem solver, author, speaker, instructor, photographer, designer, and coach. He trained as an architect but left that for a career in IT and the sociological side of technology.

He left the security of employment in Australia to move and start his own company (with his brilliant wife) in the United Kingdom. Since then he has gone on to co-author seven books, numerous courses, and the *Volere* requirements techniques and templates, which have been adopted by organizations all over the world as their standard for gathering, discovering, communicating, tracing, and specifying solution needs.

James' career is broad, both in a geographical sense and the areas and systems that he has worked with. It is fair to say that James has worked on almost every type of commercial IT project—from a start as a programmer in a software development house in Sydney, to consulting in New York, London, Rome, and most European capitals. He has earned his experience at the sharp end of both project and research work.

He divides his time between London and the French Alps. He skis for as much of the winter as demands on his time allow, and hikes all summer.

Suzanne Robertson is having a stellar career in information technology and systems engineering. She is a teacher, practitioner, writer, instructor, and guide.

Suzanne is a pioneer in adapting ideas from other domains for automated solutions. She has collaborated in workshops using experts from fields as diverse as modern music, visualization, and cookery. Ideas from these domains were adapted to make major breakthroughs in creative ideas for domains ranging from air traffic control to local government.

She is co-author of the best-selling *Mastering the Requirements Process*, among other books and courses. She is co-creator of the *Volere* requirements techniques. She was the founding editor of the Requirements Column in *IEEE Software*.

She has also made an impact in the socio-technical arena. This includes research and consulting on managing project sociology, both individually and as collaborative efforts between business, technology, and academia.

Her experience with different projects in both the private and public sectors has given her experience in a wide variety of systems and locations. She has worked in Europe, Australia, the Far East, and the United States.

Suzanne is a founder and principal of the Atlantic Systems Guild.

Her other interests include opera, cooking, skiing, and finding out about curious things.

Agile Business Analysis

• An example of agile business analysis—Bernie's Books
• People assume they know the solution
• Solving the problem for Bernie • Designing Bernie's solution
• Stories for Bernie's solution • The changing nature of business analysis

Think of the software or the website you are about to build, the consumer product you want to bring to market, the service that your organization is planning to provide, or the device that you are building to sell. Whatever it is that you're working on, let's call it your *solution*. What's the most important quality your solution must have? Or, to put it in a different way, what is the single quality that, if missed, would cause the solution to be a failure?

Of course your answer is *meeting the needs and solving the problem for the people who buy it or use it*. It does not matter how quickly you build the solution, whether you come in on time and on budget, if you use an agile approach or traditional methods, or if you build it yourself, outsource it, or assemble it from components. If you don't solve the real problem of your customers or users, your solution is worthless. Actually, it's less than worthless. You've wasted your time and resources building it.

> **agile.**
>
> When we use the word *agile* in this book, it means small "a" agile. Big "A" Agile refers to one of the Agile methods. We are agnostic as to which Agile development method you are using. We use *agile* to discuss the ability of the business analyst to respond to changing circumstances and unexpected discoveries and to deliver value.

This is a book about agility in business analysis and how it helps you discover your customer's real problem, find the real needs, and deliver better, more valuable, more relevant solutions.

Why Is This "agile"?

We are using the word *agile* in the sense of being nimble, active, lively, flexible, adaptable, or quick. We do not use the word with a big A. Big "A" Agile means that you are following one of the Agile methods—Scrum, XP, Crystal Clear, Lean, Kanban, DSDM, or any of the others. We are not going to talk about these—they are plentifully covered elsewhere—but everything you find in this book is compatible and applicable to any Agile method.

This is not about better ways to build solutions, but ways to build better solutions.

This book is about doing business analysis in an agile way—trying new things, adapting to changes, adapting to things you discover, being flexible in your approach according to your circumstances, and being quick. Experience tells us that duration matters and that the quickest way to deliver a solution is to deliver the right solution. Indeed, our projects should be as short a duration as we can possibly make them. Prioritizing relentlessly, investing only in solutions that deliver value, and ensuring that our learning is always fruitful leads to the quickest and happiest results.

Möbius Strip

Figure 1.1

Agile development has two aspects, but it is really one continuous process, so we can represent this situation as a Möbius strip. One part of this strip is the Discovery of the problem and its needs, and the other is Delivering a solution that implements those needs. This book is mainly about the Discovery side of things. This diagram is adapted from Ellen Gottesdiener and Mary Gorman's graphic in their book *Discover to Deliver*.

Figure 1.1 shows a *Möbius strip* representing the continuous nature of constant delivery. If you are not familiar, the Möbius strip—named after German mathematician August Ferdinand Möbius—is made by taking a strip of paper, making one half twist, and joining the ends to make a loop. The result is a two-dimensional entity with only one surface. Start anywhere and draw a line along the surface; your line will arrive back, uninterrupted, at the point you started.

We see this uninterrupted characteristic of the Möbius strip as an appropriate metaphor of the continuous process of Discovery and Delivery.

Discovery and Delivery are a continuous loop.

The Discovery side of the loop is concerned with discovering the customers' needs. This means uncovering the customers, their objectives and values. It involves experimenting with proposals as a way of exposing the real problem.

Once the optimal solution to the problem has been discovered, it must be communicated to the Delivery portion of the loop. This communication is done in a way that enables the Delivery team to deliver the correct product. It is also done in a timely manner that allows the Discovery and the Delivery to work synchronously. This in turn makes feedback from delivery more useful to the discoverers.

Discovery and Delivery are a continuous loop; the loop is continuous until either all the customer's needs have been satisfied or it is decided that anything remaining is of insufficient value.

But it doesn't end there; the looping continues after a suitable product has been delivered.

The world we live in is agile; it is constantly changing and then reacting to its own changes. There are always new opportunities, new problems, new technologies, and new innovations that lead to new possibilities; new laws that mean changes to our businesses and solutions; and changes that mean more Discovery and more Delivery.

Why Are We Concerned with Business Analysis?

At the beginning of many development efforts, people *assume they know the solution*. Given the number of failures in product, service, and software development, they clearly don't. Delivering a solution is not the same thing as delivering value. Sometimes it's the opposite.

Any sensible approach to solution development must involve taking whatever time is needed to work with our customers to discover what is most valuable to them, what their real needs are, and what the best solution is to satisfy those values and needs. We should also ensure that the customer's problem is worth solving and that the solution will bring value to both the customer and the provider of the solution.

Delivering a solution is not necessarily the same thing as delivering value.

One of the foundation ideas of agile development was to avoid "big upfront activities." It implied that teams should not spend too much time building a complete requirements specification before beginning development. Unfortunately, some overenthusiastic acolytes took this to mean "nothing upfront." But "nothing upfront" just doesn't work; anything meaningful has *something* upfront. If you want to drive to Baltimore, you must first find out how to get there or program your GPS. This is an upfront activity and is far preferable to setting out to drive along random roads hoping to find one that leads to Baltimore. Acting randomly is not going to get you where you want to go. You would not attempt to provide streamed music without first understanding the audience for your music and how they might use it. Nobody attempts to build a house without planning how the rooms are laid out and where the doors and windows should be.

Software projects cost the same as, or more than houses do. Why should anyone think software can be built without *any* upfront preparation?

Software is certainly more malleable than bricks and mortar. But if you are not solving the right problem, no amount of refactoring is going to save you. If you fail to understand the customers for your solution, no amount of redesign will build a product they want.

Despite the need for some upfront activity, it must not take too long.

However, despite the need for some upfront activity, it must not take too long. Nor is there a need for the upfront activity to be finished before construction work begins, to produce voluminous documentation, or for the upfront activity to be remote and unconnected to the building activity.

This book is about integrating analytical thinking into any development process. It aims to show you how to ensure that the right solution is delivered. It also aims to show you that by not heedlessly constructing an assumed solution but by taking the time the solution needs to discover the real problem, you take giant steps toward the success of your mission.

Let's look at an example to see how this works. This might seem at times a little long-winded. Please keep in mind that the activities discussed are overlapping and iterative. They can be done quite quickly, and in Chapter 7, "Jack Be Nimble, Jack Be Quick," we discuss how rapid your agile analysis can be.

Bernie's Books—An Example in Agile Business Analysis

You are a business analyst and have been hired by Bernie's Books[1], shown in Figure 1.2, to improve some of the systems. Bernie's Books is a bricks and mortar bookstore that—against the trend—is thriving while many other bookstores are closing their doors. Bernie's store is located in a well-established shopping street, with restaurants, cafés, and better-quality clothing stores, all of them attracting the type of customer Bernie serves.

Figure 1.2

Bernie's Books is a brick and mortar store selling a better class of books.

(Credit: SpeedKingz/ Shutterstock)

Bernie has an idea: he wants to offer customers who buy a hardcopy book the option of a free digital download of the same book.

Bernie also thinks he might start selling his books online. This might be done so that the customer receives an immediate digital download, and the hardcopy book is sent to the customer by mail. This, of course, opens the possibility of digital-only customers.

What Do You Do?

You could rush in and start working on the assumed solution: the automatic digital download. Or you could apply a little analytical thinking to Bernie's problem.

The problem is that we often don't know what the problem is.

Bernie has provided a solution: free digital downloads. However, he hasn't said what the problem is. Indeed, we should ask Bernie if he knows what the problem is, and if so, ask if his proposed solutions really solve that problem.

As John Carrol of Penn State College of Information Sciences and Technology puts it, "The worst misstep one can make in design is to solve the wrong problem."

It would not be the first time that someone has put forward a solution without understanding the problem. Also, without knowing more about the context and the environment, we cannot know the extent of the problem.

FOOTNOTE 1
Readers of Lawrence Block's burglar series may have guessed that our Bernie, the bookstore owner, has been named for Bernie Rhodenbarr, Block's larcenous but lovable bookseller. We thank Mr. Block for his character's name and his entertaining novels.

What's Bernie's Problem?

What is Bernie's need, or what problem does Bernie want to solve? Analytical thinking is partly about finding underlying reasons for things, usually by asking "why?" Suppose we start by asking Bernie this: "Why are you able to run a successful bookshop at a time that other brick and mortar bookshops are closing their doors?" Bernie answers:

"My bookshop is successful because I have enough loyal customers who enjoy reading. They like reading books that appeal to more intelligent people, they are more literary than the general population, and most of all, they want to read the kinds of books that I want to have in my shop. I am not a mass market seller—I don't carry the blockbusters, and my popular fiction is aimed at a better class of reader. I am not exactly upmarket—more "upbrain." I also carry better children's books and a section of cookbooks. This brings the right kind of people into my store. My clientele is pretty loyal.

"Of course, I have to keep attracting a younger audience with the same reading tastes. I cannot keep selling to the same audience forever—they are getting older and at some stage won't be mobile enough to get to my bookstore at all.

"My reason for wanting the addition of the digital download is to appeal to younger people—digital because young people are more likely to read books on their phones or tablets. I also want things to be more convenient for my traditional customers who want the convenience of tablet or phone reading while on a plane or when they don't have room in their handbag or briefcase for the hardcopy.

"I have also seen people come into my bookshop and browse through my books. When they find something they like the look of, they whip out their phone and buy it online from Amazon or one of the other online stores. I call these people "book cover bandits." I lose a sale and see no reason why they shouldn't buy their digital version from me. They're in my bookstore after all."

So now you know a little more and can see that Bernie's assumed solutions are not necessarily going to work.

People Assume They Know the Solution

They don't. They can't know the solution until they know the problem.

You could provide a free e-book version with each paper book bought, but there is nothing yet to say that customers would find any value in having both versions.

You could build a *BernieReader* app, but would anybody use it? And if they did, would it provide value to Bernie?

You could provide free instore Wi-Fi, but there is no evidence that customers would pay attention to it. Alternatively, it might encourage more people to order one of Bernie's books from an online retailer. Additionally, it might give the wrong image if too many people are wandering around using computers or handheld devices in Bernie's store.

Could an online solution harm Bernie's business? It's not unheard of.

Any solution you deliver must solve the right problem; it's the only way you can deliver value. That means that we need to turn our attention to finding the right problem. Once we understand that, we can find the right solution to it. Until then, let's keep an open mind.

Analytical Thinking

To illustrate business analysis agility and analytical thinking, let's take a brief look at the approach we would use for Bernie's Books. We shall go over the activities in detail in subsequent chapters, but for the moment, a quick run-through is sufficient. It is also appropriate; what we are proposing is usually done quite quickly.

Why do we need analytical thinking? Because we need to think rather than be led along by dogma and knee-jerk reactions. For example, one unfortunate piece of dogma is that the team should deliver only the minimum workable product and only the product that has been asked for.

That is a complete abdication of the responsibilities of solution development. It turns the development team into automatons who mechanically transform whatever is asked for (which is often wrong) into software. It is not how good solutions are developed.

Delivering only a minimal working product does not guarantee that anybody will want to use it. You can deliver what they ask for, but the truth is that the customers do not always know what they want, what they need, and what they can get. Nor does the development team.

The right solution delivers the best value. Nothing less.

To deliver *value* by solving the real problem, you need to discover what is needed and what is valuable and not just be a robotic translator.

The right solution delivers the best value. Nothing less. To deliver the right solution, the customers and the development team work together, discover the right business problem (it's usually subtler than people think), and then derive the solution that solves this problem in the best possible manner. The best solution has qualities other than minimal. It is convenient, appealing, secure, and robust. It is not—definitely not—"only what is asked for."

Bernie's Business Goals

Why is Bernie making an investment in this project? What are his business goals? Bernie wants to sell books, but more importantly he wants to keep selling books in the future. This means his objectives must include keeping the loyal customers happy, attracting a younger generation of readers, and convincing the book cover bandits to buy from him.

Of course, Bernie can only achieve his goals with the cooperation of his customers. In turn, the customers will only cooperate if there is some benefit to them. This means that we investigate the customers to learn what it is that they value. Once we know that, the problem shifts to deriving a solution that the customers find valuable and satisfies Bernie's business goals. This is illustrated in Figure 1.3.

Figure 1.3

Each distinguishable customer segment values something; you can describe it by writing a value proposition. You derive a solution to deliver this value, and this solution must contribute to meeting the business goals.

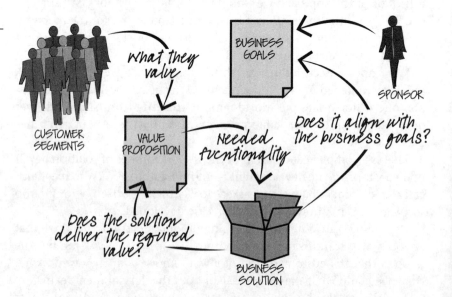

Customer Segments

In the beginning, pretty much all your client knows is the target audience for the proposed solution. You don't know yet what you will deliver, but you do know who you will deliver it to. You can categorize the target audience using *customer segments*.

A customer segment is a group of people who have a unique profile—a collection of characteristics that separate them from other customer segments in a meaningful way.

For external customers, we suggest you start by segmenting according to the customers' needs. You could also use demographics, attitudes, and tasks that they want to accomplish, and so on.

In the case of in-house consumption, a customer segment is a group of users who share the same profile. The people who inhabit the segment have a set of needs and wants and concerns that set them apart from the other segments. You might prefer to think of this category as *user segments*.

You might also at this stage begin to develop *personas* for your segments. A persona is a virtual representation of the archetypical customer within the segment. The persona is usually a synthesis of typical behaviors, skills, objectives, and so on, and it is usually given enough human touches—a name, photograph, personal characteristics—to make it real for the team. We have more to say about customer segments and personas in the next chapter.

You will probably find more accurate problems and better solutions if you segment Bernie's customers by their needs and their propensity to buy. This project is about keeping and growing customers, so understanding their buying attitudes seems a reasonable place to start. This thinking gives you three main segments, which Bernie names *loyal customers, twentysomethings*, and *book cover bandits*. There might be some other, smaller segments—people buying a gift, casual browsers, etc.—but for the moment let's focus on the three most valuable segments.

Loyal Customers

Benie's first customer segment is the *loyal customer* who likes buying books in his store. This segment cannot be ignored because this is currently Bernie's main income stream. This segment is probably middle aged, but you want to have a good look at them first and not make too many assumptions. The mention of cookbooks might suggest predominately female readers, but let's make sure before proceeding.

(Credit: kzenon/123RF)

Digital versions of books might be attractive to this segment, but you would have to consider whether you should have an automatic download or whether a simple voucher system for a voluntary download would be more appropriate. It might be completely useless to offer a digital version of a cookbook when most cooks (not necessarily female) prefer a hardcopy book to cook from.

You might introduce a loyalty card system whereby the loyal customers receive points when they buy books, thus reinforcing their loyalty. Perhaps the earned points could be used to buy coffee at nearby coffee shops.

But we are getting ahead of ourselves. *We don't know what the problem is yet and what this segment will find valuable.* There is no point guessing because our guesses are almost bound to be wrong. We have to talk to these people and discover what they value and what they need.

Twentysomethings

(Credit: Lakov Filimonov/
Shutterstock)

The next, and probably the most important customer segment in terms of future value to Bernie, is the customers that Bernie does not yet have. His loyal customers are becoming older year by year, and Bernie must replace them with younger people who like to read better books. Bernie wants to attract this audience and keep them reading his books. Bernie tells you that he has been looking at some research that suggests people form lifelong reading habits in their twenties. It is also a time when many people are beginning to have disposable income. Bernie wants to capture this group and try to get them to become regular Bernie's shoppers.

These folks receive value, or at least Bernie does, if they discover that the experience of shopping for reading matter in Bernie's book store is a better experience than shopping online, or wherever they get their books at the moment.

We'll call this segment of people *twentysomethings*, but keep in mind they could be any age from late teenager to mid-30s. Bernie stocks children's books, but kids don't buy books; their parents do. These parents are likely to be twentysomethings.

These twentysomethings become truly valuable if Bernie can convert them to buying books from him. He has to make it exciting and attractive—let's say cool—to buy books at Bernie's. This problem won't be easy to solve, but that makes it all the more attractive to a bright, innovative team. Additionally, as you get to know more about this segment, you might discover that Bernie might sell things other than books to them, including coffee, literary apparel, experiences, in-store talks, and events. However, until we know more about this segment—indeed any of the segments—speculating about solutions is not very useful.

Book Cover Bandits

The third customer segment is made up of the people that Bernie thinks of as *book cover bandits*. These are people who use Bernie's as an attractive place to browse for books. Bernie puts his books out on tables, so customers can see the books face up. This invites browsers to pick up a book and look more closely at the contents, the style of writing, and so on, and decide whether to buy the book. The problem is that the book cover bandits don't buy their books from Bernie. Most of the time they find a book in Bernie's and then go online and buy from one of the big online booksellers—sometimes while they are right there in Bernie's store.

Performing an analysis does not mean that we want to delay delivering a solution. It means we want to deliver the right solution.

This customer segment appears to want to read books on a mobile device, so offering an immediate download might seem an appropriate solution. This customer segment would probably want compatibility with existing readers—Kindle, Nook, iPad, Aldiko, Better World Books, Marvin, and so on—or maybe prefer a new *BernieReader*. But again, let's not get ahead of ourselves by guessing at solutions.

It might turn out that you and Bernie choose not to bother with the book cover bandits. If they don't provide enough value to Bernie, then you cannot justify spending time on them, and you and Bernie might decide to put them aside.

You might also consider the *gift givers*. These are folks who might not be readers themselves but those who are buying a book as a gift. You have to consider how many people are in this segment to evaluate whether it is worth providing a solution for them. You'll have to speak to Bernie about this.

We will have more to say about customer segments in Chapter 2, "Do You Know What Your Customers Value?" but we think you get the idea by now. Let's move on.

Value Proposition

In conjunction with your sponsor—in this case Bernie—and your product people, you determine a *value proposition* for each of the segments. What is it that the segment finds valuable? What *impact* does the sponsor want to make for each of the segments? And, of course, does satisfying each value proposition contribute to meeting Bernie's business goals? This is illustrated in Figure 1.4.

Figure 1.4

A value proposition sets out what each of the customer segments values. You must ensure that providing this value makes some contribution to meeting the sponsor's business goals.

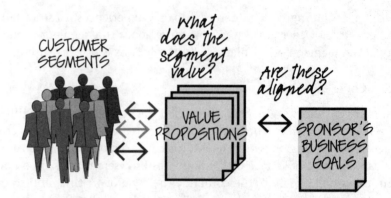

Of course, the value proposition is not a guess. You and Bernie need to interview the customers in the segment, study their work and their needs, discover their aspirations, and find out what it is they value. Keep in mind that people are not always as forthcoming as they should be when you talk to them about such things. It is often best to rely on your observations of the customers rather than simply on what they say.

Fortunately, Bernie has already spent a lot of time talking to and observing his customers and can supply you with most of what you need.

For example, with Bernie's guidance, you can confidently write the value proposition for the twentysomething segment as this:

> `As a twentysomething, I receive value when I discover that buying books from Bernie's is a better experience than buying from wherever I bought them before.`

The customer need we can identify from this value proposition is a better book-buying experience. The problem you must solve is how to offer that experience, as it is only by doing so that you will provide the required value.

You might consider adding an acceptance criterion to this value proposition. For example, if your solution results in the twentysomething buying 15% more books from Bernie than from any other source, your solution is acceptable.

Your solution must also align with Bernie's business goals and be worthwhile developing. That is, the revenue from the twentysomething market is sufficient to pursue your solution. In Chapters 2, 3, and 4, we go into more detail on how you discover the customers' needs and values.

Loyal customers receive value when they enjoy and continue shopping at Bernie's, and delivering this value aligns with Bernie's business goals. The problem you must solve for loyal customers is how to keep them coming back. This suggests you must find solutions to meet their needs by keeping Bernie's shelves and tables full of books that they want to read. You must also find other solutions to make loyal customers' book-buying experience something they want to repeat—often.

Book cover bandits receive value when they find a book they want to read. It is a business goal to have the bandit buy the book from Bernie, either online or in the store. The bandits may have other needs, which you must discover as part of finding a solution for them.

Who Identifies Customer Segments and Their Value Propositions?

Identifying the customer segments and their value propositions is a customer-facing activity, so it naturally falls to the product owner, the program or product manager, and the project sponsor. The business analyst and analytical-thinking team members are part of the observations and interviews that contribute to the value propositions.

It is important to identify your segments by talking to actual customers, not their surrogates. In some cases, at the beginning of a project your management gives you this information. We urge you to challenge that and check to ensure that the customers and their values have not been merely guessed at and that you can rely on the proffered information.

This is a crucial step in your development process, so make the effort to get it right. As crucial as it is, it does not have to take forever. Keep in mind that the time you spend is well saved when you deliver more appropriate, more valuable solutions.

How Can I Solve the Problem?

The twentysomethings segment is the one that Bernie is most anxious about, so let's start with that one. The value proposition for this segment says that these people receive value when they discover that buying books from Bernie's is a better experience than buying from wherever they bought before. This means that you should provide one or more solutions that solve the problem of enticing twentysomethings to become Bernie's customers and provide a good book-buying experience.

Bernie knows that the offspring of parents who read are more likely to read themselves. You can provide an enticement to read Bernie's books by proposing a solution whereby parents who buy a book from Bernie encourage their offspring to read it. If the offspring enjoy the book and are made aware that this is a Bernie's book, they are likely to shop at Bernie's for more of their books. Whatever solution you propose must make it attractive and convenient for parents to give a book from Bernie's to their offspring. This could be the hard copy, or it could be an e-book version.

For example, consider this conversation between a mother and her daughter:

"Hey, Sally. I'm in the middle of reading a book by Donna Tartt, and I love it. I think you would enjoy it, too. I can give you the book when I'm finished, or would you like to get the e-book right away?"

There are probably several—possibly more than several—ways of providing a solution to this problem. Here is where you, the business stakeholders, and the team discuss and generate multiple proposed solutions.

> ### Stakeholder.
>
> This term should be taken to mean a person with an interest in the solution. Certainly, it includes users and customers, but it also includes people with specialized knowledge—subject matter experts, security consultants, lawyers, user experience (UX) designers, technology specialists, and so on. Stakeholders provide input to your analysis; they do not necessarily have veto power.

How many solutions should you generate? It depends on the value that the solution will deliver. If this is a customer-facing part of your client's business that is intended to have a significant impact on the market, you should generate lots of solutions to find the very best ones. For routine, housekeeping parts of the business, don't spend too much time generating alternative solutions, but certainly have more than one.

Never stop at one solution, for as Linus Pauling says, "The best way to have a good idea is to have lots of ideas."

There is no need to elaborate on your solution proposals once you have a description—model, diagram, bullet points, elevator pitch—something that is understandable to your fellow team members. Do this quickly, but let your imagination run freely.

Each solution that you propose is just that—a proposal to solve the problem and deliver the required value. The term *hypothesis* is often used and is appropriate; at this stage, any solution is speculation on your part, and you have yet to prove it will work as required.

One note of caution here, and this was first pointed out to us by Chris Matts: people are more likely to propose solutions that they know they can deliver. These are solutions that are contained within their departmental boundaries and do not involve other teams.

He and She.

In our experience, business analysts, product owners and other team members are equally divided between males and females. However, we feel that constantly writing *he or she* or *his or hers* is tiresome. We also think (and keep in mind that your authors are one male and one female) that using *she* as the pronoun has a condescending feel to it. We could be wrong about this, and please excuse us if you disagree, but we have elected to mix *he* and *she* randomly.

On the other hand, analytical thinking means that you are unconstrained by the current departmental boundaries and thus look outward to propose solutions that span departments. If that results in a better solution, as it often does, please keep this conflict of interest in mind.

Safe-to-Fail Probes

You now have the embryo of some proposed solutions. They are, as yet, hypotheses. You are suggesting they will solve the problem. Now it's time to test those hypotheses. You can cheaply and quickly test them with *safe-to-fail probes*. You can run these probes much more quickly than you can build software or construct a full prototype. It's good to be quick because you might have to run several probes before you know you have the right solution to the right problem.

The intention of the safe-to-fail probe, as shown in Figure 1.5, is to test the hypothesis for viability, affordability, acceptability, possibility, and more. The tests are experiments and should be fast and cheap. This implies that paper or whiteboard models are used, but you could build quick-and-dirty software or hardware prototypes if needed. You might play through a proposal using team members and stakeholders to act out a business process. You could experiment with having a team member play the part of a proposed solution and have business stakeholders attempt to use it. And if the solution is mission-critical, you might build several working prototypes and test them against live customers from the segment.

As you run these probes, you are collecting evidence for or against the proposal. How much would it cost? Will costumers use it? Can the staff be trained to operate it in time for rollout? What impact will it have on current operations? Your intention is to show whether a proposal would be suitable, and if so, whether it is a desirable solution.

Figure 1.5

Team members draw and test their proposals in a safe-to-fail probe.

(Credit: Baranq/ Shutterstock)

Back at Bernie's, as an example of a safe-to-fail probe, you could work with the appropriate stakeholders to build a storyboard (or some other model) for the previously mentioned proposition of a parent enabling a twentysomething offspring to download an e-book. The storyboard for this probe is shown in Figure 1.6. Note the annotation of the estimates of usage. These estimates come from a survey of a selection of customers and are intended to provide information on the viability of the proposition. Bernie has obtained the agreement of most publishers about e-book versions, and it appears that the small extra charge will be offset by both sales and exposure to the customer segment. You, meanwhile, have run a quick survey with some of Bernie's customers to determine their take-up estimate.

Figure 1.6

An example of a simple safe-to-fail probe using a storyboard. This proposal provides for a voucher to enable the download of the e-book version of a title bought from Bernie's. The usage estimates have been added.

Your probes will no doubt be more complex than the one shown, but the point here is to give you an idea of how you go about using probes to find the right solution.

This does not go on forever. The point is to have more than one solution to overcome the original assumed solution. By generating several proposals, you are likely to show that they are superior solutions and will provide greater value. In this you would generate other solutions for passing along the e-book. Your solutions must encourage parents (they belong to the loyal customer segment) to give the e-book to their offspring (the twentysomething segment) and encourage them to read it. Your solution aims to get someone to do something—when they do that thing, they provide value to Bernie.

You also would have generated several other solutions to encourage the twentysomethings to buy books from Bernie's. These might range from opening an in-store coffee shop to social networking approaches to talks by movie scriptwriters to, well, almost anything. Each of the more likely proposals is probed.

The probes confirm that you are solving the right problem, and they help you refine your ideas on how to solve the problem. You will most likely find that your probes cause you to have new and better ideas. So much the better.

After a few probes, one of the proposed solutions will emerge as the most appropriate for the customer segment. This is illustrated in Figure 1.7.

Will the functionality of the proposed solution deliver the value shown in the value proposition?

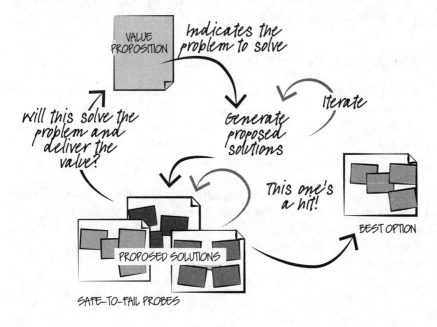

SAFE-TO-FAIL PROBES

Figure 1.7

Start with a value proposition. From its implied problem, generate multiple proposed solutions. For each of these, test your proposals using safe-to-fail probes, constantly using the proposal to repeatedly ask, "Are we solving the right problem?" Any proposal that fails to solve the problem and provide the required value becomes apparent, and the team discards it. Sooner or later the best option for a solution becomes apparent.

*Being agile means
being adaptable
and allowing
for mid-course
corrections;
to challenge
assumptions and
find better things;
and to expect to
be wrong until you
can guarantee that
you're right.*

Let's say that you have run some quick-and-dirty safe-to-fail probes. Let's also say that with Bernie's help, you have come up with some solutions that are sure-fire hits. They are appealing, attractive solutions, and they address the real problem.

We have a lot more to say about finding the right problem and safe-to-fail probes in Chapter 3, "Are You Solving the Right Problem?"

Who Performs Safe-to-Fail Probes?

Examining the problem, generating proposals for solutions, and running safe-to-fail probes involves the whole team. This must include the sponsor because it is here that you make the decision on which of the proposals to carry forward and develop. The program or the product manager is an obvious choice to participate here, either brings a knowledge of the direction that solutions should follow. For customer-facing solutions, the participation of a UX designer is invaluable. Naturally enough, the product owner and the business analysts are heavily involved in proposing solutions and running safe-to-fail probes.

Having real customers available is extremely helpful. After all, these are the people you want to use your solution. These are the people whose reactions count more than anyone else's. If you can afford it, or if it is critical, bring the actual customers into your probing team.

As with all activities, the amount of time you spend generating solutions and probing is directly proportional to the value that the solution will bring. Your probe should also reveal the estimated cost of the solution. Again, this should be in proportion to the value it provides.

Investigate the Solution Space

At this stage, you are looking at a *business solution*, not merely a technological solution. In other words, the solution is more than software. So now your analytical thinking is aimed at investigating the business processes and the people involved in your solution. You also look at the organization, the existing people and their needs, and any processes that might be affected by your solution.

You can call the area you're investigating the *business area*, the *business domain*, the *domain*, the *work*, or several other things. From here, we shall mainly use the term *solution space* to refer to the business activity (both automated and manual) that makes up your business solution.

> ## Solution Space.
>
> This is the extent of the business area, or the work area, needed to visualize the business solution. The automated product you build is usually part of the solution space. The rest of the space is occupied by the people and interfacing automated systems.

Consider the solution space needed for passing along a voucher for an e-book download. Let us say that Bernie has an agreement from the main publishers for a reduced royalty of the e-book and that this will be absorbed by the expected extra revenue. So now you look at the work of buying a book from the moment of selection through paying for the book and receiving a voucher for the digital edition. What steps in the process should you consider? Are there discounts, customer loyalty points to be added or redeemed, or book tokens to cash in?

Questions like this—and there are dozens more—are part of investigating the solution space. This is something that must be done to ensure that you deliver a solution that suits the sponsor's business.

Think of the people involved. For this solution, you have two customer segments involved. What kind of people are they? How will they interact with this part of the business? What kind of cultural norms do they adhere to? What kind of inducement should you offer to get them to pass on the e-book voucher? What would induce the twentysomething to read the book? What links to Bernie's should you provide with the e-book? Is it an assumption that the twentysomething prefers to read on a handheld device?

The purpose of this investigation is to determine whether the chosen business solution meets the customer segment's needs and delivers the appropriate value.

You might also consider the techniques available for your investigation. Depending on the complexity and the value of the work, you might use one of the ethnographical or anthropological approaches. You might use business process models, and customer journey maps (see Chapter 3) might prove a valuable tool. You also have interviews; workshops; inquiries; observation; SWOT (strengths, weaknesses, opportunities, and threats); surveys; and a remarkably long list of others. We have more detail on these in Chapter 4, "Investigate the Solution Space."

The investigation also *scopes the solution space*. That is, you build a model of the scope to determine and demonstrate the extent of the business solution. A sample scope diagram is shown in Figure 1.8.

Figure 1.8

The solution space scope
model for the part of
Bernie's business that we
are interested in.

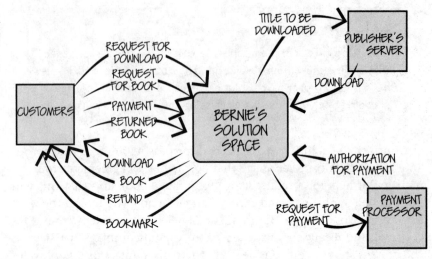

*You cannot make
the informed
change unless you
know what you are
changing from.*

Naturally enough, different people have different expectations of
the scope, which causes problems (and arguments) later. Many of the
arguments originate because the scope is not documented, which causes
people to make their own assumptions. Your scope will, from time to
time, change as you discover more about the solution space. However,
by having a clearly documented initial scope, the team can monitor
changes to it to ensure that informed changes are made as needed and
the scope does not become an uncontrolled bloat.

Who Investigates the Solution Space?

Investigation is the activity that most people think of as business analysis. This suggests that business analysts are the investigators. However,
you might not have *business analyst* as a job title in your team. Some
teams don't. The role name is not as important as having analytical skills
in the team. Anybody on the team with these skills and an open, inquir-
ing mind can—and should—do this.

This investigation is not meant to be overly comprehensive. Some of
the detailed discovery is done during the development cycles, and some
is done during safe-to-fail probing. Provided you are confident that the
developers will not be ambushed by some undiscovered cultural or environmental showstopper, your investigation should be relatively short.

Designing the Solution

Anything worthwhile is designed. The operating system that makes your
computer work the way you like it has been designed to make you like it.

The console on your car where everything is readily at hand has been designed to make it easy for you. Your office chair has been designed to make your rear end comfortable; if not, the designer, not your rear end, is at fault. The smartphone you use has been designed to be attractive and usable. The business process that is both usable and effective has been designed to make it, well, usable and effective. These products don't happen by chance; they're designed.

Armed with a knowledge of the problem, the culture of the customer segments that are to use your solution, the constraints imposed by the operating environment, and the business processes and data to be accommodated, you become a designer.

Designing business processes and automated solutions is not about flashy graphic design (we have flashy graphic designers to do that), and it's not about interfaces (we have interface designers for that), but about *designing a business solution* that will best serve the real business needs. This means that you must design an interaction between the human part of the solution and the automated part of the solution. At the same time, you must design the human and automated tasks that are needed to make the whole of the solution work. This crafting of the processes and the data is shown in Figure 1.9.

Designing the future solution concentrates on two main areas: *information* and *interaction*. As a designer, you decide the information needed for the best interaction, you plan how to present the information in the most meaningful way, and you determine how to make the interaction as convenient and effective as possible. You might think of this as UX design, and it is all to the good if you have UX designer skills in your team. If you plan on using artificial intelligence (AI) as part of your solution, this is when you design it.

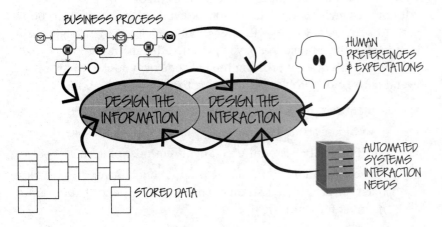

Figure 1.9

Designing the future solution means forming the stored data into useful information and the business process into a convenient and usable interaction. The informational and interactional needs of both the humans and the interfacing automated systems must be accommodated by the design.

Let's see how you could design for Bernie. Suppose the solution of passing a voucher for an e-book download to an offspring has been selected as a hit. (Never mind whether you agree with this solution; let's just suppose.) You saw the storyboard for the safe-to-fail probe in Figure 1.6. Naturally, the design must be aimed at the humans involved, and to be successful, the voucher must be presented in a way that both attracts the loyal customers and motivates them to pass it to a twentysomething offspring.

Each book needs a separate voucher to carry the book's ISBN (International Standard Book Number). We could ask the sales clerk to write a voucher, but that seems pedestrian; it would be time-consuming, and busy sales clerks would be tempted to save time by not offering the voucher.

Consider also when you are formulating your design that there is a transaction between the book buyer and the sales clerk. The sales clerk must ask the book buyer if she wants the voucher for the e-book. Further, the sales clerk must be encouraged to urge the voucher upon those customers who have someone suitable (to Bernie) to pass it to. The clerk is more likely to offer the voucher if it is convenient for him to do so and does not take unnecessary time. In turn, the customer is more likely to accept the voucher if it is presented in an attractive and convenient way.

People reading hardcopy books use bookmarks, so let's make our voucher more appealing to humans and design it as a bookmark.

Once the salesclerk has scanned the barcode on the paper book (this must be done for the checkout to work regardless of the voucher), the cash register captures the ISBN and can look up the link to the e-book version on Bernie's site. If you adapt a commercial ticket printer to print the bookmark, you can easily print a bookmark with Bernie's logo and advertising, along with the QR code for the e-book.

It now becomes a simple matter for the eventual recipient of the bookmark to scan its QR code with her mobile device, which triggers the download of the e-book. We have illustrated this in Figure 1.10.

Consider this design: printing the QR code on a bookmark is solving several parts of the problem at the same time:

- It identifies the book and provides a convenient way to download.
- It would be attractive and easy to do for the twentysomething.
- The bookmark is a semi-permanent reminder of Bernie's books.
- The bookmark is useful to the original book buyer, so she is less likely to give it to a stranger than she is to lend it to a family member for scanning.

THE SALES CLERK SCANS THE BAR CODE ON THE BOOK

THE SALES CLERK ASKS THE BOOK BUYER IF SHE WANTS THE OPTIONAL E-BOOK VERSION TO GIVE TO A FAMILY MEMBER

THE TICKET PRINTER PRINTS A BOOKMARK BEARING THE QR CODE

THE BOOK BUYER'S OFFSPRING SCANS THE QR CODE WHICH TRIGGERS THE E-BOOK DOWNLOAD TO HER DEVICE

Figure 1.10

The design of the business solution that encourages offspring (the twentysomethings segment) to read Bernie's books.

Remember that this part of the solution is encouraging parents (the loyal customers segment) to get their offspring (the twentysomethings segment) to read books from Bernie's.

You probably need to do a little more designing. For example, should the QR code expire after a pre-determined time? Can it be used only once? You must consider all the interfacing automated systems and other design solutions. We shall return to design in Chapter 5, "Designing the Business Solution," but this will do us for the moment.

You might be wondering why this solution was chosen and not Bernie's original suggestion of a free e-book with each paper book purchased. The difference is subtle but important and comes from good business analysis. Automatically giving away a free e-book would probably not work. The majority of the free e-books would go to loyal customers, and they would have no use for it. It would be harder to give a free e-book to someone once it was on the loyal customer's iPad, if indeed they had one.

By giving the e-book to offspring of loyal customers, the e-book becomes valuable. It will be sent to the correct device, it comes with the recommendation of a family member, and the bookmark is something useful and a reminder of Bernie's Books. The design makes this a special event. It's a voluntary event, not just an automatic giveaway—we attach little value to giveaways. Besides, Bernie pays the royalty on only the e-books downloaded via the bookmark and not every e-book given away with the paper book.

Who Designs the Solution?

Designing the solution is best done by one or two people, definitely not by a committee. Design is about the usefulness and the usability of the solution, how it works with the infrastructure of the business, and how the product becomes part of a larger ecosystem. If the design is to be optimal, then it must incorporate a wide range of viewpoints and needs. The designer receives input from any stakeholder with a genuine interest in the end result.

The product owner and other product people are certainly involved. Operations people, usability experts, UX designers, and human behavior people would all provide valuable input. Intended users of the product should be part of the consultation circle, as should other stakeholders. Design should not be unnecessarily rushed but must be limited by available resources and available time.

Opportunities

Part of being agile (small "a" agile) is looking for *opportunities*. You can think of opportunities as the converse of problems. There is nothing to fix, but there is the chance to make something better. These opportunities arise during your normal business analysis activities.

Suppose, for example, that you are talking to some of the customers at Bernie's Books. You talk about what they do when they buy books, their activities, their desires and fears, and you discover that cookbooks feature largely in the conversation. Let's further suppose that several of your interviewees mention how much time it takes to find recipes in their cookbooks once they have decided what they want to cook.

Say, for example, a customer bought a swordfish steak and wants to cook it in an interesting way. The problem is that this customer knows there are swordfish recipes in Bernie's cookbooks, but the customer doesn't usually know where in Bernie's cookbook collection the recipes are.

This apparent problem presents us with an opportunity, as shown in Figure 1.11. Bernie could provide a service that keeps track of the cookbooks sold to each customer. (This can be captured at the cash register.) Then, by analyzing lists of ingredients for the recipes in the books (an automated process), Bernie can provide a service whereby a cookbook owner merely has to mention the main ingredients ("I feel like having duck tonight. Perhaps duck with pomegranates"), and the service will provide him with recipes from the books he owns that mention duck and pomegranate. Perhaps this service could be extended further to include other cookbooks not bought from Bernie's, but we should talk to Bernie about that.

Figure 1.11

An opportunity to provide a search facility for the cookbooks bought from Bernie's.

There's the opportunity: a recipe search facility for cooks. Good idea or not? To find out, go back to the beginning of this chapter and determine if this provides real value to the target customer segment. Is this a problem worth solving, does this proposal solve the customer's real problem, and does it provide value to Bernie's Books?

Write and Manage Stories

In Figure 1.10 we illustrated the design of a business process using a storyboard. Although this is convenient for showing your design to the stakeholders, it might not enable the developers to build the right solution. Here is where you start to write stories.

There is no hard and fast rule about the size of the story, but from the storyboard in Figure 1.10, you could do a lot worse than writing a high-level story for each of the panels.

```
As a sales clerk, I can capture the ISBN of the book
for the cash register so that I can charge the cor-
rect amount for the book and identify the equivalent
e-book.
```

Then continue with this:

> As a sales clerk, I can determine whether the customer wants the optional e-book so that I can enable someone to download the e-book.
>
> As a sales clerk, I can produce a bookmark containing a QR code that identifies the e-book link so that I make the download as convenient as possible and encourage the customer to use it.
>
> As a recipient of the bookmark, I can download the e-book so that I can read it on the technology of my choice.

Stories at this level might have to be sliced to make them fit with the iterations of the developers. But let's put slicing and estimating aside for the moment. This way of handling stories is shown in Figure 1.12.

We urge you to write your stories starting with higher-level ones as in the examples above. It is simple enough to derive the details from this kind of story. It is sometimes very difficult to read anything meaningful from a random collection of low-level stories. Additionally, when written at a higher level, your stories are about business needs, not assumed solutions; they don't talk about buttons and menus or other implementation trifles. This way your stories are more meaningful to the big picture and for ensuring that you are solving the right problem and producing something useful and valuable.

It is here that the product owner coordinates the activity. She is prioritizing the stories, helping the developers to select the story (or stories, or parts of stories) that is to be the target of their next development cycle

Figure 1.12

Stories are a convenient way to communicate discovered information. Each development iteration implements its selected story or stories.

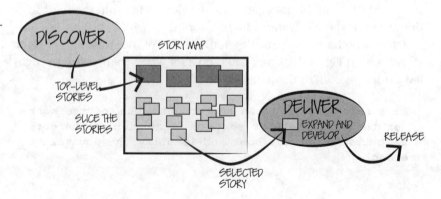

(sprint), and is directing the business analysts as to which parts of the problem need more exploration, and more clarification. Thus, the activities shown in Figure 1.12 are iterative and coordinated, with both the discoverers and the deliverers synchronizing their efforts to deliver the right parts of the solution at the right times.

We discuss stories and development cycles in Chapter 6, "Writing the Right Stories." We also look at *story maps*, which are probably the best way to manage your stories.

Stories are about the real needs, not just assumed solutions.

agile Business Analysis

We have described—quite briefly—the conduct of business analysis in an agile environment. Our intention in doing so is to give you a brief overview of what to expect in the rest of this book. The activities we have just described are laid out in Figure 1.13.

When you look at this figure, note the connections between the activities and the feedback from one activity to another. We would like you to think of these activities not as *transformational* activities, but as *exploratory* activities.

As a business analyst, you are a researcher, or student, of the problem space.

- A *transformational activity* is one that takes its input and uses that to produce an output with the expectation of never seeing it again.

- *Exploratory activities* are about discovering the real needs and the reasons behind the needs.

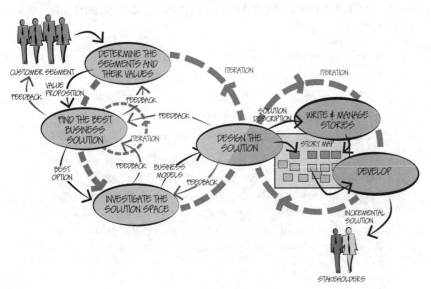

Figure 1.13

The activities of agile business analysis are iterative; the feedback and iteration loops are an important part of the model.

Naturally enough, explorers find things that they did not necessarily expect to find, which in turn means looping back and iterating.

Figure 1.13 shows the activities as separate entities with feedback between them. It is better to think of these activities as *overlapping*. That is, you are never fully engaged in one activity, but switching rapidly between them.

Analysis does not mean paralysis. Analysis is meant to be fast and should run in tandem with implementation. You have prioritized the customer segments, so the first thing you build is likely to be the most valuable. You might consider building a skeleton product as a proof of concept or a way of testing your ideas. However, any product built at this stage should be looked upon as provisional; your analysis might still reveal some better approach, so please don't treat this skeleton as a production system simply because you have written some working software.

It might be fashionable to start building something and rely on a redesign if it turns out to be the wrong thing, but this is little more than hacking, and we have learned that in the end it produces an inferior result. Some issues are hard to compensate for if you get them wrong. Architecture decisions, environment decisions, and UX decisions must be well established and considered immutable if your project is to be a happy one.

The great consumer products you use in everyday life are not hacked together, the great buildings you see and go into do not come about by blind experiment, and the great software that powers your computer was analyzed, designed, and implemented once the team knew it was building the right solution.

Business Analysis for Traditional or Sequential Projects

What's the difference between agile and traditional business analysis? Both are intended to discover the right problem to solve, and both discover, one way or another, the needs that the product has to satisfy.

> ### Traditional or Sequential Business Analysis.
>
> This means that you are assembling a requirements specification before development. There is nothing wrong with doing that, and in many cases, there is a real need to do so—outsourcing, government, medical, and military projects come to mind. We assume that about half the readers of this book work on traditional projects. Almost everything in this book also applies to traditional projects.

The biggest difference is that traditionally a requirements specification is produced before construction starts. This arrangement is shown in Figure 1.14.

The traditional approach is also known as the *waterfall* approach, or *sequential* or *predictive*, and has been much derided over the years. Most of the criticism is wrong; there are valid reasons for using it provided it's used well.

In some organizations, there is a need to have a completed specification. This is tested and certified as being correct before any construction can begin. There may be industry standards that mandate this approach, and certainly if your work involves the military, medical, pharmaceutical, aeronautical, or some government work, you are obliged to produce a complete requirements specification and be able to prove that you have built and tested all the requirements.

If you are outsourcing your construction, most contractors require that you have a complete specification before they start work. Indeed, if you are outsourcing, your specification must be complete, correct, and unambiguous so that the contractor can adequately price and deliver the work to be done to specification.

We have colleagues who serve as expert witnesses on legal cases involving outsourcing. They tell us that the number-one cause of disputes and litigation is poor requirements specifications. Court cases such as disputes over nondelivery of software often have millions of dollars riding on them. We can assure you that doing astute business analysis is far cheaper than lawyers if you are considering outsourcing.

We are suggesting that business analysis can be done iteratively and incrementally and that an agile mindset is crucial for producing the right requirements and specifications.

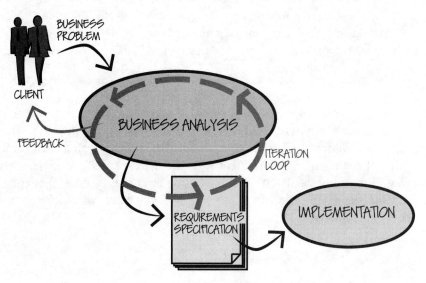

Figure 1.14

The traditional approach to business analysis. The specification is built iteratively and is completed before implementation begins.

In this book, we are suggesting that analysis can be done iteratively and incrementally and that an agile mind-set is crucial for producing the right requirements and specifications. The techniques we talk about are applicable regardless of whether you work in an agile or a traditional organization.

We have more to say about this in Chapter 7. However, let us leave this for the moment by saying that the actual business analysis—that is, the study of the business problem and finding its optimal solution—is done much the same way regardless of whether you are using agile or traditional implementation.

The Changing Emphasis of Business Analysis

The title *business analyst* is relatively recent, dating back a mere decade or so at the time of writing. During that time, the role has evolved considerably, and so have the tasks of business analysis. This evolution has become more dramatic and far reaching as organizations have come to understand the value of business analysis and have begun to invest in it.

> ### Business Analyst, or Business Analyst Practitioner.
>
> This term should be interpreted to mean anyone doing the analysis regardless of their job title. Our experience has been that business analysis is not the sole province of business analysts but is undertaken to various degrees by product owners, business stakeholders, agile team members, sometimes developers, and almost anyone in the organization who is studying the work with a view to improving it.

In the beginning, business analysts were little more than stenographers, faithfully writing down (and believing) everything the users said they wanted and then equally faithfully turning that into some form of requirements document that was fed to the developers. This way of working persisted until it became abundantly clear that turning *statements of want* into *statements of requirements* was more or less counterproductive.

In the beginning, business analysts were stenographers.

Business analysts learned that what people were asking for was not always what they needed. They learned that assumed solutions were not always the right ones. They learned to challenge assumptions and the conventional wisdom. They learned that discovering the right problem to solve and designing the best solution was the fastest way to get the right result.

Business analysts today are often found not in the IT department where they have traditionally lived, but attached to the business divisions. It's a healthy trend. However, this sometimes leads to a silo mentality, where the business analyst tends to ignore things outside his own business division.

Even healthier are the business analysts who operate independently from both the business and IT. These fortunate people—and at the time of writing, these few people—can operate far more effectively because their personal objectives are not aligned with any department, but with the organization as a whole. These business analysts move from their resource pool to become part of a project team. They must ensure that they establish a meaningful working relationship with the team and with the business stakeholders to ensure that they (the analysts) are seen as family members and not remote outsiders.

The business analyst's goal is simple: to craft the most effective business processes and to guide projects that produce solutions that are precisely what the organization needs. Moreover, the solutions are correctly aligned with organizational goals.

By being independent of any department, the business analyst is unencumbered by the status quo, does not have a vested interest in existing solutions, and is not swayed by existing processes and procedures or by departmental or political boundaries. In short, the business analyst is both detached from the people who run the processes and systems and yet involved in how and why they exist and what can be done to make them better.

The lesson we can take from the evolution of the business analyst is clear and applies to all members of an agile team. The product owner is expected to represent the business and the customer, and therefore should possess business analysis skills. It is important that the product owner not let the product part of the role name overcome the need to be looking toward the real business problem. Agile team members need analytical skills for both the pure analytical activities and for ensuring that, during the development cycles, the correct requirements are derived from the stories.

Business analysis skills should be present in several members of the team, regardless of the names of their roles.

None of the Agile methods prescribe the role of business analyst, yet all of them, one way or another, acknowledge the need for business analysis. However, it is crucial that regardless of their job titles, you should ensure that several members of the team have business analysis skills. It is these skills that ensure you are always solving the right problem.

So now that we have taken you on a brief tour of business analysis agility and told you what meanings we have attached to some words, we invite you to explore the remainder of this book. We hope you enjoy it.

Do You Know What Your Customers Value?

2

• The problem versus the solution • Customer segments
• Priorities • Value propositions
• Talking to the customers • Impact of the solution
• The moving target

Here's the situation: You work for Gotham Office Furniture, which has been in existence for several years. It sells office furniture and fittings, a lot of it via the web. It also has showrooms in most of the major cities.

Several of the top managers at Gotham have noticed the growing trend of people to work from home. Some people work from home because their company has agreed that they need not be in the office for some or all of the week. Others run their own business from home. And sometimes it is simply convenient to have an office in the home for those office-like tasks that families have.

The Gotham managers see the trend for working from home as an opportunity to sell home-office furniture and fittings. In some cases, this is as simple as selling a desk. In others (and this could be the major part of the business), there is an opportunity to fit out spare spaces around the home: an attic, an area beneath the stairs, a garage, an unneeded bedroom, and so on. Gotham believes that most people need help envisioning space and what they can do with it and would welcome a service that could provide this planning. A cleverly fitted home office could be small yet still effective (see Figure 2.1).

Gotham has set up a new subsidiary company, *HomeSpace*, and you have been assigned to work for them. Your management wants you to start work and find the solutions needed to support this business.

You are required to use any of the existing Gotham systems either as they stand or modified for your purposes. The web selling site would be reusable, as would some of the back-office stuff.

Figure 2.1

HomeSpace offers custom home offices. These range from selling a desk and a chair to fitting out a spare space at home.

(Credit: Denis Ismagilov/123RF)

So, what do you do? Clone the Gotham website and replace the office furniture with home-office stuff? Put up some photos of successful home conversions of spaces previously thought unusable?

Or, before you commit too many resources, do you ensure that this is a worthwhile project?

Let's assume that you answered "yes" to the last question. We shall proceed to look at the intended beneficiaries of your project.

Problem Versus Solution

Solutions are valuable only if they solve the right problem. That much is obvious. So why do so many development efforts rush into a solution without first considering the problem the solution is meant to solve? Probably because solutions are easier than problems.

Consider this. You are building your solution for an organization or group of people. For simplicity's sake, let's just say you are building for customers. These customers exist in an ecosystem that changes from time to time. When the ecosystem changes, so must the systems, products, or services the customers use. Sometimes the change to the ecosystem is forced by external factors—changes to the law, changes to technology, changes in the marketplace—and sometimes by changes in the behavior, or the demographics, of the customers.

When the ecosystem changes, so must the systems, products, or services the customers use.

Each time the ecosystem changes, you must rework your solutions so that they fit with the new state of the ecosystem. For example, the customers of Gotham Office Furniture are now behaving differently. Some of them are working in their homes rather than in an office. To restore fit with the ecosystem, Gotham must adapt its systems and products to accommodate this new behavior.

The problem exists in the ecosystem. It's what the home workers are doing, how they see their needs, their aspirations, and what they want but don't yet know it. It is the organization's task to understand the ecosystem and its problems and provide a suitable solution—a solution that restores the correct fit between the organization and its ecosystem.

So blindly rushing into a solution—such as building a website—is probably not going to be productive. The reason is simple: to be an effective solution, it must solve the right problem.

And if you think at the beginning of the project that you know what the problem really is, you're probably mistaken. Problems have a way of disguising themselves, hiding under assumptions, camouflaging themselves with proposed solutions, and secreting themselves. It needs some determined analytical thinking to wipe away the shroud of secrecy and bring the real problem, kicking and screaming, into the sunlight.

Problems have a way of disguising themselves.

Any solution you deliver must provide value to a *customer segment*. These are people either in the ecosystem interacting with the organization or inside the organization interacting with the ecosystem (see Figure 2.2). We can put them into segments because they have common characteristics that make them a unique group.

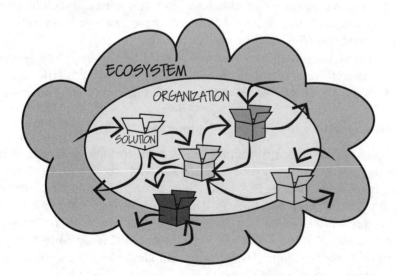

Figure 2.2

An organization's solutions interact with each other and the ecosystem. If the ecosystem changes, solutions have to be adjusted to match the new reality.

For our purposes here, *customer segment* should also be taken to mean *user segment*. We prefer to call them *customers* because focusing on pleasing a customer with specific characteristics expands your thinking more than pleasing a generalized user.

Identify the Customer Segments

The task is to identify the customer segments and discover what it is that they value. This might sound simple, but it is more than guessing. To state the obvious, you are building a product that will succeed only if it brings value to your customers. Therefore, you must be certain of your customers and what it is they need.

Let's start with a reality check: we are talking about people. These are live flesh and blood people—people with a pulse and a brain. Their brain is just like yours, and just like you, these people have needs, wants, and fears, and they are trying to get things done. Like you, they will respond positively if you provide what they need. If you present a solution that resonates—it solves a problem, it gives them an advantage, it opens an opportunity—then the customers in the segment will respond positively. They will buy what you are offering or will use it willingly, will be more productive, will do their work more effectively, or will react in some other beneficial way.

Continuing with the reality check: someone in your organization has already told you the segments and values. Treat this information warily. People sometimes tell you about segments and needs that fit with what they want to supply or are able to supply. You must also consider that customers in the ecosystem might well have changed their behavior from the expected.

Customer segments and their needs must be seen from the demand side: the customers' point of view. The reality is that most of the customers' values are discovered when you are talking to the actual customers.

> 66 *Who are we designing for?* 99
>
> —Andrew Kendall, transport systems designer

How to Identify the Customer Segments

We suggest you start with your best guess at the customer segments, or the segments as identified by your organization. Find people who belong to the segments, and talk to them. You are looking for insights into their problems and what they need, and these insights come only from real people.

A customer segment is a collection of people who share the same need. Some of these needs are not apparent at the beginning, so you will probably find yourself reforming your ideas about the segments and their needs as you study them.

> *A customer segment is a collection of people who share the same need.*

People don't, and can't, always tell you what they need. Sometimes they simply don't know or don't understand what they need. Other times we don't realize what we need until we see it. And then other times someone's need is not apparent until you spend time with them talking in some depth.

The need you are looking for is what your customer wants to achieve. Don't look for tasks—a need is not what people do, but the outcome of what they do or why they do it. My task might be to buy a ticket, but my need is to travel legally. My task might be to generate a business intelligence report, but my need is to understand sales trends of my consumer products.

Sometimes people don't know what they need. People ask for what they know they can have or what they have seen. People do not ask for things unless they think it is possible. However, some of the most valuable solutions we have are those that nobody asked for but once produced created a need for them. Social media, smartphones, ride sharing, self-driving cars, mobile banking, text messaging, and so on are examples of solutions creating needs. In this case, you must assess whether a customer segment would have a need for your proposed solution if you delivered it.

Look for needs and outcomes, not tasks.

You might find that segments decompose themselves when you look into them. Despite a shared need, some customers' demographics might mean that you should consider them as a separate segment, as most likely you would develop a separate, or modified, solution to accommodate them. For example, if you hark back to Bernie's Books in the previous chapter and the twentysomethings segment, you might consider that twentysomethings who use mobile devices are a separate segment to those who prefer paper books and want to be in the bookstore. Similarly, socioeconomic factors, attitudes, cultural differences, or the jobs they are doing might bring about a divided segment.

Be patient when your first ideas for customer segments start to fragment and reveal other segments.

At the moment, you are looking at the customer segments and their values. These are qualitative values, such as, "I value being kept up to date on the status of my flight." Of course, this has to have some value to the sponsor providing this service, so we shall soon talk about quantitative values for the customer segments.

When you find your customer segments, give them a name—preferably an informative one that indicates them and their need. "Freshman enrollees" is more useful than "Students." "High net worth investors" is a better segment name than "Rich people."

HomeSpace

Let's go back to HomeSpace and consider its customer segments and their needs. Starting with the obvious, the segments would be people running their business from home; employees who work from home one or more days per week; and casual customers who are not working but want some office space in their home. We can start with those, and as we look more closely at their needs, other segments might emerge.

If we ask a casual customer what she wants to do, the answer is probably along the lines of this:

> "Not much. I need somewhere to set up my laptop, pay a few bills online, send a few emails, organize my recipe collection, gather information for the article I'm writing, and if I get a little time, write my blog."

Let's call this segment the *laptopper*. This person needs a simple setup, but not just the kitchen table. Given the stated tasks, there is probably a need for a bookshelf or a small amount of storage, and preferably a workspace that is a little out of the way of the normal household traffic. Think about what the laptopper is doing, what kind of experience she wants to have when he is working, and what she needs to have the best experience.

Next, we look at the people who work from home. Their needs are an isolated or quiet space, enough comfort and space to be able to spend the entire day without feeling claustrophobic, and probably the need to have a printer and possibly other equipment within a convenient distance. They need a way of communicating work products between themselves and their company's office.

Let's call this segment the *nine-to-fivers*. This segment is probably prepared to pay a little more for a more elaborate solution, but we should allow for people on different budgets within the segment.

There may be a need to subdivide this segment, depending upon people's willingness to self-select their office components or whether they want HomeSpace to do it for them.

Another segment is the people who run their own business out of their homes. We'll call this one *homebusiness*. The homebusiness segment needs a more complete solution, space, and storage for work-related items, and sometimes housing for special equipment used for the particular business being conducted by the homebusiness worker. Some of the homebusiness segment will be start-ups and need economical solutions; others will be better established and have more generous budgets.

When you talk to real customers, you'll discover another customer segment; let's call this one *grandfathers*. Grandfathers—they might actually be grandmothers—are retired people, and they need to feel good about themselves. Although they are retired, they want to spend time doing something relevant, surrounded by an office-like environment, a desk, lamps, bookshelves, and so on. The need is not so much concerned with functionality as it is to provide a warm, den-like appearance where they can spend a great deal of time reading and sending off the occasional letter. This might be a lucrative customer segment.

You should also consider the *infrastructure* segment. These are people who work for HomeSpace and are needed to support the external customers. (You might prefer to think of this segment as internal customers or users.) It doesn't matter *how* you think of them, provided you think of them.

The designer at HomeSpace is the obvious infrastructure segment. This is made up of the people who are designing the conversions and fitting the furniture into the home office. Your project must provide value to this internal customer segment; it is likely to be key to the success of the venture. Value to this infrastructure segment is providing convenient and effective tools for them to do their jobs.

(Credit: Cathy Yeulet/123RF)

Other Stakeholders

There might be other customer segments than the ones already identified, but you can be confident that by now you have the major ones. It is better to move on with what you have rather than delay delivering a solution to the most important segments.

If you are working on an internal project—one to be deployed within your own organization or that of your client—the principle remains the same. Form your customer segments according to the needs of the people, sometimes by what they do, where they do it, or by whatever segmenting theme you find is appropriate for finding a unique set of needs. Whether they are internal or external customers, you still need to know who they are, what they value, and what they need if you are to deliver a worthwhile solution.

Get together with your customer segments; talking to them brings you closer to your target audience. Your audience must feel that your solution is aimed specifically at them and that it is solving their problem.

Prioritize the Customer Segments

Your customer segments are not all equally valuable to your organization, so do not treat them equally. Let's say, for example, that HomeSpace management and research tell you that the homebusiness segment is projected to contribute about 45% of expected revenue. Naturally enough, you pay a lot of attention to this segment. You probably develop the earliest releases for this segment, you put more effort into design and testing for this segment, and your discovery is weighted toward this segment that provides more value to your organization.

Figure 2.3 shows the segments and their expected contribution to profit. This is a fairly clear indication of priority. The infrastructure segment is not shown on this diagram because these people do not contribute directly to profit, and their priority depends on the part they play when you look at solutions for each of the segments.

The laptoppers segment is judged to be about 5% of expected revenue, and that's about how much attention this group should receive. The grandfathers, on the other hand, must be given a higher ranking because there is a lot of potential value in that segment.

We are talking about prioritizing by expected contribution to profit. You might also think about the number of customers in the segment, the potential for growth of the segment, the desire to attract a segment, or any other value that a segment could bring. If you feel that there is a segment whose exploration would almost certainly reveal valuable discovery knowledge—knowledge that would benefit the remainder of discovery—then it should move higher on your priority ladder.

Figure 2.3

The customer segments for HomeSpace. The size of each segment indicates the expected contribution to profit, or value of the segment, which plays a large part in prioritizing the segments.

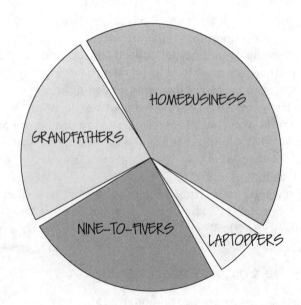

You might also consider using risk as part of your prioritization criteria. If a segment is associated with a high risk—you are uncertain if you can build a solution for it—think about giving the segment a high priority from the point of view of working on it early. If you are going to fail to deliver a solution, it is preferable to fail early.

Although the infrastructure segment doesn't directly bring revenue into the company, it is quite important to the success of the venture, so it should receive a relatively high priority ranking. It might seem strange to give an internal segment a high priority, but a lot of the homebusiness revenue is a result of the company's infrastructure, so you must ensure that the internal workers—the designers, logistics, web sales team—have enough help from your solution for them to do their work.

Prioritizing the customer segments is a joint effort involving the product owner, marketing (if appropriate), and other stakeholders. Prioritize as early as possible because doing so reminds the team of the relative worth of the work they are doing. It is always good to get early wins; demonstrably valuable early wins are even better.

If your project is an entirely in-house affair, you will find that some user groups are more important to the organization than others and receive a higher priority.

You should consider progressing with only your highest priority customer segment; the others can be picked up later. There is not a lot of point in proceeding with too many customer segments because that usually results in too many potential solutions to be evaluated, which will build up a backlog of items to deliver and most likely delay delivering product to the more valuable segments.

Let's say you have a list of customer segments and you have prioritized them. Now you need to know what each customer segment values.

Value Propositions

Value is what your solution delivers to your customer segments. The reason for looking closely at the customer segments is, simply and obviously, that value is only valuable if your solution solves a problem that the segment wants you to solve. A *value proposition* describes the value the customer receives when you solve his problem.

A value proposition describes the value the customer receives when you solve his problem.

For example, your customer is an online retailer who tells you his problem is that he is losing business to competitors because of slow fulfilment. The value proposition would say that he receives value when 95% of orders are delivered the next business day after the order is placed. Your solution must contrive a way to meet the next-day target if it is to be valuable to the customer.

Write a separate value proposition for each customer segment—each has a different need and a different problem. You can write the proposition any way you like, but we have found a variation on the story format to be as good as any.

```
As a [customer segment]

I receive value when [outcome for the customer]
```

This outcome—might be that a business condition is met:

```
As a delivery service to distribution centers

I receive value when all my deliveries are completed
within 15 minutes of the scheduled time.
```

or some new capability is provided:

```
As a subscriber to a music streaming service

I receive value when my family can share the music.
```

or some facility is provided:

```
As a householder

I receive value when I can correctly, quickly, and
conveniently install my security system.
```

Note that the value propositions are technologically agnostic. You are describing an outcome, not how something is to be done.

Additionally, the value must be real, not imagined, assumed, or over-optimistically wished for. As an example of assumed value, a Dutch initiative, Standard Business Reporting, was adopted by the Australian Tax Office. The intention of the system is to allow businesses to report their financial information in any way that is convenient to the individual business.

This seems like a good idea because it allows businesses to conduct their financial affairs any way they choose and not have to convert the information when it comes time to meet their statutory reporting obligations. However, after spending one billion dollars, the Tax Office were chagrined to discover that the take-up rate from businesses was a mere 2–3%.

The failure? Not understanding that the proposed reporting system held little or no value for the customer segment it was aimed at.

Talking to the Customers

As well-meaning as we might want to be, we cannot guess what the customer values. We have to talk with the customers and observe what they are doing. The reason is simply that people—and we're talking about the people in the customer segment—are not always able to express what it is they need and what they are wanting to do. People can be misleading—they say one thing but do something else. Sometimes they simply don't know what it is they value. You have to extract it.

We are not suggesting that you beat it out of them (as tempting as that might sound) but interview them long enough to discover their real needs and ambitions. Some teams use workshops to take their customers through the work they would do with a proposed solution. This is fine, but one must be careful to ensure that the team's enthusiasm for the proposed solution does not override the objectivity and skew the results. If it is possible to interview and observe at the customers' workplaces, do so. You are more likely to get an insightful result.

The product people—product owner, product manager, program manager and the like—are responsible for knowing what the customers value. In some cases, they will have already done their homework and will be able to provide you (a business analyst or a team member) with accurate information about the customers. In other cases, you will work with the product people to interview and observe the customers.

Whatever you do, don't guess. Understanding the customers' real needs and values is far too critical—get it wrong, and your solution is doomed. We do not mean to sound unduly alarmist, but consider those thousands of projects that deliver the wrong results.

Back at HomeSpace, the homebusiness customer segment has the highest priority, so it is appropriate to begin by interviewing this group and uncovering what these people find valuable. Let's say that you and your product people interview enough people in this category to learn that the homebusiness worker does not want to work on the kitchen table. People in this segment are running a business from home, and many have set aside part of their house or apartment for their office. Interviews uncover that they are serious people and want a business-like feeling for their office space. They also tell you that this is their home; they don't want the boring, low-cost office furniture and mass-produced fittings you find in the offices of many large organizations.

While this segment wants an ergonomic office, the people in the segment might not be good at designing and making the best use of space, or skilled at selecting the most comfortable, workable, and cost-effective furniture.

From interviewing the segment, you get this value proposition:

`As a homebusiness`

`I receive value when I have an office in my home that makes best use of space, makes me more efficient, and is a better, more complete design than I could do myself or find elsewhere.`

We are using the first person here even though a customer segment might be hundreds of people or different organizations. It is more connected and personal this way; it stresses what we must do to satisfy a human.

The "complete design" from the above proposition must provide features that give the worker privacy and isolation from household noises. It's hard to concentrate when a vacuum cleaner is running, your daughter or girlfriend is using the hair dryer, your husband is watching sports on TV, or you're looking at a pile of dirty clothes waiting to be washed.

You talk to some people in another segment, and you get this value proposition:

`As a laptopper`

`I receive value when I have an inexpensive workspace that provides me with a comfortable place to work and a fast Internet connection.`

Value can be gained in many ways. Keep in mind that simply delivering software, or any other solution, does not mean you are delivering value. Value is delivered when your solution enables your customer to do something useful or pleasurable that he could not do before.

A customer segment might, for example, be able to achieve certain levels of trading, sell goods and take orders from anywhere on the planet without leaving home, or process a mortgage application in 15 minutes when it took 2 days before.

You can only deliver value if you know what your customers value.

Value comes in many forms, but it must be a real value. If it is real, it is also measurable. In the next chapter, we look at measuring when we talk about safe-to-fail probes. In the meantime, you must ensure that the value to be delivered is sufficient for the organization to warrant the development of your solution and that enough value can be delivered to make the project worthwhile.

The value proposition for the homebusiness customer segment is not exactly easy to measure. However, a combination of questions would tell you if you have delivered the required value. For example:

- How satisfied are you that you have the best use of space?
- Is it quiet enough for you to work effectively?
- Could it have been better designed by yourself or some other company?
- Would you recommend your installation to other people?
- Do you enjoy working in it?
- Is there anything significant you want to change?

There is no realistic quantification for this kind of value proposition—it's not like "reduce the cost per unit by 5%," but if there are enough subjective questions, those serve to make the value measurable.

What Impact Will Your Solution Have?

Another way of thinking about delivering value is to consider the *impact* that your solution will have. Will it change the behavior of the intended audience for the better? For example,

- Will it make the audience spend more money with your organization?
- Will it enable the dispatchers to manipulate their fleet of trucks more effectively?
- Will it convince people to stream music from your source rather than from another's?
- Will it entice policy holders to renew their insurance early?
- Will it alter someone's behavior in a way that is valuable to your organization?

Alternatively, will the solution enable your audience to do something that was previously not possible? Will it, for example, enable householders to securely accept deliveries when they are not at home? Or cause deliveries to be made only when they are at home?

Without an impact, the solution is unlikely to deliver much value. Think about these topics when you consider the impact:

- **Marketing**—Will the solution be more attractive to customers or make them more likely to buy it?
- **Compliance**—Will the solution comply with a new or changed law?
- **Problem solving**—Will your solution solve a business problem for your customer?
- **Behavior**—Will the product make your customers behave in some beneficial (to your organization) way?
- **Improvement**—Will the solution make a business process cheaper, faster, or more efficient?

Whatever the impact, it must exist, it must be beneficial, and preferably, it should be measurable. You should be able to look at your value proposition and assess the impact it has on the target audience. For example:

```
As a small bar

I receive value when I have minimal liquor inventory
and can still satisfy all demands.
```

The impact here is that it solves a problem for the small bar customer segment. This segment cannot afford to have much money tied up in inventory but knows how unsatisfactory it is to regular patrons if they cannot have their favorite tipple. Any solution that has this impact is likely to entice small bar owners to sign up for your service.

You should also assess whether your impact could be detrimental. For example, in Australia, cane toads were introduced as a solution to control cane beetles, a pest that blighted sugar cane production in the north of the country. The detrimental impact came when the cane toads eliminated the beetles and then began to spread out over other parts of the country looking for other sources of food. Cane toads are prolific breeders that are highly toxic to other animals. Having no predators, they themselves have become a pest with seemingly no solution.

On the other hand, there can be unintended beneficial impacts. Aspirin, originally produced as a painkiller, also works as a blood thinner. Millions of people take a daily aspirin to lessen the chance of stroke or heart attack. This is quite a long way from helping with a headache.

It is worth spending some time exploring the intended and unintended impacts of the value you propose to deliver.

Business Value

Of course, providing value to your customer segments is one thing; making sure that your organization receives value is just as important. Let's now look at this from the point of view of your employer, the Home-Space organization.

The organization wants to make a profit; that's obvious. It will only make a profit when its customer segments buy goods and services from it. These goods and services must provide a value that they, the customer segments, want and value. It also requires that HomeSpace be able to supply their goods and services at a cost that yields a profit.

For example, suppose your solution can persuade the nine-to-fivers to buy an office from HomeSpace. You now ask if there are enough nine-to-fivers, with enough spending power, to make it worthwhile pursuing them. Is the cost of providing the office—not just the financial cost, but the disruption cost and the risk—justified by the outcome?

The laptoppers are expected to contribute about 5% of revenue. How much can you spend on solutions for them? Is there a business case for proceeding with this segment?

There are some things that are now possibly out of your (as a project team member's) control. Selling a desk profitably means being able to buy it from the manufacturer at a price that the customer segment is happy to pay after your margin is added. Finding a cost-effective supplier and haggling over prices is not something that normally falls into your remit, but it might mean that part of your eventual solution must provide functionality to support this activity.

Business value is a product of the potential gain tempered by the odds of success and the cost of producing that gain. Keep in mind that the odds of success are not 100% despite us wishing them to be so.

To summarize, the value propositions for each of the customer segments should align with the sponsor's business goals; the business value must make it worthwhile to proceed with the project.

Is It Risky to Deliver the Value?

All worthwhile projects contain an element of risk. As our partners, Tom DeMarco and Tim Lister, said, "If there is no risk, the project is not worth doing." At this early stage, it is well to take a quick look at risk. Traditionally, risk analysis has not been part of the business analyst's charter, but because so much of the information needed to assess risk is now present, it is practical if you have a quick look at the risks and raise alerts if any risk appears to be potentially crippling.

The two most common risks in software development are the risk of not building the right solution and the risk of insufficient budget or time.

We can significantly reduce the risk of building the wrong solution by using safe-to-fail probes and short discovery-delivery cycles, and by understanding our customers—what they value, what will solve their problem, and whether they want us to solve it.

The risk of insufficient budget can be addressed by careful prioritization—don't waste resources on stuff nobody wants—and partitioning the problem and solution into slices small enough to estimate accurately. Rapid, incremental delivery of small slices of the solution also reduces risk.

Let's return to HomeSpace and look at its risks. A serious risk is that people are not willing to pay for custom-fitted office space in their homes. There is also the risk that where it is necessary to measure a space prior to designing custom fittings, the measurements will not be accurate, resulting in incorrect installation. (This risk is there because HomeSpace installers cannot get access to measure, or the customer does the measuring incorrectly.)

Note that you are not yet attempting to overcome these risks, but they must be borne in mind when you are designing a solution.

Team members are the people most likely to understand the risks of a project. They are also the people most likely to first realize that a risk is about to become a problem. Risk management is largely a collaborative effort between the product owner, the team members, the business analyst, and the project manager.

The Moving Target

Many development projects act as if they are aiming at a fixed target. The assumption is that when the solution is delivered, it will fit perfectly into the intended environment. However, that environment has probably changed between the beginning and the end of the project.

Things change. Technology is constantly advancing and bringing with it new possibilities, some of which could be incorporated into your solution. Laws change frequently. New regulations mean changes to solutions, regardless of whether the solutions are years old or still under development. Businesses change as new opportunities and new markets appear. People change. No matter how inconvenient to our plans, our solutions must adapt to fit the changing reality.

Change is inevitable. It is one of the few things that we know—with absolute certainty—will happen. And if we know with certainty that change will happen, it defies logic to begin projects without contingency built into the project plans.

Change is one of the few things we can rely on.

You do not know the extent of the changes that will be needed before the end of your project, but there is enough evidence to say that for projects longer than a few months, you can count on about 2% of your business requirements changing each month. For longer projects, this implies that a significant portion of your development will be discarded because one change or another has made it redundant.

When you build contingency into your plan, you are ready and able to adopt changes as they appear. You should also be constantly looking over your shoulder to see if the ground you have already trodden on has changed, and be prepared to revisit it. By delivering your solution in small increments and constantly reprioritizing, you should reduce waste caused by change. Your budget should always contain a contingency for change; if you don't spend all of it, it's a bonus.

When we are talking about change, we do not mean changes that are necessitated by building the wrong product, either partially or wholly, and then correcting it. That's not change; that's poor business analysis.

Wrong Until Right

Our colleague Mike Russel writes about projects being *wrong until right.* Mike's analogy is the archer who aims at the target and releases his arrow when he is satisfied that he is aiming dead center. At that moment, he is right. However, if the target moves, the arrow misses and the archer is wrong.

The alternative approach is the heat-seeking missile that constantly monitors the moving target and adjusts its trajectory to suit so that it is right at the moment of impact.

So far you have determined the customer segments and what they value. This information was right at the time you gathered it, but the customer segments and their problems are moving targets. This is illustrated in Figure 2.4.

Anyone doing agile business analysis must constantly monitor the customer segments for signs of the target shifting.

Anyone doing agile business analysis must constantly monitor the customer segments for signs of the target shifting. If it is a significant shift, you must revisit the segments and their value propositions. This is undoubtedly irksome, but nevertheless necessary if your project is to deliver the right solution.

Figure 2.4

Your eventual solution solves the customer segment's problem and thereby delivers value. However, if the segment changes, what they value changes, or their problem changes, your solution must also change.

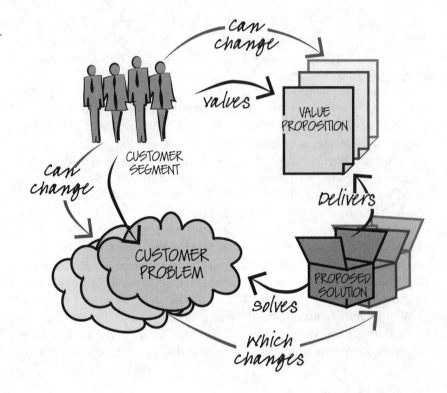

In the next chapter, we talk about safe-to-fail probes where you test your hypotheses for solutions. It is vital that part of each test is to assess whether this solves the problem and to revisit the problem and assess whether it has changed. As you incrementally deliver your solution, it is also vital that you check whether the problem is changing under you.

You will also find that you discover things other than changes that cause you to loop back to previous activities and adjust the findings.

This suggests very strongly that prioritization and iteration are necessary. The core activities of the business should be implemented as early as possible. The remainder of the solution is developed iteratively in small increments such that feedback from each iteration is available to influence upstream activities.

Note the feedback arrows in Figure 2.5. These are here to suggest that as each activity learns more about the problem and the solution, it feeds back to the previous ones. And sometimes the feedback goes back more than a single activity.

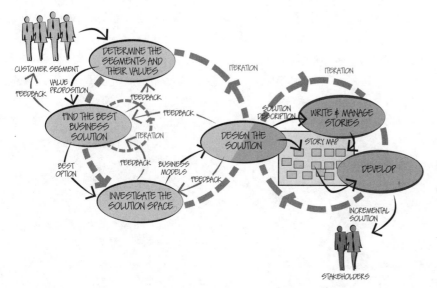

Figure 2.5

The agile business
analysis activities.
Each of the activities
is iterative, and also
provides feedback to
previous activities.
Constant monitoring
is necessary so
that changes are
incorporated as rapidly
as possible.

Summary

By now you know the customers who are the target for your solution.
You have divided them into segments and determined what each of the
segments values. The value propositions point you at the problem to
solve and what your solution must do to solve the problem and deliver
the value.

Generally, we are pretty good at solving problems. Unfortunately, we
are less good at solving the *right* problem. Let's look at how we find the
right problem in the next chapter.

Are You Solving the Right Problem?

3

• The customer's needs • The essence of the problem
• Disguised problems • The real scope of the problem
• How might we solve this problem? • Generating solutions
• Safe-to-fail probes • Choosing the best option

The problem is usually the problem. In other words, the problem solvers don't have enough understanding of the problem to deliver the right solution. Insufficient information is made available, the problem is incorrectly or badly defined, or the real problem is ignored and instead, an assumed solution is proposed. Naturally enough, it is impossible to deliver the correct solution with any of the above scenarios. Here, we look at how you discover the right problem and ensure that you deliver the correct solution.

> 66 *We fail far more often because we solve the wrong problem, than because we deliver the wrong solution to the right problem.* 99
>
> —Russell Ackoff, Professor of Systems Sciences and Management Science, Wharton School, University of Pennsylvania

The Problem

The problem normally arises because of some change in the ecosystem. It means something has happened that is beyond the control of your client—a change to the law, technology, customer trends, and so on—that requires a change to one or more of the client's solutions. You can think of the problem as a disruption to existing solutions, and your solution must restore the equilibrium between the solutions and the ecosystem.

However the word *problem* may also mean any combination or variation of the following:

- A desirable business condition to be met
- A significant change to the technology that your customer's solutions use, or could use, that necessitates some product development or redevelopment

- An opportunity or a new idea that your client can take advantage of
- A malfunction that necessitates some development actions

For the sake of simplicity, let's say that *problem* means any of the above. When we talk about "solving the problem," we also mean taking advantage of the opportunity, or adapting to the change. That it is a problem does not necessarily mean that something is wrong; it's just something for which you will find a solution.

> ## Customer problem.
>
> This is a misfit or malfunction that, if solved, provides value to the customer segment. The problem might be a badly functioning business process, a desired change, or an opportunity.

Are You Solving the Right Problem?

Figure 3.1 shows the components that we are dealing with. However, you must always keep in mind that the customer's description of the problem, and the value the customer places on its being solved, might not yet be correct.

Figure 3.1

The situation: the customer segment has a problem, and it puts a value on this problem being solved. Your solution must solve the problem and, by so doing, deliver the value.

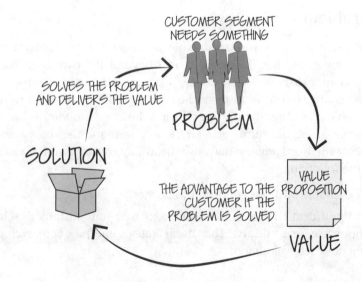

We *think* we know what the problem is, but we are keeping an open mind to the possibility of its changing as it becomes clearer.

What can go wrong? Plenty.

- What if you have misidentified the customer segment?
- What if there are subsegments, each of which has a slightly different problem?
- What if the value stated is indeed valuable, but there is something even more valuable?
- What if initially the segment has indicated something is valuable, but there is little or no value to your organization?
- What if there is a mismatch between the problem and the customer segment?
- What if the segment needs something more than the needs already stated?
- What if the need you based your value on is not the most important need?
- What if solving the problem has inadequate benefit for the customer or your organization?
- What if solving this problem will result in a vanity product, when more fundamental needs (to do with the customer's continued wellbeing) are ignored?
- What if solving this problem is contrary to your organization's strategic direction?

"Am I solving the right problem?" is a simple enough question and one that, surprisingly, is not asked nearly enough.

Clearly, we need to spend a little time looking closely at the problem. Solving the wrong problem is of no use to anyone.

It might take a little effort to find the right problem, but consider the alternative. Every year, the results of tens of thousands of software projects, and countless more product and service development efforts, are abandoned because they failed to solve the right problem. It is hard to imagine teams deliberately building something nobody has any use for. We can only conclude that the teams failed to discover the right problem to solve.

We must also ask whether we are heading in the right direction. If your customer's business is losing sales, building a point of sale system is not going to solve the problem. A business intelligence system is not going to help much if you cannot fulfill your customers' orders. Sadly, we see this kind of thing all the time—projects that set out to build solutions that will do little or nothing to alleviate the real problem and do not provide anything of real value.

Maslow's Hierarchy of Needs

As bizarre as it might seem, you might consider Maslow's hierarchy of human needs. In case you need a refresher on Maslow, please look at Figure 3.2, while we describe how his hierarchy of human needs also applies to organizations.

The thing to note about Maslow's hierarchy is that it is necessary for a human to attain one level of need before being able to move up to the next level. For example, you are not concerned about a feeling of belonging to a community if you are being shot at or bombed. Similarly, personal safety is not of great concern if you're starving or without water.

Many companies have learned Maslow the hard way.

If we apply this hierarchy of needs to organizations, we see that at the bottom level, the organization's need is for some form of revenue (organizational food) if it is to survive. Similarly, an organization cannot expect to achieve respect from peer organizations if its products are not being loved by the market. Nor would producing a well-loved product work if the logistics, product, and distribution are not firmly in place.

Consider the problem that your project intends to solve and ask where in the organizational hierarchy it fits. Keep in mind that you must attain one level before moving upward to the next. Is your project attempting to improve security when you have no (or incomplete) infrastructure or revenue to protect? Is your project intending to produce a vanity product aimed at one of the higher levels when the organization has not yet attained the basic low levels? If so, you're not solving the right problem.

The Outcome of Solving the Problem

There is a need to step back and understand the needed outcome before you start construction. This is not a plea to return to the big upfront specification, but a suggestion that without knowing the required outcome, without understanding the real needs of the customer, your project is likely to flounder. We have seen that building software and testing

Figure 3.2

Maslow's hierarchy of human needs and how it applies to organizations.

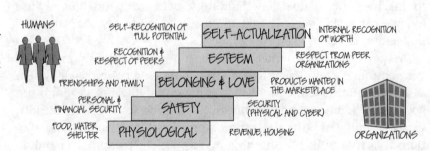

it on its users can be counterproductive. Much of the time, individual users are not in a position to assess the outcome for their organization as a whole. They can see that the software does something they asked for, but the chances are that they have asked for the wrong thing, or there is a better solution than the one they asked for.

However, if you have correctly understood the customers' needs and know the right problem to solve, you will produce a better solution and do it more efficiently. Until you solve the right problem, your project remains unfinished.

The Customer's Needs

Talking about needs is another way of talking about the customer's problem. But it's worth doing, as sometimes you find different insights by approaching from a different angle.

Needs are subtle and aren't always the first thing to appear. Chris Matts, an agile coach, told us about an experience he had where the need was initially perceived to be for large-print books for older people. After a little digging around, it was discovered that some older people are embarrassed or reluctant to have their eyes examined. While large-print books would help, there is also a need to make it easy and not embarrassing for old people to receive eye examinations and, if needed, treatment or reading aids.

Needs are not the same thing as solutions. For example, you don't need health insurance, but you need to be able to afford the healthcare you need. Whether that need is met by insurance; free or cheap healthcare; becoming incredibly wealthy; or becoming incredibly healthy and reducing the lifetime need for healthcare is irrelevant. The need remains the same—you need to be able to afford whatever care you need.

Talking about needs, not solutions, is a better way of talking about the customer's problem.

Obviously, unless we understand the needs of the customer, we are unlikely to build products that they will use.

However, sometimes seeing these needs is difficult. First, we tend to see other people's problems through a filter built around our own existing products and solutions or around what solutions we think we can deliver or indeed want to deliver. So we must step away from our own internal reality, get out of our own way, and embrace the reality of the customer segment whose needs we want to fulfill.

Consider this. Customer segments were probably determined by needs. That is, the segment is made up of people with the same need, and they receive value if you can satisfy that need. So now we can say that the real problem is how might we deliver real value by satisfying the real need.

Customer Journey Maps

Customer journey maps (perhaps you might think of these as *customer experience maps*), first written about by Ron Zemke & Chip Bell in their 1989 book *Service Wisdom: Creating and Maintaining the Customer Service Edge,* are used to show how a customer interacts with your organization. Keep in mind that customer experience has emerged as one of the most important factors in achieving success for any organization. As a business analyst, you must be concerned with how your customer sees your organization, and thereby determine her needs.

The customer journey map is drawn from the customer's—that is, the external—point of view. It does this by breaking a significant transaction into the steps that the customer (not the organization) makes to reach her objective. Having made the map, you go through the steps and identify the customer's needs for each of the points and the points where her needs might be unclear.

Consider the customer journey map shown in Figure 3.3. We've taken a reasonably simple scenario by way of illustration. There is no need to have anything more complex to see how this works.

Note the symbols beside each of the stages of the customer journey; they indicate the potential needs of the customer or the happy or painful points. You can travel the journey, and as you do, consider the needs for each of the stages. The customers might not tell you about their

Figure 3.3

A customer journey map of having your refrigerator (or any major appliance) repaired.

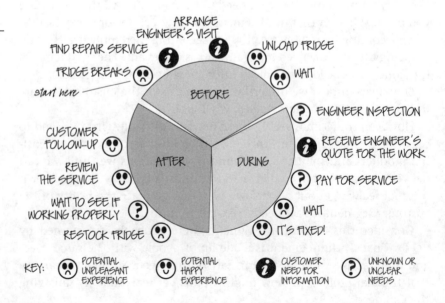

needs at each step. You might have to observe the customers in action to see them. The advantage of the journey map is that its discrete steps as the customer sees them, make it easier to find all her needs.

Let's look at an example. Suppose you work for a repair service. Your management wants to improve the service experience. The customer segment receives value when the refrigerator is once again in good working order, and it is made so at a cost the customer considers reasonable.

Use the journey map in Figure 3.3, and for each of the points, consider both the needs of the external customer and the internal organizational needs. We'll do it briefly here.

Start at the point where the *fridge breaks*. This is an unhappy experience, but there is little that you as a repair service can do about the fact that it broke. You didn't make the fridge, but you will fix it. Next up is the customer *finds a repair service*. At this point the customer has a need for information. Consider what kind of information would be most useful and what you, as the repairer, should supply. Makes and models of fridges and the most likely quick fixes for them would be top of the list. You might also consider warranty conditions. Think about other informational needs—if you supply this information better than the competition, your service becomes superior to theirs, and presumably attracts more customers.

Arrange engineer's visit also has information needs. The customer needs to arrange a mutually agreed time, find out what repairs will cost, and determine if she should do anything before the engineer arrives.

Unloading the fridge is never pleasant because the customer must find a place for all that food, and unless she can borrow space in neighbor's freezer, a lot of her frozen stuff is going to be wasted.

Next is the *engineer's inspection*. This has been tagged for unknown or unclear needs. Think about what the customer is doing when the engineer is inspecting the refrigerator and assessing the repairs. Is there any useful information that can be given to the customer? Is there a need for the customer to arrange entry for the engineer if the customer is not at home? Is there a need for clear explanations of what has to be done? Does the engineer need additional material or information to explain things to the customer?

Receive engineer's quote for the work. For this step, put yourself in the place of the customer. What do you need to know? How should the quote be delivered? What additional information would it be beneficial for the customer to receive: time to complete; alternatives to repairing the appliance; warranty; payment options; cost of replacement appliance; access conditions for the engineer; and some others that you can think about.

We'll leave you to follow the remainder of the journey to the end but want to touch on one point: *waiting to see if working properly* has unknown needs. Is there a need to give the customer information to help test whether the fridge is working? Or perhaps information on how to correctly adjust the fridge now that it is in a working state again?

Travel the Same Journey as Your Customer

A customer journey map illustrates how a customer sees your organization. While there is no need—in fact, it's not desirable—for your customers to understand the internal workings of your organization, but you need to. The journey map gives you a structure for discovering both the customer's, and your organization's, needs.

If you, as a service organization, are serious about finding all your customer's needs, and through that improving your service, be your own customer. Make calls to your own customer support team. Try to sign up for an account at your own service. Disable your own fridge and call the company. Be the customer and critically consider each step of the way, asking what processes your organization initiates, whether you could make the customer's experience better, whether the process could break down, what risks you and the customer face at each step, what is needed to make the journey better and more effective, and what can be eliminated or changed to make the path smoother.

At the very least, shadow the engineer and observe how customers react to what they are being told and asked to do. You should learn this stuff firsthand—you cannot guess it.

Talking to the Customers

The more you talk to your customers, the better. There are two situations when a conversation with the customer is critical. The first is when you are determining the customer segments and their value propositions. The second is when you are questioning the customer as to what he needs and why he needs it.

Customer segmentation is done mainly on need; the more accurately you established the need, the better. You should understand what's going on in the customer's world—what does he do now that causes this need? And if he has this need, what barriers exist to stop him from satisfying it?

Your intention is to understand what's happening in your customer's world. You question the customers about their current situation, but your motivation in doing so is to understand their future situation, one in which they are using your solution.

The next critical time when you need customer conversation is during the safe-to-fail probes (more on this in a moment), where the questioning is slightly different. During the probes, you are determining if a proposed solution satisfies the need and solves the customer's problem and whether this is the right problem to solve.

Keep in mind that during these conversations, your customers do not always know what they need. Marketing people understand that consumers are generally unaware of what they want until they are told they can have it. It is only by careful, patient, iterative questioning and listening that you can gain the insights into the customer's world needed to understand the right problem and to deliver the right solution for it.

The better your questioning, listening, and observation, the more empathy you build and the more accurate your understanding of the real problem becomes.

> *The better your listening and observation, the more empathy you build, and the more accurate your understanding of the problem becomes.*

Uncovering the Essence of the Problem

The problem should be thought of as an abstraction, free of any implementation technology, including human or organizational participation. This abstraction is the *essence* of the problem; a pure statement of the problem with no suggestion of a solution. Or you could say that the essence is the soul of the problem but not its body.

For example, you can stream music; download it; play music on a CD, iPod, phone, vinyl, or cassette tape (ask your parents); or attend live music. The essence of any of those is that you *listen to the music*.

> *The essence is the soul of the problem, not its body.*

Of course, without some implementation technology, the essence cannot exist in our real world, but it can exist in your mind and your models. To see the essence—the real problem to solve—you must look past the real-world machinery and organizations.

Let's see how this could work. Here's what you are told by various people who work for a beer distributor. Beer distributors are wholesale organizations that supply bars, restaurants, and hotels, but not retail drinkers.

Sales representative:

"I am spending too much time on the phone with my customers who think they are not getting the freshest beer."

"I also have to spend time calming customers who cannot get all the beer supplies they want for special events, like the World Cup or the Super Bowl."

Warehouse manager:

"We spend a lot of time moving stocks around in the warehouse. We do this so that the oldest beer is in the front. It must be in front so that when the drivers load the trucks, we get rid of the oldest beer. This means that we don't get stuck with beer that's past its use-by date."

"I need an iPad so I can run an app to tell me what beer I have and what age it is."

"I want the app to tell me if any beer is getting close to its use-by date."

Company manager:

"I had lunch with a salesman who showed me some warehousing software. It looks promising. I think we could manage the warehouse better if we had it."

"I don't want to get a bad reputation by selling beer too close to its use-by date. Our customers hate that."

"It is very important that we are always able to meet the demand."

"We are paying the truck drivers too much. Their job is not that hard to do, and I am sure that we could find cheaper drivers."

Truck driver:

"My loading sheet just tells me which brands and how much to load. I don't have time to go looking for the oldest beer. I rely on it being at the front."

You find the essence of all this by removing the solutions currently being used or being proposed. You are not interested in *how* they do things, but *why* they do things.

Ask Why Again and Again and Again

Why do the warehouse workers move the beer around the warehouse? Because it is their solution to the essential problem of keeping the beer as fresh as possible. Any serious beer drinker will tell you how important it is that beer is not allowed to become too old. The warehouse manager wants to reduce the average age of beer being delivered, and by putting the oldest at the front, he makes it convenient for the drivers. Why? Because the manager knows the truck drivers are not interested in hunting around the warehouse reading the use-by dates, and they want to load the nearest stock. By loading the oldest beer first, they ensure (as far as possible) that the oldest beer is not left in the warehouse to age beyond its use-by date.

Why does the warehouse manager want to know if any beer is getting close to its use-by date? He didn't tell you this, but if any beer is close to the use-by date, he tells a sales representative, who sells it off cheaply to one of the low-end bars. And that begs another question: why are low-end bars willing to take almost-expired beer? Suppose the response is about price; low-end bars want to reduce costs and think their low-end customers won't notice that the beer they are drinking is getting a little old. You could now ask if high-end bars would be willing to pay a little more to get even fresher beer.

The iPad app is a solution, but the warehouse manager has no idea if it solves the real problem. The essence here is knowing that some of the beer is approaching its use-by date, but that indicates a systemic problem with warehouse quantities or management, and that should be given priority over new iPads.

Finding the essence means that you should look for causes and not simply treat the symptom.

The company manager has proposed a warehousing software solution. However, there is no indication whether it would solve any problems, so until you determine exactly what it does and what problem it is meant to solve, it should not be seriously considered.

Finding the essence means that you should look for causes and not simply treat the symptom. For example, the sales rep says she spends too much time on the phone; this is a symptom. The underlying cause is beer that is too old. Customers not getting the supplies they want for special events is a symptom; the cause is that the distributor cannot adequately anticipate customer demand.

When finding the essence, you also eliminate anything that is out of beneficial scope. For example, paying the truck drivers is something that your project is unlikely to be able to do anything about. As a business analyst, your only concern here is whether the drivers' pay rate has any effect on the distribution business or whether there are some skills needed that require higher payment to the drivers.

But let's go back to the employees' statements and their underlying meanings. From those we can conclude that the essence—the real policy of the company—is straightforward: to deliver on average the freshest beer possible, and to anticipate and meet all demands from customers. Without this clear understanding of the problem, any solution is unlikely to be useful.

Referred Pain

Referred pain is a medical term. It concerns pain that is felt in one part of the body when the cause of the pain lies elsewhere. The most common example is sciatica—the symptom is a pain felt in one or both legs, but the problem is a slipped disk pinching a nerve in the spine. Treating the leg will do nothing to eliminate the problem.

Take this example of referred pain. The staff at a large organization are complaining that they are on hold for far too long before they can speak to the internal helpdesk. You could attack this problem by hiring more people to man the helpdesk. You could eliminate waiting on hold by implementing a register-and-call-back system. You could play calming music for the caller.

These solutions address the symptom and leave the cause of the problem untouched. The root cause of the problem has nothing to do with the helpdesk; it is with people *needing* the helpdesk. By investigating why staff need help, you could, or should, be able to improve the organization's systems. Making the systems easier to use and more comprehensible, you reduce the need for help. Perhaps your investigation uncovers a lack of training. If the staff were better trained, they would be more productive, need less help and, as a bonus, not waste their time on hold waiting for the helpdesk.

Disguised Problems

Sometimes problems are deeply disguised. Consider this example:

Store managers at a supermarket chain are concerned with the age of their point of sales (POS) system. Some of them say that customers have been complaining about long checkout lines (see Figure 3.4). The IT department has suggested developing a new POS system.

What is the disguised problem here? You will recall what we said earlier about solving the problem that you want to solve. The IT department is keen to develop a new POS system, but it is far from clear that it would do much to alleviate the real problem.

Figure 3.4

What causes long supermarket lines?

(Credit: RubberBall/Alamy Stock Photo)

Why would it not? The POS system is old, but does that necessarily mean it is slow? And would that be the only cause of long checkout lines? Probably not. Consider these causes of long checkout lines:

- There are not enough checkout registers.
- There are not enough checkout clerks.
- The checkout clerks are too slow.
- The barcode scanners malfunction frequently.
- The people hired to pack the customers' bags are not fast enough or are in the parking lot fetching abandoned shopping carts.
- The design of the checkout area is slowing things down. (We have observed a checkout line where the shopping carts were too wide to fit through the checkout, causing shoppers to carry their goods some distance to the belt.)
- The lines are long but fast moving. This still qualifies as "long checkout lines" even if it does not inconvenience customers.
- The environment in which shoppers wait in line is unpleasant, which causes them *think* they spend a lot of time in line.
- There are sweets and candy displayed near the lines, and mothers have trouble restraining their kids from grabbing the sweets.
- People in individual lines always think that other lines are moving faster than theirs. This might lead shoppers to complain of "long lines."

This list could be longer, but let's stop there. Admittedly, this list is speculative, but it points out that until the cause of the "long lines" is known, it would be folly to spend money rushing into a new POS system. The right problem to solve might well still be hidden, and the right solution to the right problem might well be far cheaper than a new point of sale system.

Suppose you interviewed the supermarket's customers and found that "long checkout lines" means that people perceive that the lines move too slowly. You might solve this quite easily by having one feeder line that branches to individual checkouts as they become available. This system of queuing *appears* to be faster and might make people stop complaining. It would be worth trying—the cost would be little more than a few retractable queue barriers such as they have in airports. If complaints lessened where it was tried, then you're on the way to solving the problem.

You might also consider approaching the problem laterally. People are complaining about the time spent checking out, so why not consider slowing it down and have one lane designated as the "slow lane"?

The objective is to cater to people—usually old people—who feel pressured once they get to the checkout to do it as quickly as possible. A lot of old people have anxieties that they are "in the way" and want to avoid keeping people behind then in the queue waiting. Some of them simply want to take as long as they possibly can so they can have a conversation at the checkout. Customers for this lane might also be people with a mental impairment that slows them down, people who suffer anxiety attacks, mothers with several young children to control who want extra time, or people who simply don't care how long checkout takes and welcome a leisurely approach.

By having a dedicated slow lane, staffing it with somebody who is sympathetic to the people using it, warning people in a hurry that this is a slow lane, you might remove other sources of friction and cut down on the number of complaints. It is worthwhile spending a little time exploring a solution such as this.

Without observing the situation, interviewing real customers, and unmasking the disguised problem, any money spent is likely to be wasted.

The Real Scope of the Problem

We have been discussing the problem and how to recognize it, but there is one factor we haven't yet mentioned: the scope of the problem. Indeed, it is impossible to find the real problem without knowing its scope. If you want to find the essence, you must ensure that you have included everything that is rightfully in scope. There is little chance of delivering the right solution if you fail to study the complete problem. You must consider scope to be your first decision.

Let's look at a scope example. Figure 3.5 shows a request from a user.

Figure 3.5

The user is requesting a solution. However, we do not yet know the scope of the problem he is trying to solve.

This user is a fulfillment manager, and he wants to know about unfilled orders. But simply having a list of unfilled orders, whether on a screen or anywhere else, is not going to solve his problem. However, by knowing *why* the orders are not being filled, he would be able to rectify the problems that are causing the delays. Presumably, that is his intention. The essence of the manager's problem is to be able to identify the reasons for orders not being filled. There are probably several, but looking at the real scope of the problem is the necessary first step.

Finding the reason for orders not being filled means you should include inventory shortages in the scope. Shortages are the most obvious problem, and they're closest to the fulfillment manager. But it is not enough; shortages in inventory might be caused by seasonal variations catching the warehouse unaware. Or perhaps the problem lies with production bottlenecks where components are not being made quickly enough, and that in turn has led to the suppliers not being able to get the goods to the warehouse in sufficient volume to provide adequate stock. Figure 3.6 shows the activity that should be considered to be within the scope of the problem.

If you are to find the essence of the problem, you need to see all of the problem, not just selected parts of it. Don't be too concerned that the scope is ballooning. Not all of it needs to be investigated to the same level of detail, but some of it will contain elements that are crucial to uncovering the real problem.

If you want to solve a problem, you must be able to see the whole of the problem.

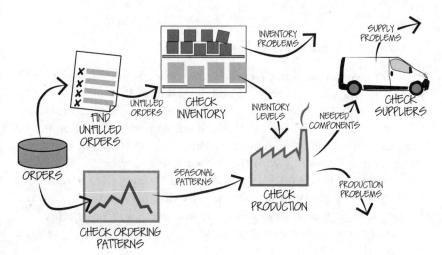

Figure 3.6

The real scope of the unfilled orders problem. To see the essence of the problem, you must cast your net widely enough to view everything that contributes to the problem.

Are You Solving the Problem That You Want to Solve?

Or are you solving the problem that you think you can solve?

There is a temptation to see only what we want to see and to hear only what we want to hear. People read newspapers and watch news services that present only the news they want to hear, the news that corresponds to their view of the world. We all have examples of left- or right-wing media bias. When it comes to hearing our customers' problems, your authors have observed a tendency for some people to hear only the parts of the problem that they know how to solve or think that it would be interesting, or cool, to solve. You are no doubt familiar with the saying about small boys and hammers.

There is a temptation to see the problem through the lens of a solution that you want to deliver.

There is also a temptation to see only the parts of the problem that fall within one's own department or area of authority.

However, the greatest temptation is to see the problem through the lens of a solution that you want to deliver. A web developer sees only the part of the problem that is most readily solved with a website. The security expert sees only the security aspects of the problem and doesn't worry too much about whether the rest of the customers' problem is solved.

Step back, and look again at the problem. Think about its essence, and forget any assumed or personally desired solutions. Is the problem what you first thought it was or want it to be, or does it have some deeper implications that are yet to be uncovered?

Now You Need a Solution

There are several things in play. You know your customer segments and what they value. You know—at a high level—what the customer needs. You understand the essential problem. Now what's needed is a solution.

We must be clear that we are looking for a business solution. It will likely contain automated elements—computers, devices, AI, networks, clouds, and so on—along with the needed human elements.

For software projects, the business solution means the software and the surrounding people and devices. For consumer products, it means the product you intend to produce and any needed infrastructure. For services, it means the service to be provided to the customer, along with any needed support and infrastructure.

If you think only of the product, it's too restrictive, and you miss out on the most important aspect of all—what does the customer do with your product? What is she doing that she needs your product to help her with? Without thinking about a business solution, you are bound to miss important needs.

Note that in Figure 3.7, the solution is shown as a shipping box. Please accept this to represent the whole solution—automated, human, and anything else you choose for your solution.

The Solution Is a Hypothesis

When you propose a solution, you do not really know whether it will solve the problem. You are proposing it because it *might* solve the problem, or it *looks* like it could solve the problem. Until you prove its viability, you continue to think of it as a *hypothesis*.

"Hypothetically, this will solve the problem."

Despite the uncertainty, this is quite a useful way of thinking about your solution. You are not yet committed to it. If you are not committed to one solution, you're more likely to go looking for another. The next one is also a hypothesis, so you look for yet another. For any of these hypothetical solutions, you are less likely to invest ego in them and far more willing to accept changes and improvements to them.

Off-the-Shelf Solutions

We are not treating off-the-shelf (OTS) solutions any differently from custom-made solutions. If you include an OTS component as part, or most, of your solution, it remains as much a hypothesis as any other until you prove it's viable and it works.

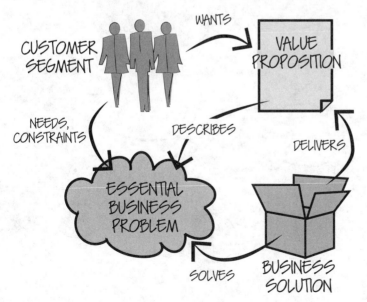

Figure 3.7

Each customer segment has a value proposition that describes an outcome that the segment values. The customers have needs and constraints that are the problem. The solution—note that it is a business solution— delivers the value when it solves the problem.

Options for Solutions

There are several approaches you could take at this stage.

The first, and certainly the riskiest, is to go along with the assumed solution from day one. "We can solve this with a website upgrade," or something similar. All too often, teams leap to the assumed solution, and without looking up, develop it. This usually results in an inferior solution or a solution to the wrong problem.

Another approach is to embark on an exhaustive study of the alternatives. This will eventually produce a result, and it will be the right result, but it will come at a tremendous cost of time, money, and resources.

Instead, we suggest that you go in a different direction, shown in Figure 3.8.

The first thing is a reminder that you are interested in *business solutions*. A business solution will almost certainly contain automated elements, but it also has human elements and probably other stuff as well.

With that in mind, you and the team generate solutions—as many as you can within a reasonable timeframe. You generate multiple solutions—by doing so you almost certainly find better solutions. You also give yourself the opportunity to show that the assumed solution is

Figure 3.8

Once the problem is well understood, the "How might we solve this problem?" question is asked. This generates multiple hypothetical solutions, which are probed for viability and outcome. The best option for a solution is chosen from the candidates as a result of the probing.

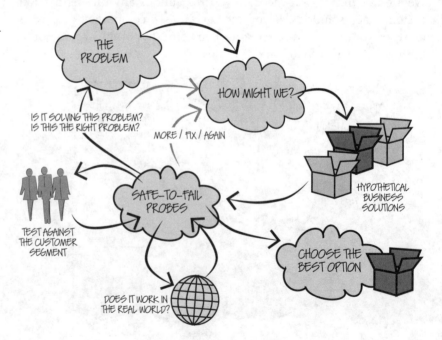

either worthwhile, or that it is inferior and should be discarded. These solutions are, as we mentioned, hypotheses. You don't yet know if they work, but you will soon.

You are about to test your hypotheses using safe-to-fail probes. The safe-to-fail probes determine whether the solution works with the environment, solves the problem, is acceptable to the customer segment, and so on. Eventually the probes reveal the best option for a solution to be developed.

But we are getting ahead of ourselves. We don't have hypothetical solutions to probe. Let's look at how we generate them.

How Might We?

As a team, you ask, "How might we solve this problem? How might we provide this value?" You are looking for creative ideas; asking "How?" gives you the widest latitude for any solutions. "Might" implies that there are lots of possibilities. You are not asking "Can we do this?" or "Is it possible to solve this?" but what might we do to solve it. There is no judgment on whether it can be done or how it is done, just the opening of possibilities. The "We" at the end says that everybody is involved.

Answering the "How might we" question is likely to produce some unusual and imaginative solutions. It will almost certainly produce some wonderful but completely impractical solutions, and some pedestrian ones. The point is not yet to find the best solution, but to find multiple solutions, and through experimentation with safe-to-fail probes (more on these later) find your ultimate winner.

This might be messy, it might be hard, it might be exhilarating—it depends on you and your team. You might find it frustrating to generate solution ideas and then see them discarded, but such is the nature of innovation. You will almost certainly generate some unworkable ideas, but again, that is the nature of what you are doing. You do not have to be right the first time. Almost nobody is. But you'll find that having a wrong idea usually leads to a much better idea.

> If you're not prepared to be wrong, you'll never come up with anything original.
>
> —Ken Robinson

If possible, include customers from the segment when you ask "How might we?" They are the people who will use your product, and they have ideas and reactions that you will find immensely useful.

In short, this is a group activity with the objective of finding the most beneficial, imaginative solution.

Willingness to Be Creative

The most important quality that you can bring to the "How might we?" session, is *willingness*. This means a willingness to try to generate ideas. A willingness to listen to others. A willingness not to criticize, debate, evaluate, or in any other way try to prevent the flow of creative ideas. You must be willing to suspend disbelief for the moment and accept that *any* idea, no matter how bizarre, has the potential to be a good idea.

You must be willing to participate, to cooperate and interact with your fellow team members, to generate ideas, and to encourage them to generate more, and better, ideas.

Techniques for Generating Ideas

There has been a lot written about generating ideas; much of it is useful. We have found that no single technique is more valuable to you than your attitude and approach. Figure 3.9 shows the four elements that we have found contribute most to generating ideas.

Hard work is important. There are some people who, given a problem to solve, can instantly come up with several brilliant and workable solutions. Most of us are not like that, and we need to work at it. That is, we need to keep searching for new solutions when we have already found several. But it's also hard work to be willing to listen to criticisms and improvements for our ideas.

Figure 3.9

The factors that contribute most to generating ideas for solutions.

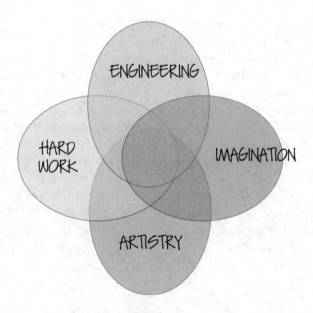

Engineering is making something work, and work well. Making your ideas workable and functional is part of finding new solutions. *Imagination* is what gets you your ideas. The ability to think and imagine what might be is how we find new solutions. If you look at the best apps and the best consumer products, there is a certain amount—sometimes lots—of *artistry* built into them.

You are not expected to be good at all these things. But you must expect to apply some of them to your creative work. Having good ideas is not all that difficult when you are sparking with your team, and you'll find that you touch each of these areas, one way or another, whenever you generate new potential solutions.

There are lots of techniques to help generate ideas. Many books have been written about innovation and creativity techniques and strategies. We do not intend this to be an exhaustive treatise on innovation techniques, but we feel it's worth mentioning a few techniques—the ones that we have found most useful over time.

Innovation Triggers

These are called *innovation triggers* because they prompt you to think about an aspect of your solution. Consider the following partial list of innovation triggers.

Participation

People like to participate in the work; they like to be much more hands-on with their automated products. If you prefer, you can think of it as self-service—people doing for themselves something that previously was done for them. Online banking is the obvious example. The questions to ask are, "How might I get the customer segment to participate? What solution would maximize customer involvement?"

Connections

People like to be connected. Look at the immense amount of time people spend online with social media and other forms of communication—they want to be connected most of the time. "How might we connect to our customers?" Loyalty cards that offer some kind of discount spring to mind, as do reminder emails, "You asked us to remind you when it's time to come in and be fitted for your wedding tuxedo." Keeping credit cards and delivery details make it easier for customers to return to you to buy yet more stuff. They also keep the customer connected.

Speed

Whatever your customer needs to do, ask how he might do it more quickly. Speed does not have to be absolute speed, but the appearance of speed. For example, having your boarding pass on your mobile phone may not actually be faster, but it appears to be faster when you're passing through the airport.

Service

Good service does not always generate repeat business, but it certainly helps. Conversely, poor service is highly likely to repel customers, and they are almost certain to tell at least one other person of their experience of your poor service. This means that you need to aim for your service to be average or above, and if you want to be favorably spoken of, it should be excellent. Ask how you might provide a service your customers enjoy and want to repeat.

Grandchildren

The question here is, "What will my grandchildren do? What kind of product will my grandchildren use?" Obviously, we have no real idea, and attempts to predict the future are generally wrong. The intention is not to be accurate, but to open people's minds to the potential. Project yourself forward in time and speculate on the technology that might be available to you and the things that people might be doing. Does it suggest a solution that would please your grandchildren?

Constraint Removal

Constraints are restrictions on the problem space. These are not physical restraints like a pair of handcuffs, but some stated or unstated limitation on your solution. Constraints often appear as barriers to you finding a better solution.

For example, there might be a constraint that the organization must make a profit, that the product must be cheap, that it works on mobile devices, or that it runs in the cloud.

Some constraints are real, and some are assumed. All of them reveal interesting insights when removed.

However, if you pretend for a moment that the constraint can be removed or significantly altered, you often find a new solution. What if you ask if customers can have a credit card without the constraint of carrying a card? What if they need a ticket, but you remove the constraint of a physical ticket? What about commuting by road without the constraint of a car?

What if you take the profit constraint and ask, "What if we gave our product away?" This might just work because lots of stuff is given away to generate larger profits downstream. Social networks give away access to their sites to get people to post, and then the people are advertised to. Prior to Facebook, people paid to go online and post their thoughts.

Some music artists give their music away. This generates followers (who doesn't like free music?) who in turn pay for concert tickets or stream the artist's music from a service that in turn recompenses the artist.

At the time of writing (and please keep in mind that by the time you read this, things will have changed), electric powered cars are making inroads into traditionally fueled cars. Attention is beginning to switch to long-haul road freight using trucks. The argument is that trucks cannot be converted to be electric powered because, on an average in the United States, a truck travels between 300 and 600 miles a day. A battery to power a truck over this range would be prohibitively expensive and weigh over 16 tons, thus reducing freight capacity by 50% or more.

However, this argument is predicated on two constraints: a) the truck must travel the full day's distance on one charge, and b) the battery is an integral part of the truck. By removing those two constraints, we can have a situation where the size of the battery is such that it interferes minimally with cargo capacity. The distance it can travel on one charge is shorter, which allows for a smaller, lighter battery.

Now let's say that our truck stops every 100 miles. Let's also remove the constraint that the truck must be driven by a human, so now nobody minds the frequent stops. The truck robotically switches out its used battery, replacing it with a freshly charged one (billed to the truck's owner), and continues on its way to the next charging station 100 miles down the road.

This truck could cross the long part of the United States stopping about 30 times and arriving about two and a half days after setting out, travelling day and night. That's a pretty good result in return for getting rid of a couple of constraints. (Dear reader, by the time you read this, standardized vehicle-battery swapping might be commonplace. We hope so. Currently it's unheard of, so you read it here first.) This solution does not overcome the problem of the cost and limited supply of lithium, but because we don't need a high-performance battery, perhaps these batteries could be made using something other than lithium.

Combining Ideas

This is simply combining existing ideas to make a new idea. For example, putting a camera into a telephone—previously completely unconnected devices—made one far more useful device.

Guttenberg combined the coin stamp and the wine press to give us the movable type printing press—perhaps the best innovation of all time. The hybrid car is also a combination—this time a petrol engine and an electric motor.

The foundation of combination is that you do not have to invent everything. You just have to find existing components that, when plugged together, form some new solution. Keep in mind that many of the components you want to combine might be found outside your own organization.

You might also consider deconstruction—that is, taking part of another solution and making that your solution.

The Slogan

When you come up with an idea, summarize it into a one-sentence slogan. You might also do this as an elevator pitch. The slogan or pitch must include a benefit—a one-line statement that tells your audience what your solution does for them.

- **"The ticket you don't have to buy"**—This would be some alternative to a ticket buying system, perhaps using debit cards, smartphones, or fingerprints.
- **"Renew without renewing"**—This would be a convenient way for policyholders to renew their insurance with little or no effort on their part.
- **"Think your blog, don't write it"**—This might be for a blogging site where the solution entices bloggers to make use of it by providing a way of inputting the content without having to type it.
- **"1000 songs in your pocket"**—This was the slogan for the original iPod. The benefit was so appealing that the iPod went on to make Apple a wealthy company.

Note that none of the above make any mention of technology. It's all about the benefit, or the impact of your solution. The benefit sells, so sell the benefit.

Personas

A persona is an artifact made up of a specific narrative about an archetypal customer or user. The narrative comes from the characteristics, limitations, and demographics of your customer segment. In most cases, a study of the target audience is made, and the persona is synthesized from the collected data.

The persona has enough characteristics for the team to understand the audience for their solution. Thus, the persona guides discovery and helps make decisions about functionality, usability, appearance, and prioritization.

To make the persona accurate enough, most teams write a one- or two-page description that sets out the persona's behavior patterns, goals, skills, attitudes, and environment. There are downloadable templates and online forms that help you generate your persona. It is usual, and desirable, to include enough personal details—including a name—to bring the persona to life. For example:

> Harry is 27 years old, drives a hybrid car, and uses social media for about 30 minutes each day. He regularly meets his friends at their favorite coffee shop. Harry reads a lot of fiction—normally on his tablet device. Harry is educated to degree level, likes sports, and enjoys good food. He is doing well at his job as a financial analyst. He has a girlfriend of 3 years standing, and they are quite serious about each other. (There could be much more, but you get the point by now.)

We suggest having a photograph to represent the persona, such as the one shown in Figure 3.10. A photograph encourages people to relate to the persona's character and predict its behavior. Some teams, on a rotating basis, have one of the members play the part of the persona. This member states his needs and aspirations, but from the point of view of the persona. One team we came across has a mask that the "persona" wears while role playing.

Figure 3.10

A stock photo used to illustrate Harry, a persona derived for Bernie's books (see Chapter 1). Harry is representing the twentysomething customer segment, and the team is generating solutions to persuade Harry that buying books from Bernie's is a preferable experience.

(Credit: Rostislavsedlacek/ 123RF)

The persona makes it easier for the team to think about and relate to their customers' needs. When they can see a photo and speak about the persona as someone real, it puts a human face on what otherwise would be abstract data about potential customers. The question they ask is not what a set of data needs, but

"What does Harry think is cool? What cool things can we offer?"

"What does Harry need?"

"What would persuade Harry to buy paper books from Bernie?"

"What time of day is Harry available for book buying?"

"What could we do to entice Harry to the bookshop?"

"Would Harry respond to the handed-out bookmark carrying a QR code?"

"What is Harry's problem? How might we solve it for him?"

Having a persona avoids the "elastic user," whereby different team members assume the customer to be whatever they have in mind. It also prevents team members from defining the customer as themselves. This "self-referential" approach almost always yields idiosyncratic results, with one team finding the solution easy and intuitive, but the target audience having little idea of how to operate it.

The "realness" of the persona gives the team a target to aim their solution at. Details such as computer literacy, attitude to technology, cultural taboos and viewpoints, gender bias, and so on guide the team as they search for solutions. The persona "tells" the team its needs.

Portraying Your Solutions

There is no right or wrong way to record and present your proposed solutions. We have used sketches, wireframes, elevator pitches, slogans, a process model, a screenshot, a story—in fact, anything that allows you to communicate your ideas to others.

Rather than getting hung up on format, we suggest you use whatever seems easiest and most natural to you.

Safe-to-Fail Probes

Safe-to-fail probes were proposed by Dave Snowden as an adjunct to the Cynefin Framework developed within IBM. The framework talks about different states of systems and how to reach a decision on how to proceed. That is what we want to do here. For complex systems—those with no repeating relationships between cause and effect—Snowden proposes safe-to-fail probes as a way of judging the effect of small-scale changes on the system at large. We have borrowed the idea and propose you use it in a slightly different manner.

Safe-to-fail probes, as we are using them, are quick and nimble experiments, done quickly and cheaply, on the proposed solutions from your "How might we?" session. As the name suggests, it is quite okay if the solution being probed doesn't work out. These experiments must be time boxed and can be done any way you like, but we suggest that you use storyboards, sketched prototypes and scenarios, and perhaps role playing as a way of modeling your probe and making it more real. See Figure 3.11 for an example.

Let's have a look at the kind of things you would probe for. As we are doing this, please refer to the handwritten annotations on Figure 3.11. These are the kinds of things that you would add as part of your probe. You would also ask questions along the lines of these coming up.

Does It Work?

Is the process sound? Can it produce the required books? Is the technology capable of meeting the expected demand? Do you have a fairly good idea of the demand? Is the book produced to a standard that will satisfy Bernie's discerning customers?

Figure 3.11

A safe-to-fail probe that uses a storyboard to explore the idea of customers printing books while in the bookstore. The advantage to the bookstore is the ability to supply out-of-print books, or those not stocked. The advantage to the customer is the almost infinite catalog of books available for immediate on-demand printing. The storyboard has been annotated with the findings from the probe. This solution appears to be viable and to solve the problem.

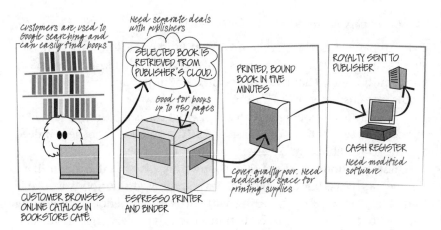

Need separate deals with publishers

customers are used to Google searching and can easily find books

SELECTED BOOK IS RETRIEVED FROM PUBLISHER'S CLOUD.

Good for books up to 450 pages

PRINTED, BOUND BOOK IN FIVE MINUTES

ROYALTY SENT TO PUBLISHER

CASH REGISTER
Need modified software

Cover quality poor. Need dedicated space for printing supplies

CUSTOMER BROWSES ONLINE CATALOG IN BOOKSTORE CAFÉ.

ESPRESSO PRINTER AND BINDER

What Is Its Outcome?

Can you demonstrate that the functionality contained in your solution solves the customer's problem? Your investigation should reveal the outcome of the solution and that it contributes to the value proposition.

The outcome you are looking for would be along the lines of the customer having a book she would otherwise not be able to get. Further, the transaction is such a good experience that the customer is likely to recommend it to others and do it again herself. It's not just about being able to sell a book; the outcome goes beyond that.

What Are the Economics?

Cost is almost always, naturally, an important consideration. There is no point proceeding if the costs exceed the potential benefits or if you cannot afford it. You must consider the upfront development cost, the operational cost, and the cost of refreshing the solution every five years or so for a couple of decades.

You should also look at the economics of doing nothing. What is the cost to your organization in lost opportunity if you do not develop the proposed solution?

Does It Solve the Right Problem?

The storyboard shows the solution printing on-demand books in the bookstore. This can only be valuable if the customer segment places a value on being able to buy the books that are only available on demand, or are otherwise unobtainable.

Will Customers Accept It?

Refer to panel 1 of the storyboard. What kind of person wants this service? What motivates people to use this service? What kinds of searches (title, author, era, characters, associated or similar authors, and so on) would the customer use? Finding the right answer to this last question might be critical—you need to discover what she is looking for and how she sees the search task. You must also assure yourself that she is indeed willing to search for an otherwise unobtainable book.

These questions need not take a long time. The point is not to have detailed answers, but to determine if the proposed solution is workable and that it is worth proceeding with it. Naturally enough, anything that is not viable is discarded without the loss of very much time and resources.

There will be times where you choose to go beyond the quick experiment that uses some graphic representation of the solution. In some cases, the complexity of the solution and the number of unknowns cause you to build some software prototypes or simulations. Software mockups can be particularly valuable when you feel the need to probe your proposed solutions using live customers.

A colleague, Andrew Kendall, tells us of how he participated in the construction of a full-sized mockup of a railway station entrance to probe commuters' reactions to the layout. High throughput was essential, and probing with live commuters and realistic station entrances was cost effective and successful. Ellen Gottesdiener used a "man behind the curtain" simulation (someone pretends to be the automated solution, but the responses are partially manually generated) used to probe reactions to a carpool initiative. Other probes have used software, cardboard boxes, and whiteboards; there are no rules.

Safe-to-fail probes test the hypothesis that the proposed solution solves the customer's problem and provides the required value.

Note that safe-to-fail probes are different from *spikes*. A spike is done so that a story can be estimated, but the story itself is not in question. In other words, a spike is not about whether the story will solve the problem, but how much effort we need to implement it.

Safe-to-fail probes are for you to test and modify your options. We suggest that you conduct your probes jointly with your team members. Additionally, having people from the customer segments is invaluable. It is the reactions from these people who tell you whether your proposed solution is a hit or a miss. It is also these people who can answer the question, "Is this solving your problem?"

The question to ask is not, "Will this work?" but "Tell me about your problem and how this solution would affect it. Tell me if the outcome of this solution is what you are needing to achieve."

If you are involving customers, as you would with some of the examples in this chapter, then care must be taken to select a good representation of the customer segment so that the results are not biased in any direction.

Lean thinking: Do any of your probes indicate that some of the problem can be ignored or postponed or if some of the proposed solutions can be simplified?

If live customers are unavailable to you, thoughtful use of your persona will be a suitable alternative.

For in-house development, always involve as many users as possible. This way the chosen solution emerges from a cooperative effort and is more likely to get buy-in.

We suggest that you use small teams to conduct your probes. Obviously, several probes can be going on at the same time, but there is no need for the one team to do all the probes.

For each experiment, the outcome must be observable and demonstrable with a reasonable degree of certainty. For example, if you are using a storyboard to describe your experiment, the panels making up your story should be coherent such that the team and the customers can follow your reasoning and agree with the outcome. While it is desirable, it is not always entirely necessary to add costs at this stage. However, showing cost estimates on your probes makes for better comparisons between options. For example, see Figure 3.12.

Note that although technology appears in the illustrations (see Figure 3.11 for an example), they are showing a business. You might end up selecting an alternative technology for the final development.

Right Outcome?

When you run a probe, you determine the *outcome* of the proposed solution. Please note that this is the outcome and not the output. You now should determine whether the outcome of the solution satisfies the customer's needs. Additionally, it must deliver the value specified in the value proposition and solve the other parts of the customer's problem.

You now should interrogate your customers:

"Is this the outcome you want?"

"Does this outcome satisfy your real business need, or should we revisit that?"

"Is it solving the problem you want solved?"

"Tell me again about the problem."

"Tell me again why you value having this problem solved."

And so on.

These questions are crucial to your success because it is quite possible that the problem first voiced by the customers is not their real problem. When customers see a demonstration of your proposed solution, they get a better understanding of what they are trying to achieve. Be prepared to restate the problem and adjust your proposed solutions accordingly. Whatever happens, you must ensure that your proposal solves the right problem. Otherwise, there is no point to your project.

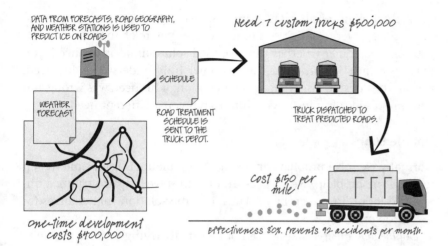

DATA FROM FORECASTS, ROAD GEOGRAPHY, AND WEATHER STATIONS IS USED TO PREDICT ICE ON ROADS

WEATHER FORECAST

SCHEDULE

ROAD TREATMENT SCHEDULE IS SENT TO THE TRUCK DEPOT.

Need 7 custom trucks $500,000

TRUCK DISPATCHED TO TREAT PREDICTED ROADS.

cost $150 per mile

one-time development costs $400,000

effectiveness 80%. prevents 92 accidents per month.

Figure 3.12

A safe-to-fail probe exploring the possibilities of treating the problem of ice on roads with salt or some other de-icing compound. The sketched proposal shows estimated costs. This solution will solve the problem if it is affordable for the road authority.

"Failed" Probes

Sometimes the probes fail. That is, they reveal that a hypothesis won't work. This is to be expected—it's part of the technique, and it's why they are called safe-to-fail probes. If a probe fails, the loss in terms of cost, time, and personal involvement is negligible. A failed experiment should not be seen as a failure, but simply as eliminating an alternative from consideration. It means that you have learned something more about the problem and its possible solution.

> ❝ *I have not failed. I've just found 10,000 ways that won't work.* ❞
> —Thomas Edison

"Trial and error" is sometimes used to describe this kind of experiment. But that is not the right thing to say because "error" implies that there was a "right" outcome in the first place. This is experimenting quickly—if something does not work, learn from it and move on. There are no right answers, just some that are more promising than others.

For each failure, consider whether there is an alternative that would not fail. Let's say that your probe modeled a new selling system for custom-fitted cars and failed because the time delay between order and delivery was too long. The things to look at here are the order and the delivery. Is there an alternative to customers ordering custom-fitted cars? Could they, for example, take options on several different cars, and when one of those became available, the customer would be invited to take up his option? Or could there be an alternative to delivery? Could the customer collect the car himself? Could the pre-sales service be changed to make it faster and so deliver earlier? Is it feasible to manufacture each car to the customer's specification set at ordering time?

Be willing to admit that you might be wrong, question everything, and revisit your assumptions about the problem you're trying to solve.

Lastly, and most importantly, probes are iterative. You are asking questions, the answer to which sometimes causes you to change direction. If you ask a customer whether the proposed solution meets his need, you must also question whether the customer fully understands his need. Perhaps he doesn't, or perhaps his perception of his need was wrong and your proposed solution triggers him to tell you a different need.

Double Loop

Normally we solve problems in a single loop manner. Each time we fail to solve the problem, we go back and try to solve it again, trying a different solution to the problem. Thus, it is the solution that changes for each loop of the cycle.

Double loop means that instead of repeatedly trying to solve the same problem, you loop further back to the original problem and question it. Could it be that we are trying to solve the wrong problem? Could it be that there is a better problem to solve? Could the original problem be incorrectly defined, and by correcting it, could we have a much better problem to solve? Or could it be that our attempts to solve it prompt the customer to realize that this is not the right problem to solve? Figure 3.13 illustrates this double loop.

The double loop means that instead of being locked into a trajectory, you're looking around to see if there is something better on offer.

Figure 3.13

Double loop. The attempt to solve the problem using a safe-to-fail probe reveals that the problem was not solved. A single loop will go back and probe a different solution. A double loop goes back and questions whether we are trying to solve the right problem.

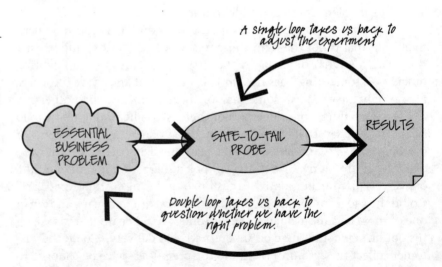

Outcome and Impact

We see outcome and impact as much the same concept, so from here we will talk about outcome.

This goes right back to the value proposition. The outcome is what your customer values, and you would have recorded this in your value proposition. We mention outcome here because your probes are revealing the outcomes or your solutions. You can also think of the outcome (or impact) as the change brought about by your solution.

For example, the outcome could be along the lines of any of these:

- **Improvement to a business process**—It is now faster, easier, cheaper, or more effective.
- **Money**—Your solution sells more of your client's product.
- **Saving money**—This is usually done by improving a business process.
- **Opportunity**—Your solution takes advantage of a business opportunity—it provides the means to operate in a new arena.
- **Technology**—Your solution improves something by using a new technology.
- **Enablement**—People can now do new things.

There can, of course, be other outcomes, but the preceding list is sufficient for the sake of example.

You have to be aware of the outcome of your solution, and usually as part of your safe-to-fail probe, you are measuring the outcome. You can think of the outcome as the change between the previous state of the business and the new state when your solution is deployed. If the change is insufficient or not desired, you abandon that proposed solution and move to the next. If you cannot measure the change, there is little point in building the solution. After all, the point of your project is to bring about a change.

Measuring the change usually requires that you have a measure of the current performance—throughput, revenue, speed, level of service, number of customers, customer satisfaction, or whatever measure is appropriate. This is measuring the business process you aim to replace. (Sadly, too many projects and businesses do not have this kind of measurement to hand.)

Figure 3.14

There should be a change in performance brought by your solution. Part of the outcome is the disruption caused by the change you are bringing about. The impact of your solution is the difference between current and future performance. You should allow for the disruption period to be longer, and harder, than you think.

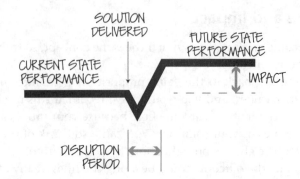

The impact (or change) is the increase in performance that your solution will bring about. This is shown in Figure 3.14. Admittedly, it is only an estimate at this stage, and you should have qualified people in the team help assess this future performance. Prudent management would follow up and remeasure when your solution goes live.

In some cases, value is delivered, but there is no applicable quantitative measurement. You just achieve the value or not. For example, your solution enables the organization to obey a new or changed law (this applies to a considerable proportion of IT development effort), and the outcome is binary—it complies or it doesn't.

A technique called *impact mapping* is available. It is a little more than we need here, but in case you are interested, we have shown an example of an impact map in Figure 3.15. We think we can leave it to you to assess the contribution of this kind of diagram to your own efforts.

Figure 3.15

Impact map. The goal here is similar to the value proposition; the actor is the main player involved in achieving the goal. The diagram shows the impact that the deliverable (part of the product you are building) brings to the actor.

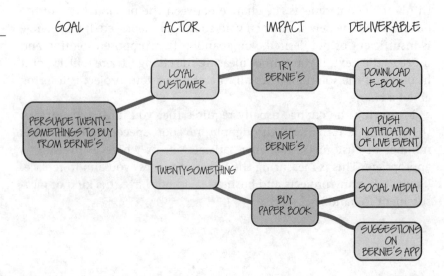

Systems Thinking

Systems thinking, also known as *systemic thinking*, is a discipline that business analysts should be familiar with. Much has been written about systems thinking, and we shall not attempt to replicate it here. However, a brief introduction might be sufficient to point out the advantage of thinking systemically.

A system is an organized collection of components and subsystems that are interconnected to accomplish some objective. The system has various inputs that go through certain processes to produce certain outputs, which taken together, accomplish the desired goal for the system.

Systems thinking is, in one way, the opposite of analysis. Analysis is concerned with partitioning and studying individual pieces. The word *analysis* comes from the root meaning "to break into constituent parts" or "the process of separating something into its constituent elements."

On the other hand, systems thinking is concerned with the system as a whole—it is concerned with how the interaction of the components combine to produce the system's outcomes.

Suppose your client, a busy metropolitan subway system, has a problem with long queues and congestion at the ticket counters. The client tells you that value will be delivered if your solution can sell tickets 15% more quickly. That percentage is the client's estimate of the improvement needed to clear the queues. You deliver your solution, and voilà! the queues at the ticket offices disappear. Now there is a new problem: people are moving more quickly through the ticket halls, and the platforms are dangerously overcrowded. Train drivers are reporting near misses as commuters are jostled close to the edge of the platforms. The strangling effect of slow ticket sales was keeping people off the platforms and safely in the ticket halls.

Failure to consider the system as a whole has led to a new problem—this time one with potentially serious consequences.

Systems thinking tells us that if one component changes such that it produces a different output, and this output becomes input to another component, the interaction has changed, and it probably affects the outcome of the whole system (see Figure 3.16).

We should think of *the system* as the whole of your solution—that is, the product you are building, the people in your organization who use it set in the context of their outside world environment. The systemic

> 66 *Systems thinking is not worrying about the first or second consequence of an action, but the third and fourth and fifth.* 99
>
> —Steve McMenamin, CIO and Senior Vice President, Hawaiian Electric Company

> 66 *Does the flap of a butterfly's wings in Brazil set off a Tornado in Texas?* 99
>
> —Edward Lorenz, meteorologist

Figure 3.16

An illustration of a complex system. The effect of a change to one component might have an impact on any number of other components (shown as darker). Systems thinking is directed toward the interaction between the components and their effect on each other and the system as a whole.

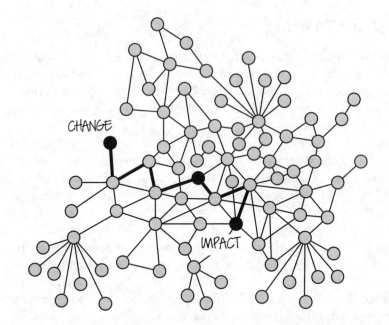

question is not, "If I change this component, what happens to my product" even though that is an excellent thing to ask. Instead, the systemic question is, "If I change this component, what effect does it have on my users and customers and anything relevant beyond them?"

The point of systems (or systemic) thinking is that the effect of any solution is not just its output, but the resultant *outcome* or consequences on its customers and its environment.

Coming back to the question of "Are you solving the right problem?" the systemic question becomes, "If I solve the customer's problem, are all the outcomes beneficial, or does my solution create new problems?"

Choosing the Best Option

You have been probing several potential solutions. Ideally, you have been working with real-life customers from the customer segment, others in your team, in-house experts such as user experience (UX) designers, security, and so on. It is important to have anybody with a stake in the outcome participate in the probe. You are about to select a winner, and everybody must be able to see that this is an objective decision; it must be clear why the winning proposal is better than the others.

So far, we've spoken about the probe achieving two objectives: one is to determine if the solution works, and the other is to determine if it solves the right problem.

Now we add a third: of your several candidate solutions, which one is the best? Which one should you develop?

There can be no precise formula for selecting the best option, but there are guidelines.

Your customers are paramount, and if your customers love one of the solutions, and they tell you that it is solving their problem and doing so in the best possible way, then this one is the winner.

Moreover, the team loves it, the product owner loves it—everybody loves it. It feels like the next iPhone, Photoshop, Android, *Harry Potter*, *Star Wars*, and oxygen rolled into one. Perhaps we are getting a little carried away, but your winner should generate excitement. The solution is elegant, it offers the best user experience, and most importantly, it provides the best possible outcome.

We don't have a lot to say about picking the winner. The winner will be obvious when you see it.

Summary

We have been discussing the problem you must solve if you are to provide real value to your client. It is all too frequent that teams or management assume a solution, and the team rushes to develop it. The result is wasted effort and delays before the correct solution can be produced.

It need not be this way. We have shown quite a few ways to determine if the right problem is being addressed. Starting with a value proposition and working from there, quickly generated, sketched solutions can be tested against customer expectations, and importantly, against the customer's view of the problem. The customer's problem is not always apparent, is not always well understood, and is sometimes cloaked in assumed solutions. Testing your hypotheses against the problem always brings the real problem to light.

And solving this problem—the real problem, the right problem—is the only way you can deliver value to your customer.

Investigate the Solution Space

4

• The scope of the solution space
• Why business events make your investigation easier
• Investigating the business events
• Why don't I skip analysis and just write stories?
• Creative observation • Classifying the culture

We want to start this chapter by saying that investigation is not necessarily a separate activity. When you were doing your safe-to-fail probes, you would have investigated the processes and the environment to ensure that the proposed solution both solves the problem and is feasible to construct. When you are designing your solution (next chapter), you'll find it necessary to investigate other aspects of the solution space to make your design seamless with its environment. During backlog refinement and development (Chapter 6), more investigation might take place as you tease out the fine details of the stories. If you were to think about this in an agile way, you would look at the investigation as a distributed activity that overlaps and iterates with other activities (see Figure 4.1).

The reason for having a separate chapter is to make it easier to talk about investigation; however, our intention is to talk about *what* you do, not *when* you do it.

We also want to start by saying that investigation need not, and should not, be a lengthy process. It is, of course, important to do enough

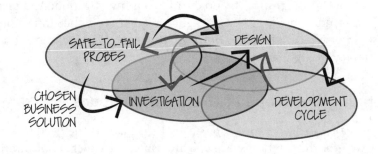

Figure 4.1

Investigating the solution space is not a separate activity, but something that overlaps other activities.

investigation to ensure that you are getting it right, but it's also important that you do no more than is needed to ensure that your solution is solving the right problem.

Why Are We Investigating?

You arrived at your proposed solution space by generating alternative potential solutions, and you found the most feasible and acceptable one by running safe-to-fail probes. One of your probes picked out a solution that seemed the most likely to succeed.

It is important to reiterate here that the solution we are talking about here is a *business solution*. It probably involves more than hardware and software, and you need to understand its environment, the people involved as part of the solution, and the people who are affected by the solution.

The solution space is what you must understand if you are to learn whether the proposed solution solves the customer's problem and does it in the best possible way.

Because of the complexity of most solutions we build these days, it is crucial that there are no nasty surprises lying in ambush that might derail or delay later development. You need to understand how all the parts fit together, how your solution fits into the wider ecosystem, how the people involved are expected to react, and other factors that affect the success of your solution.

How detailed is your investigation of the solution space? It depends on several factors. Is this solution mission critical? Is it completely new for your team or your organization? Is it routine stuff? Is a lot already known about the domain? How much can you leave to the development cycles, and how much do you need to investigate before even thinking about development?

It is, of course, necessary to strike a balance between spending too much time investigating the solution space with the possibility of bloated specifications and potentially late delivery, and spending insufficient time resulting in a solution that does not solve the problem or is inappropriate to the work and the people doing it.

Let's look at the things you do during your investigation. And please keep in mind, some of this you might already have done, and some of these things you might delay. However, the scope of the solution should be attended to right away.

Defining the Scope of the Solution Space

Scope is a two-edged sword. One edge of the blade is the need to know the extent of the solution space you are using; the other is not wanting to unnecessarily restrict yourself by locking into an unchangeable scope and denying yourself the opportunity of beneficial changes to your solution.

Let us look at how you might define the scope and why you would do that. Keep in mind that you might find reasons to change it later, but if there is no initial definition of scope, much of your time will be taken up with discussions and arguments about whether functionality is included or excluded. So let's fix the scope but allow controlled changes to be made later.

You need to define the scope of the solution space, but the scope should not be considered entrenched.

To reiterate on an earlier point, you might be defining the scope during a safe-to-fail probe of your solution. There is no need to make this a discrete activity done in its own time slot; you can determine scope whenever you need to.

You define the scope because it would be unfortunate, or probably neglectful, if you discovered later, when you were well down the track, that there is something that was not considered, and this something has caused substantial backtracking or rework. It might be that this something is a showstopper. If there are to be showstoppers, let's find them as early as possible.

You also need to know the scope to ensure that it is within your power to deliver everything inside it. For example, when the true scope is revealed, are there parts of it that you or your project sponsor are not authorized to change? If you need to negotiate territorial rights, then again, let's do it as early as possible.

The solution you propose is a business solution, with multiple roles, devices, and dependencies. Your scope must include those.

The solution that you have proposed is a business one. That is, it includes some human activity, some software, possibly some hardware, and possibly other devices. Yes, there are some software-only solutions, but mostly there is human involvement as part of the solution. Outside of the embedded systems world, software—and hardware for that matter—doesn't stand alone untouched by humans. And there's usually more than just a single user sitting in front of a computer. In most business solutions, there are multiple roles, multiple devices, and multiple dependencies. Your scope must include those.

Our preferred way of showing scope is to use some kind of graphic model. The *context diagram* is the one we have found to be the best at precisely and clearly showing the extent of the solution space. The context diagram is a functional model that demonstrates the functionality that is both inside and outside the solution space.

This model shows the part of your client's business that you intend to develop or redevelop; this is your *solution space*. This solution space is shown in the sample context diagram in Figure 4.2. This diagram

Figure 4.2

The scope of Bernie's
solution space shown as
a context model.

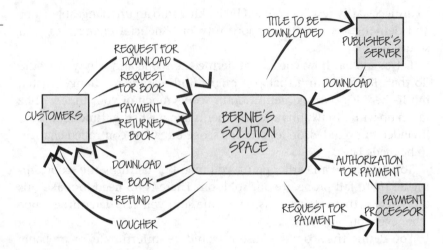

demonstrates what you consider to be your solution space. It intention-
ally ignores any other parts of Bernie's business—payroll, reordering,
inventory control, and so on.

The context model in Figure 4.2 illustrates the *data* that enters and
leaves the solution space. The incoming data flows in from the outside
world because it's needed by the solution—*request for download*, *request
for book*, *payment*, and so on. This incoming data is needed to produce
the outgoing flows, including *download*, *book*, *refund*, and *voucher*.

The solution space is the central activity, and for the moment all its
details, processes, and internal data are hidden. This is intentional; you
are defining the extent of the solution space, not the way it works.

*Define the scope
by determining the
data flows that
cross the boundary
of the solution
space.*

The squares outside the solution space are *adjacent systems*. These are
external entities that you have no authority to change. However, you
may negotiate with adjacent systems if there is some mutually beneficial
reason to change. The adjacent systems are there to show the source of
your solution's incoming data/material and the destination for its outgoing data/material.

The important thing to remember is that the arrows are named. The
reason for the name is that the arrow represents a flow of data (or sometimes material), and its name indicates its content. And that, in turn,
shows the solution's functionality. For example, there is an incoming
flow called *returned book* and an outgoing one called *refund*. Obviously,
there must be a process within the solution to put the returned book
back into stock (if it is not damaged) and give a refund to the customer. If
you look again at Figure 4.2, you can see other pairings of flows entering
and leaving the solution space.

When you draw a context model, start with the central activity to represent the extent of the solution space. That much is easy. You should know some of the functionality contained by the solution space, so ask what data is needed to feed the functionality and if that functionality produces outgoing data. Then ask where does the data come from, and where does it go?

Show these incoming and outgoing flows, together with the adjacent systems that are either the source or destination of the flows. Suppose you have some other flows that are leaving the solution space. Ask if there is any incoming data that is needed to produce them. The converse works for any unattached input flows: what output, if any, is produced as a result of the incoming flow?

Answering these questions might produce a few more inputs and adjacent systems. Then ask if there are any other outputs that might be relevant to the option you have chosen. Add any to your context diagram, and keep doing so until you are confident that you have all the flows entering and being produced by your business solution.

Use the context diagram to demonstrate how the scope is sufficient to deliver the required value.

The intention of doing this is to show the extent of the business solution that you have chosen: what's in it, and what's out of it. You might want to spend a little time with the business stakeholders to ensure you have captured the chunk of functionality that can produce all the required outputs. The main question now shifts to, "Does the functionality contained by the solution space solve the customer segment's problem?" You use the context diagram to demonstrate how the scope is sufficient to deliver the required value.

Business Events

Business events are things that happen, and that happening affects your solution. For example, when one of Bernie's customers requests a download, that's a business event. You do not know when the customer will request the download, or why she requested it, but you know that the request has been made because there is an incoming flow on the context diagram in Figure 4.2 called—wait for it—*request for download*.

When a business event happens, it happens in the adjacent system. The event produces a flow of data that informs the solution of the happening. When this data arrives at the solution, it triggers a response. The response from the solution is to carry out some processing, which might result in an outgoing flow that delivers whatever has been requested by the incoming flow.

Let's consider a couple of examples of business events:

- *A policy holder paying the premium to renew an insurance policy* is a business event. The trigger is the arrival of the payment with an identification of the policy, and the response is to record the policy as renewed and send the final policy document to the policyholder.

- *A passenger checking in for a flight* is another business event. This one is triggered by the passenger either going online or arriving at the check-in desk. The response is to check the passenger's reservation, check that the flight is available, allocate a seat taking into account any preallocations or passenger's recorded preferences, acquire the number of bags to be checked, record the passenger as checked in, and print the boarding pass or send it to the passenger's phone.

There are also *time-triggered events*. These happen when it is time for the solution to do something. Most solutions have reporting functionality, and this is usually done on a timed basis—the report at the end of the day, renewal reminders sent one month before the anniversary of an insurance policy, and so on. Your bank prepares a statement of your account activity on the last day of each month and either sends it to you in the mail or sends you a text or email to tell you that it is ready for you to log on and browse. Either way, there is a flow of data that leaves the work and travels to the outside world.

> *A business event is an external or time-triggered happening that triggers a business response.*

By using business events, you see the solution space as outsiders see it. This is your customers' view of the business, for it is your customers who are causing business events when they ask for things—information, services, whatever—from your business. The activities that are triggered by a business event form a cohesive partition— an independent, isolatable subset of the solution's activities that collectively contribute to the solution's response to the business event.

Is there anything else? Does the solution space do anything except respond to business events? Not at the business level. That's all there is. Everything it does has a connection to the outside world. Either there is an incoming request for a service or information, or there is an outgoing flow of information. Some business events have both. If there is no connection to the outside world, it might be for technological reasons, but it is hard to see that there would be any business benefit.

Once you have discovered all the business events (regular projects would have 20–50 events; enterprise projects would have several hundred) and studied the responses to the business events, you have completed your task of investigating the solution space. However, let us hasten to add that there is no need to investigate all the events before you do anything else. We suggest that you investigate the highest priority event first, do as much of the investigation as you need to do to decide your plan of action, and then move on.

Scoping by Business Event

Another approach to scoping is to use business events. As an example, let's revisit the beer distribution business you saw in the previous chapter. In the beer distribution business, the problem is to supply retail customers with the beer they want. If you consider this solution space and collude with a range of stakeholders, you can derive the business events.

This beer distribution business wants to have a warehouse to store the beer before it is sold to customers. (Yes, there are alternatives to a warehouse, but none of them is considered practical for various commercial reasons.) Because warehousing is an integral part of the solution, we put it inside the solution space and then look for things that happen to that warehouse. Or we could say that we look for flows of data to or from the outside world. One of the outside world entities would be a brewery, or importer, of beer. A business event happens when one of the breweries/importers delivers a beer shipment to the warehouse. Clearly, this event is necessary; it must happen if the warehouse is to have beer to distribute to the customers. You can investigate the activity triggered by this event including the checking of the delivery, the positioning and storage of the beer in the warehouse, the recording of the delivery for payment, and so on.

That's one business event, but there are more. Given a little time with your stakeholders, you would derive a list of business events like this:

- The brewery delivers a shipment of beer to the warehouse.
- The customer orders beer.
- The bartender submits his estimates for consumption.
- The bartender scans his stockroom.
- A delivery arrives at the customer's address.
- It's time to restock the warehouse.
- The customer returns some beer.
- Etc.

Consider the business event *It's time to restock the warehouse*. This is a time-triggered event, which means it happens inside the solution space. It results in the *Supplier Order* data flow going to the outside world. This event happens periodically—probably once a week. When it is time, the solution determines the stock on hand, looks at the predictions of what is needed for the coming weeks, and places orders with the appropriate suppliers.

When a customer orders beer, it's another business event that produces the incoming flow *The customer orders beer*. The response to this business event is to process the order, collect the required beer to be loaded into the driverless delivery vehicle (DDV), and send the delivery instructions to the vehicle. You can see these flows in Figure 4.3.

As we are talking about scope, it is appropriate to mention that the DDV is considered outside the scope of the solution space and is thus shown as an adjacent system. The reason for this decision is that the vehicles are unchangeable by your project, and they are not owned by the beer distributor. Therefore, there is no point including them as part of the solution space; your responsibility ends when you have sent the beer and the instructions to the DDV. You must, of course, negotiate with the manufacturer that the data you are sending is suitable for that model of DDV.

Figure 4.3

The scope of the solution space. The incoming and outgoing data flows are there because business events happened. You can correlate the flows with the list of business events shown above.

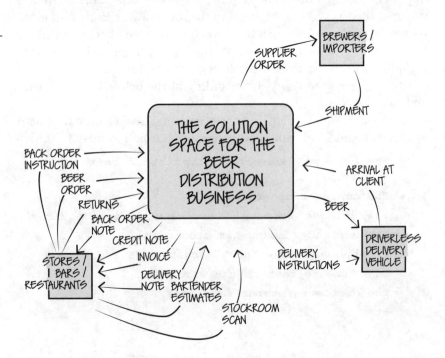

In other circumstances, you might have determined that the DDVs were within scope. If, for example, the DDV was partly under development and your solution was to program the DDV, get feedback, and make corrections to deliveries while the vehicle was doing its rounds, it should be included.

Another business event happens when the DDV arrives at the bar; it sends data to the solution space, which in turn triggers more business activity.

Each of the business events on the list triggers activity, and as part of that activity, receives data from the outside world, sends data to the outside world, or both. If you draw each of the flows and the origin or receiver of the flow, you would get the context diagram shown in Figure 4.3.

Please keep in mind that the list of business events shown above is incomplete. You might care to take a few moments to complete it for yourself.

Look at your scope model. Are there things that you can add to it to make it a more comprehensive and better solution? What can you delay developing parts of it or subtract from it?

You need to work with the rest of the team and the business stakeholders to build the list of business events and the context diagram. Important decisions are made when you determine the scope; you are deciding what is inside your solution space and must be studied and what is outside your control and cannot be changed. Sometimes these decisions are the most difficult ones that the project team makes.

Please don't let your project proceed too far without knowing the scope with a reasonable degree of certainty. Although the scope can be changed if there is some benefit to be had, it is desirable to have a communicable model of it. We understand that some practitioners advocate that scoping is not necessary, but our experience is that few projects work at their maximum potential while constantly revisiting scoping decisions and not knowing if something under discussion is part of the solution or not.

Finding All the Stakeholders

You don't perform this investigation on your own; you need help. Most of this help comes from your *stakeholders*. Stakeholders are not necessarily the same people as those who inhabit your customer segments, and they are not necessarily the people you call users.

A customer segment is made up of people with a problem that you want to solve. There is a reward for both you and the segment for doing so. Stakeholders, on the other hand, are people with an interest in the solution, but their interest is not necessarily one of being rewarded. For example, your security specialist is just doing his job when he provides his security requirements. The operations stakeholder is just doing her job when she tells you about operational needs.

You need these stakeholders, and you need to find them.

There is no hard and fast way to find the stakeholders, but we suggest that the simplest thing is to make a checklist, and for each business area, run through the checklist looking for applicable stakeholders. You might not have a checklist now, so use the following as a starter:

- **Customers for your service or product**—These people interact with your solution. Include each customer segment.

- **Internal users of your proposed solution**—Some have different business needs, and some have different cultural needs.

- **Subject matter experts**—These are specialists in the business area under investigation.

- **Managers**—These managers are affected by your solution. Don't forget your sponsor.

- **Consultants**—These might be external, such as security, user experience (UX), auditors, and so on.

- **Operations**—These include both internal ops and external ops for outward-facing solutions.

- **Legal**—There are too many laws, and it is too easy to fall foul of some. Your legal department has helpful stakeholders.

- **Inspectors**—These include government regulators, industry bodies, and standards bodies.

- **Cultural**—Your HR people might help; otherwise, look at the culture of your customer segments and users.

- **Special interest**—This might be public opinion consultants or special interest groups applicable to your industry.

- **Marketing**—These are your company marketing people as well as market-forces experts.

If you would like a more comprehensive list, please look at the Stakeholder Analysis spreadsheet and Stakeholder Map at www.volere.org.

You'll also find that if you are modeling some of the business processes, the models have a way of attracting stakeholders. "How do they know where to put stuff in the warehouse?" invites you to find the warehousing people, the people who retrieve stuff from the warehouse, a stakeholder with knowledge of storage and retrieval, and perhaps a mechanical handling guy. Each of these has the potential to tell you things about the problem that you might not otherwise have discovered.

And that's the point of it all: the more you discover, the better your delivered solution, and the higher its value.

Investigating the Business Events

You have a list of the business events that affect your solution space. We shall use these business events as a partitioning theme for the investigation (see Figure 4.4).

We suggest that you investigate the solution space one business event at a time. In other words, you study the activity triggered by an event and restrict your studies to that single event. This gives you a smaller, self-contained slice of the solution space to investigate. You can think in an agile way here and study as much as you need. Once studied, either move on to investigate another event, or take the event you have just studied and develop it (see Figure 4.5).

It is worthwhile to consider the effect of the business events on your eventual product. Every organization works by responding to business events. If an organization did not respond, it would quickly go out of business. The automated product that you build is simply part of the organization's response to a business event. We shall revisit this theme later in Chapter 6, "Writing the Right Stories."

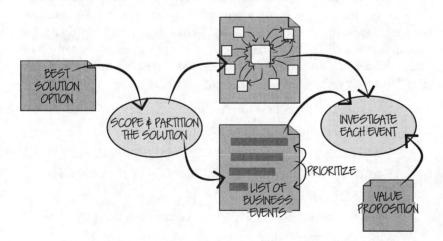

Figure 4.4

The chosen business solution is scoped and partitioned into business events. The response to each business event is investigated to ensure that its functionality delivers the required value.

Figure 4.5

The solution space is investigated one business event at a time. The investigation produces artifacts such as models, stories, and requirements (your choice). These artifacts are progressively communicated to later development activities. The shaded area of the diagram highlights a more sequential approach.

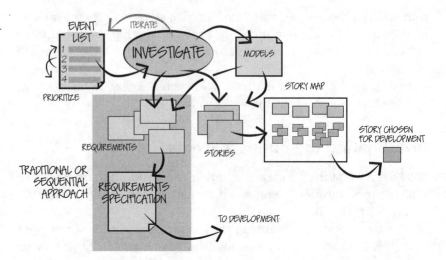

If you approach the investigation one business event at a time, you do not have to cope with the entire solution space at once, but an independent slice of it. This is convenient for modeling, which we shall talk of shortly. The business event gives you well-defined boundaries for your model. Your model starts with the business event happening; it ends when all the data has been stored or retrieved and all notifications have been sent to the outside world.

Prioritize the Business Events

Before leaving this, we must mention that you should prioritize your business events. You can think of this as triage if you prefer. You work on the highest priority events first and leave the low priorities until later (or perhaps never). Different teams have different priorities, so we cannot be prescriptive when discussing the factors that drive your event prioritization. However, we suggest you use factors such as the following:

- Legal demands (it's best to stay out of jail)
- Contractual obligations (avoid being sued)
- Value to the customer segment or to your organization (profit)
- Contribution to the value proposition (satisfy the customers)
- Risk (do the high-risk things early)
- Market impact (people have to notice your solution)
- Stakeholder availability (grab them while you can)
- Damage from not developing (the risk of getting further behind the competition)

- Need for visibility (make your project important in the eyes of the organization)

- Politics (keep the CEO, or someone else, happy)

Keep in mind that it is quite normal for 80% of your revenue to come from 20% of your activity. Prioritizing that 20% at this stage is extremely beneficial.

You might also consider clustering the business events by the adjacent system they interact with. This allows you to prioritize the adjacent systems and capture all that is needed to satisfy each one.

Also, remember that the scope is not standing still. Changes in the world might mean new events or changes to existing events. Whenever a new business event is selected for investigation, the choice of event reflects the priority of what is really happening in the business now, not what was considered the most important a few weeks ago.

Revisit your priorities from time to time. They change remarkably quickly.

Using Models for Your Investigation

All too often, modeling is seen as an end unto itself, but it's not. Modeling is undoubtedly useful, but we have observed too many times teams spending an inordinate amount of time building detailed models, when a few simple models would have been adequate for the purpose. Modeling can be a lot of fun to do, so we are urging you, dear reader, not to get carried away.

Keep in mind that the purpose of building a model is to understand and communicate. You might build a model in isolation and afterward show it to the stakeholders for their confirmation, but you'll get a better result by sketching your model in their company.

A lovely example of this came when your authors spent two days at a healthcare fund with the team leader, ten assessors, and some technical people. We gave the assessors rudimentary training, and they began to build the models of their work. These models were invaluable. They revealed parts of the work that everyone agreed were not at all obvious and might have been overlooked or not discovered without the modeling effort. They also discovered repetitions of the same work in different parts of the organization. Most of all, people who had never realized connections between their work started talking to each other. The project manager was happy that so much discovery could be done so quickly. The technical team members understood more of the problem, and importantly, it became their problem, too. That all this was modeled and visible contributed greatly to the success of the effort.

Modeling Business Processes

Process models are intended to show, well, business processes. We suggest using one of these models when the business process is complex, not completely understood, involves multiple people, or involves several departments. You are modeling to confirm you have understood the business process, the process works, and it solves the problem. You would also use the model to highlight potential problems with the solution, or to confirm the solution is acceptable to the customers and future users.

An example of a sketched process model, using part of the beer distributions solution, is shown in Figure 4.6.

Figure 4.6

A sketched process model showing a typical business process. This model has been annotated with questions and comments. It will be refined with the participation of the team and the business stakeholders.

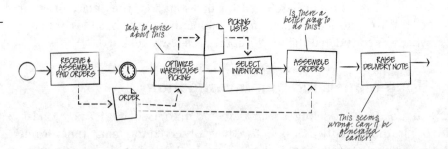

Business processes are made up of activities arranged in a sequence of some kind. Business process models use various notations to mirror the flow of these activities. The most commonly used notations are UML (Unified Modeling Language) and BPMN (Business Process Modeling and Notation).

However, there is no need to adhere strictly to any notation. A quickly sketched model, done in the company of stakeholders, is usually preferable to a perfectly formed model using correct notation, perhaps done with a modeling app drawing tidy diagrams onscreen.

Let's take the example of the business event that happens when the beer is delivered to the warehouse and sketch a model of the response to this event. After a few minutes with the dock manager and the warehouse manager, you draw the model shown in Figure 4.7.

Figure 4.7

A sketched model of the process that results from a brewer or importer delivering beer to the warehouse.

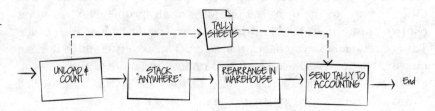

This model is useful because you can see the flow of the activities and question them. You are looking for ways to improve the process and to question the order of activities and their relevance. For example, why is the tally sheet sent to accounting after rearranging the warehouse? Can something happen during the rearrangement that could change the tally? Would this be the time that they discover damaged beer and don't want to pay for it?

Let's look at each of the activities.

Unload and Count

- The beer arrives on pallets and then is offloaded from the delivery truck by forklift. Is there a better way?

- The operator cannot see if all the beer on the pallet is the same. Some cartons are hidden inside the stacking on the pallet, and there is no time or desire to pull the pallet apart while it's on the dock. Does this cause problems later if there is different beer on the same pallet?

- The arriving beer must be counted for the accounting department. The counts are kept on the tally sheets.

- The barcode on one carton is scanned to give the beer type. Would a different technology such as radio-frequency identification (RFID) work better?

- Pallets come off the trucks in reverse order to that in which they were loaded. Is there any advantage in changing this order? Can the breweries load them in an order more advantageous to us? What would that order be?

Stack "Anywhere"

- The intention of this activity is to get the pallets off the truck as quickly as possible. There is only one forklift available, and the emphasis is on clearing the truck quickly. The pallets are put wherever there is space. Is this efficient? Could we avoid double-handling by relocating dock space or loading in a different order?

- Stacking "anywhere" frees up the dock for the next delivery. Is this necessary? How frequent are the deliveries? Could it be advantageous to take longer to unload by placing the pallets in their correct warehouse location while the delivery truck is held in the dock?

Rearrange in the Warehouse

● When a delivery happens, the forklift must move the oldest beer of each type to the front. The new beer is placed at the back. This is so that beer is not accidentally left beyond its use-by date. The forklift driver must read dates on the cartons to ensure that the oldest is being moved to the front. Could this double-handling be avoided?

● Is there a better method for selecting beer for delivery to our customers? Could we leave the beer wherever there is available space? We could if we have some way of remembering where this is and are able to retrieve the oldest beer when assembling a customer's order.

● Robotic warehouse equipment might solve this problem. Is it worth investigating? Or do we know it is too expensive? Possibly using RFIDs attached to each carton, or each pallet, might go some way to solving the problem. Should we investigate this?

Send Tally to Accounting

● We do this so the accounts people can reconcile their orders and invoices with the deliveries before paying.

● Is this done after the warehouse rearrangement so that any damaged goods can be noted on the tally sheets?

● Could we pay on delivery as soon as the incoming beer has been counted? We might get a significant discount for paying promptly and avoid a lot of paperwork.

Finally, there is the overarching question: "Is this solving the right problem?" For example, could the distributor not take delivery at all, but distribute directly from the brewery/importer? Is the central warehouse solving the problem? Could warehousing be distributed to make delivery more local?

These are the kind of questions—there would be many more—that you ask when investigating the response to each of the business events. Some of these might have a significant impact on the business process, and some may lead to a significantly different solution to that which has been proposed.

Figure 4.8

Modeling with the
stakeholders and the
team is always fruitful
and insightful.

Live Modeling

Our personal preference is to model on whiteboards and flipcharts.
We find this creates an immediacy between you and your stakeholders that is harder to achieve if you're hunched over a laptop screen.
Having people gathered around and participating as your model takes
shape and coalesces into a clear picture of the process is a lovely thing
(see Figure 4.8). We hope you enjoy it as much as we do.

Business Rules

Business rules set down the conditions under which people and automated solutions must operate in the organization. They are in effect the
internal laws of the business. If a decision is made, either by a human or
an automated process, that decision must conform to all applicable business rules. Obviously, this means that you must discover the business
rules so that any solution you propose is compliant.

Business rules can be written in several ways, but in their simplest form they look like this:

- **Driverless delivery vehicles may only be operated in approved cities.**
- **Airline cockpit crews must have a minimum of 12 hours between flights, measured from briefing room departure time to arrival time.**
- **Applicants must be at least 18 years old to open an account.**
- **Tweets may contain up to 280 characters of text.**

Business rules are not the same thing as requirements or stories; the latter specify the implementation of the rules. You will find that most rules need multiple requirements/stories for a successful implementation. Think of the rules as a source for your stories and requirements.

A response to a business event usually involves one or more business rules. You will find the rules when you work with the business stakeholders to discover the appropriate processes and data. The rules govern the processes, so they become embedded in your process models. Sometimes—perhaps often—one business rule is invoked by the multiple processes responding to several business events.

For each business rule, do you have all the business events that are needed to implement that rule? For each business event, do you have the business rules that govern the processes and data connected to the event response?

You find business rules almost anywhere in the business. Some organizations have a library of business rules, which makes it easy to identify which rules apply to your solution space. More commonly, the rules are scattered in user manuals, in operational procedures, and in people's heads.

If the rules are not currently documented, you might consider writing them yourself. They are, after all, the foundation of the work, and you must be clear about them if you are to propose and specify a compliant solution. We already suggested that business rules can be written as a single sentence:

- **Driverless delivery vehicles may only be operated in approved cities.**

Where necessary, this can be expanded by an elaboration:

- **An approved city is one that Bellingham's logistics department deems appropriate for ddvs. The city,**

> regional, and national laws allow driverless
> vehicles with no human aboard. ddvs may operate
> only within the geographical city boundary.

Or you might refer to where further information can be found:

- Driverless delivery vehicles may only be operated
  in approved cities. For approved cities, see
  https://ddv1/rules/147062.docx

In any event, when you discover a business rule, please document it. Too much depends on business rules to leave them roaming in the wild.

And while you are at it, make sure that the rule is a real business rule, not just another example of "We've always done it that way."

Why Don't I Skip Analysis and Just Write Stories?

Why don't we just brainstorm some stories instead of going to the trouble of identifying the customer segments and their value propositions, probing some proposed solutions, and investigating those solutions? The answer is that much of the time, the brainstormed stories turn out to be the wrong stories simply because the team members *assumed* they knew the solution.

Additionally, stories are granular. Almost always there are so many stories that it becomes difficult, if not impossible, for the team to have a coherent view of the product to be built.

Stories started with Kent Beck and extreme programming (XP). Beck suggested the story, or user story, as a way of describing a chunk of functionality that would be expanded and detailed at the time that the functionality was being developed. We won't call them *user stories* here, because *user* suggests that you have assumed an automated solution and who will be using it. Until you have understood the customer's needs and the problem to be solved, there is little point in thinking about automation and users.

The story is often described as a "placeholder for requirements" or "an invitation to a conversation." In other words, it is a marker for a chunk of functionality. We have described the response to a business event as a well-defined slice of functionality, so it makes sense to write a high-level story to keep a place for a business event. This approach means that you can trace the business event story back to the overall problem. We shall make use of this kind of story when we get to Chapter 6.

Mike Cohn wrote a good book on user stories called *User Stories Applied: For Agile Software Development*. Unfortunately, it has a flaw: it pays too little attention to the business side and what typical businesses would want for their development investment. We believe that we are being fair and not taking Cohn's words out of context when we quote:

> "The entire BigMoneyJobs site is probably described by these two stories:
>
> ● A user can search for a job.
> ● A company can post job openings."

These stories are at the highest level and obviously would have to be broken into finer detail before the site could be developed. The author said exactly that.

The real problem is not the level of detail but that the stories are about an assumed solution. They lead in the wrong direction and will result in a mediocre solution that in today's competitive world would not be good enough.

Suppose that, instead of rushing into some stories, you started with some investigation and analytical thinking. Questioning the users—in this case the jobseekers—you would quickly discover that people don't want to search for a job; they want to *find* a job. There's a difference. Searching is how a developer sees the problem, and finding is how the customer sees the problem. Searching for a job means that the jobseeker must repeatedly return to the site, do yet another search, and then sift through the results for something suitable. Finding a job means that the solution would do the matching, probably find a better match, and inform the jobseeker. This way the jobseeker is freed up to pursue other avenues for finding employment.

Suppose that instead of leading off with stories about an assumed solution, you asked enough questions to come up with a value proposition. It is reasonable to say that it would be something like this:

```
As a jobseeker,

I receive value when I find a position that matches
my interests, abilities, salary expectations, and
location.
```

This strongly suggests that jobseekers would be better served by providing their credentials and expectations and allowing the most appropriate job to be found for them. Matching would be more accurate and requires almost no more activity on the jobseeker's part. This approach would better solve the employer's problem by matching with a larger pool of talent and not being restricted to candidates who happened to search the site that day.

If you had started with a value proposition for the employers, it would be along the lines of this:

```
As an employer,

I receive value when I find candidates with the
correct qualifications and expectations.
```

The story "A company can post job openings" suggests that the companies would post their opening and then sit back and see who responds. The respondents will be both suitably qualified applicants, and those wannabes who are applying for jobs for which the salary is attractive but they are not.

Both value propositions suggest an approach more valuable than the original stories. The problem with the original stories is that they are product-centric and have the potential for either misleading the team or producing an inferior solution.

Resist the temptation to start writing stories until you have discovered enough information to understand the business needs.

Furthermore, your investigation can now step back and consider what kinds of things job candidates value. For example, is the commute distance critical? Should it be part of a candidate's posting? Should candidates be able to set a limit to commute time or means of travel? Are there other attributes that employers look for in candidates that you have not yet considered? And if you are to deliver value, there are many more questions to be asked before you fully understand the problem and can start thinking about a solution.

Contextual Inquiries

Let us say that you are on a project to build a music streaming service. We know there are already many of these in existence, so it is not too hard to find people who use them. Suppose your streaming service is targeted at a specific audience and is intended to be an improved musical experience. It won't get there by simply having more features, but by being closer to what people feel is the natural and instinctive way to play their kind of music.

Your contextual inquiry starts with customers of existing streaming services and other people who play music online. Let's sit down with one of these people—we'll call him Walter—and watch and talk to him while he operates his existing streaming service, be it Apple, Spotify, Diagio, Pandora, or whatever. For every step, for every click, for every thought process Walter goes through, ask him about it. Talk to him, and get him to talk to you and tell you what is good and bad about each step.

- How easy is it to search for new music?
- Does he find all the music he wants?
- Does he think he is missing out on music that he might like because the existing service makes it too difficult to find things?
- Does he feel engaged with his existing service?
- Does he appear happy with it?
- Does he like the music?
- Does it operate the way he wants?
- Does it hurt anywhere?
- Is there something missing from his music service that you could provide?
- Does he have a musical itch he needs to scratch?

66 Mankind's greatest achievements have come about by talking, and its greatest failures by not talking. It doesn't have to be like this. Our greatest hopes could become reality in the future. All we need to do is make sure we keep talking. 99

—Stephen Hawking

Be there—wherever your customers are.

The more time you spend with Walter, the better.

Even the most limited budget does not mean you skip talking to the customer; instead, you do it in the most productive manner. Being there—in the office, the home, the shop, or wherever your customers are—is the best place to study their environment and observe their work. Most importantly, you see what they don't do, where the awkward moments are, where they have needs that, so far, have not been recognized.

Creative Observation

You need to know the people in your customer segments if you want to learn what they need. You can talk to them; and you can look at them. But there is a difference between looking at something casually and looking at something with the intention of learning from your observations.

We were struck with the way that IDEO, an American industrial design firm, sends its people into the field to "observe human behavior and see where the opportunities lie." Business analysts can—and should—do this. Instead of watching the material and the devices being used, watch the people using them. Watch to see the process through the eyes of the person doing the job.

Processes always seem logical and reasonable to the people who are doing the processing. But if that process is providing a service, we must also see the process through the eyes of the person receiving the service.

There is a lovely IDEO story of one designer who pretended to be a patient at a hospital and managed to make a video of his experience. The service provided by the emergency room staff, while orderly and rational to them, was bewildering and frightening to the patient. The observations of the IDEO designer were used by the hospital to change its process and approach, to the acclaim of its patients.

Creative observation means that you watch the people doing the work or using the product (or a wireframe of it) to see where the problems lie. You are creatively observing to see what you could do to solve these problems.

The customer journey map that we spoke of earlier can come into play here. You can either develop it as you observe the action, or you can observe the differences between the actual journey and what you might have planned using a map.

The fields of ethnography, sociology, family therapy, and anthropology can contribute many ideas about how to do more effective creative observation.

Consider the Culture

The provider of a solution almost always has a different culture from the customer segment that receives the solution. Culture, as we speak of it here, is a set of assumptions and habits that guide our behavior. If your solution is to be of real value to the customer segment, then understanding the segment's culture helps you to know what it is that they value, what they won't tolerate, and what they don't want.

For example, in Western culture, we assume that red means stop or danger, and green means go or safety. We assume that pink is feminine, that white means purity, that black means death. We assume that reading is done left to right, and any progression, such as a model of a business process, moves from left to right.

These assumptions guide our behavior and subsequently the way we approach and use the solutions we are offered. We have assumptions about the meaning of words, about what links to other pages should look like, about the way that things should be. If we impose our culture—our assumptions—on our customers who have a different culture, results might not be as we would like them to be.

Let's look at a couple of cultural examples and see what we can learn from them.

The first of these is the attitude to change. Are we assuming this customer segment is willing to accept new things that might disrupt an established way of working? Is this segment at the leading edge of technology or at the back of the pack?

The second assumption, or cultural attribute, is the segment's acceptance of hands-on or hands-off. Are the people who make up this segment wanting to manipulate their solutions themselves, or are they more likely to appreciate a solution where they can sit back and watch it happen? Some people appreciate technology that requires manual input, and every aspect of it can be controlled by the operator. Some people like to program their own phone; others want to simply take it out of the box and turn it on.

There is nothing wrong with any of these cultural attitudes, but you must be aware of them if you are to deliver the appropriate solution.

These attitudes give us four quadrants in the predictable two-by-two diagram. We show this grid in Figure 4.9.

The intention is to have a way of thinking about the type of audience for your solution. Can it be a radical solution breaking with past traditions? Is your audience willing to accept significant change? Or is your audience more resistant to change, which suggests that you provide a more conservative solution? Do audience members prefer an autopilot solution that does most of the work for them? Or is this group very hands-on, preferring to twiddle the knobs for themselves?

The lower-left quadrant in Figure 4.9 is called cat. As you have probably observed, cats hate change and don't want to do much for themselves.

Figure 4.9

Culture of your intended audience. The horizontal axis measures willingness to accept change, and the vertical axis measures the segment's willingness to be hands-on.

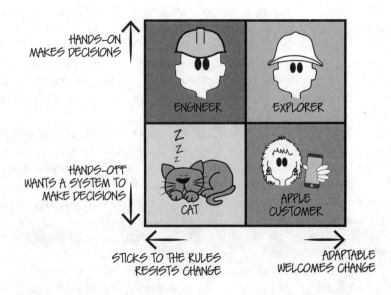

The engineer wants to be hands-on but wants a stable, predictable environment. The explorer is a hands-on kind of person who is always looking for change and therefore willing to accept it. The Apple customer readily accepts change but is happiest when the solution does almost all the work for her, as do most Apple devices and similar products.

We suggest that for each of your customer segments, you think about the culture and match it to a quadrant. This is by no means scientific, but it is sufficient to guide the kind of solution that you provide for each of your customer segments.

Of those segments willing to accept the change, your solution can be quite disruptive. For the cat and engineer quadrants, your solution should not cause significant upheaval to the work. The engineer and explorer quadrants prefer a solution that gives them a significant degree of control. Please keep this in mind when you are designing your solution, which we talk about in the next chapter.

Of course, that is not all there is to study about culture. Hundreds, if not thousands, of books have been produced on the subject, along with university and college courses, video courses, and other media ways of studying a subject.

The extent to which you study people is really a product of how known or unknown your customers are to you and the criticality of the solution you propose to deliver.

If this is a mission-critical solution pushing into a new market for you, then understanding what the customers will expect and accept is crucial to your success. In this case, we strongly suggest you hire some professional help: psychologists, ethnographers, anthropologists or whoever else can help you to understand your customers.

On the other hand, if you are the engineering company building engineering software, the chances are that you already know the culture of your engineer customers.

Culture is important. Nobody ever succeeded by producing a culturally-inappropriate solution.

Summary

Your investigation is about understanding the problem and the needs of the solution space. You are investigating the solution space to ensure that the proposed functionally is feasible—it works, the necessary data is available, and the processing can achieve its intended outcome. You are also investigating the people involved so that your solution can fit seamlessly into their thinking and their approach to their jobs.

Although we are not in any way advocating that you generate a huge amount of documentation while you are investigating the solution space, it is worthwhile considering that anything you do produce is business knowledge that can be useful for future development efforts. After all, would your own investigation have been easier if you started with knowledge from previous investigations? There is more on this theme in Chapter 7, "Jack Be Nimble, Jack Be Quick."

It's one thing to know that the solution can fit into the customer's world, but now we want to make it into the best possible fit. We do this by designing, which we talk about in the next chapter, "Designing the Business Solution." Read on.

Designing the Business Solution

5

• Useful, useable, used • Good design • Designing information
• Designing interaction • UX design • Convenience design
• Incremental, iterative, and evolutionary design

Design. This word scares a lot of people. Design is often seen as bolting on a pretty interface, laying out elegant graphics, or shaping attractive consumer goods—tasks that are done in trendy, colorful design studios by designers wearing trendy, colorful clothing.

Not here in the world of business analysis and solution delivery.

Design for us means designing the business solution, designing how all the components—the people, the hardware, the software, the organization, and so on—come together to provide the best, most effective experience for the customer.

> **Design is making things work properly.**

Design is about deriving the best incarnation of the essential problem; about finding the best way to present the needed information; about using the process and data that you discovered during the investigation activity in an imaginative way; and about devising the solution that fits most comfortably with the users' mental models and cultural assumptions.

The best solution does not come by simply analyzing the old work; nor does it come from merely listening to what people say they want. Rather, the best solution comes from looking at the problem in different ways, from having ideas, and from using those ideas to form the most elegant, convenient, beautiful, usable, desirable, satisfying solution. Simply put, the best solution is the one that is designed to be the best.

> 66 *Design is not just about what it looks and feels like. Design is how it works.* 99
>
> —Steve Jobs

Designing

So far in this book, we have been looking at collecting information or, more accurately, learning about our customers, their problems, and their needs.

Designing the solution should be seen as a transformational activity, done in conjunction with the activities just mentioned. The *safe-to-fail probe* has determined that this solution will in fact solve the customer's problem; your *investigation* has uncovered the needed functionality and the people involved in your solution. The *design* activity transforms what came before by forming the gathered knowledge into a workable business solution that not only solves the customer's problem but also presents a useful, usable solution that the customers want to use (see Figure 5.1).

Some of the design will already have been done. The major architectural decisions, graphics conventions, and user experience (UX) design guidelines will have been made early, as will major technological design decisions.

Designing: An Example

Let's look at a simple example of designing. We'll note the difference between the needs and how the designer accommodates those needs.

Gotham AirPort Express is a shuttle train that runs from the city center to the airport. Some of the passengers are tourists who make only one or two trips a year, but many are business travelers and airport workers who make multiple trips throughout the year. Passengers currently buy one-way or roundtrip paper tickets from machines or human ticket sellers at the stations. This way

Figure 5.1

Design overlaps and is concurrent with, the other activities. It is not seen as a separate activity, but as an enhancement to the other activities. The gray arrows represent feedback. The dark arrows represent connective artifacts.

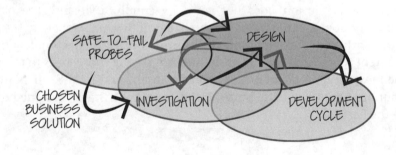

of selling tickets is expensive to run and is seen as old-fashioned by business travelers.

Management wants to sell prepaid multitrip tickets. The value proposition for this proposal is that the company receives value when it receives its money earlier and generates loyalty from passengers holding multitrip tickets. Even though they will not publicize this, there is the probability of a cash flow advantage from tickets that are lost or abandoned before all the paid-for trips have been taken. As an enticement, travelers receive a discount when buying a multitrip ticket.

How might you solve the problem of selling multitrip tickets?

There are different ways to solve this, so you must not rush at any assumed solution. Let us say that you have probed different proposals, and travelers appear willing to buy multitrip fares. This indicates that it is worthwhile to go ahead and solve the problem. Your investigation reveals that the target audience is business travelers catching a flight from the airport or airport employees going to and from their work. You have also learned how much money passengers would be willing to invest in a multitrip fare to get the discount.

How might you design the solution for selling multitrip fares?

The good people in marketing have jumped in with their idea of an app (see Figure 5.2). Passengers can download the app to their smartphone and then use it to buy their tickets. Each time they travel, the conductor scans the QR code displayed by the app, and the app debits the trip from the passenger's account.

MARKETING

GOTHAM AIRPORT EXPRESS

Figure 5.2

Marketing assumes it knows the solution.

Any intelligent fool can make things bigger, more complex, and more violent. It takes a touch of genius—and a lot of courage—to move in the opposite direction.

—Ernst F. Schumacher

However, as a designer, you must ask, "What's the simplest way of doing this?"

The simplest way is often to make use of something that people already have; for our business travelers, one possibility is a debit card. Cards are already linked to payment systems, so Gotham AirPort Express travelers can use an existing capability to buy a multitrip fare. Of course, everyone already has a smartphone or a smart watch, but these require extra steps, as well as the need to persuade people to download and install yet one more app on to an already overcrowded device.

The debit card solution means that there is no need for an additional artifact such as a ticket or an app—the traveler simply uses his existing card to buy a multitrip package. Although there are other ways to pay, any solution to the problem needs a way of identifying travelers who are using the multitrip system. The conductor on the train can do this by scanning the card, or it can be done by travelers scanning in and out at the train door or platform barrier. The cardholder's account is retrieved, the trip is debited, and the traveler is informed of the number of remaining trips. Perhaps the conductor could also pass out Gotham airport express stickers that passengers can affix to the card to remind them which of their many cards they are using for this trip, as shown in Figure 5.3.

Selecting a debit or credit card is designing a solution. And, like all good designs, this one is simple and close to the essence of the problem. Additionally, because most business travelers use their cards for business expenses, it fits well with the culture of the intended audience. It gets even better if the traveler is using a company card because there is no need to claim back expenses. A receipt can be emailed if an address is linked to the card.

Figure 5.3

The analyst selects a debit card as the solution design.

There's more. If the debit card solution is adopted by Gotham Airport Express, it is easy enough to adapt it for single-trip travel. This means casual users need not buy a ticket but can use their card and pay the standard price.

The simplest way to achieve simplicity is by thoughtful reduction

—John Maeda, The Laws of Simplicity

Simplest solutions are usually the best. Or perhaps we should say that the best solutions are usually simple.

Useful, Usable, Used

Think about the consumer products you enjoy using. They are probably visually attractive, but it's *the way they work that makes you enjoy them*. Think about websites you enjoy using, or apps that are among your favorites. It's the content and the way the websites present their content that make you use them. It's the way they anticipate what you want to do and then do it in a way that pleases you, satisfies you, that makes you continue to use them.

Of course, we want our solutions to be used. Nobody wants their solutions to languish, gathering dust on the shelf. But if they are going to be used, they must first be both *useful* and *usable*. A solution is useful if it meets the customer's needs and does something that the customer thinks needs to be done. It is usable if it provides the right information and the right functionality in a manner that is convenient and fits with its user's perception of how the task should be done.

If a solution is to be used, it must first be useful and usable.

The solution will be used if it does its useful tasks in such a manner that its users cannot imagine doing the task any other way.

For example, take a moment to visit the home page of Google.com. A search engine is useful when, for example, you want to find someone who is selling a vinyl copy of The Beatle's *Sgt. Pepper's Lonely Hearts Club Band*. Google is usable: simply type whatever you want to know in the obvious search box. Its search engine is so effective it can answer almost any question you can dream up. Do these two qualities make it used? Google processes about 3.5 billion searches each day. Being useful and usable make it used.

But useful, usable, used solutions do not come about by wishing them into existence or by leaving it to the solution builders and hoping for the best. These solutions must be designed.

What Is Design?

Design is the shaping of needs, facts, and ideas into solutions suitable for the intended audience. Sometimes this shaping is done well, and we are pleased with, and attracted to, the solution. Sometimes the shaping is haphazard, downright awkward, or not seriously done at all, and the solution's audience either suffers it in silence or, more usually, abandons it in favor of a better design.

Making Decisions

The first thing that separates design from analytical activity is that design requires you to make *decisions*. You decide what information is most appropriate at each stage of the interaction. You decide the sequence of the interactive functionality. In some cases, you decide what functionality the product is to have.

There are usually options—options on how things can be done, what technology to use, what to automate, and what to have the user do. You, or your product person, make decisions on these. Usually your decisions align with delivering the best value, and sometimes your decision is founded on other considerations such as constraints, familiarity, qualities of the users, house standards, and so on.

This does not mean that you're making it all up. You must still solve the customer's problem, but you decide how to solve it. You still accommodate the needs and the constraints, but you decide how to accommodate them.

Meeting the Essence

Even though you are making decisions, you never get away from the *essence of the problem*. Your solution, no matter how well designed, must meet and solve the customer's essential problem.

We have spoken in previous chapters about finding the essence—the solution space without any implementation technology—the soul of the business but not its body. We urge you to spend as much time as you can afford to ensure that you have arrived at the essential core of the real problem.

Something almost magical happens when you find the essence of the problem: the solution becomes apparent. When you have stripped away all the technological clutter belonging to the current or assumed implementation, you get a clear view of the essential problem. When you and your customers see the essence, you see the best solution for it. The best solution is simply the solution closest to the essence.

> *The first thing that separates design from analytical activity is that design requires you to make decisions.*

Meeting Constraints

A *constraint* is a restriction placed upon the way that you solve a problem. For example, you may have a constraint that your solution must work within the Visa credit card system, or your solution must work on iPhone and Android phones; or it must work on an airplane, underwater, or without the Internet.

This means some of the design decisions are taken out of your hands. For example, if manufacturers print barcodes on their products, a constraint on your point of sale solution is that it reads barcodes. As much as you might think it is preferable to use QR codes, RFIDs, or some other means of identification, you are constrained to use barcodes.

However, you must always challenge constraints to ensure that they are genuine constraints, not someone's assumed solution being put forward as a constraint.

Think of a constraint as a design decision that you do not get to make.

Meeting Architecture

Architecture—both enterprise architecture and systems architecture—is a constraint. The solution designer must shape the solution to incorporate the restrictions imposed by the architecture. Enterprise architecture imposes one lot of restrictions—for example, other systems that interact with your solution—and systems architecture imposes restrictions on the mechanisms available for your solution. Neither of these can be ignored.

Some architecture decisions should be made early in the project. These are actually quality requirements like interoperability, scalability, availability, security, and so on. These, like most of the quality requirements, apply to the entirety of the solution and determine some of your later architecture decisions. The last responsible moment for these decisions comes early in the project.

On the other hand, there are architecture decisions that can be left until implementation time. If these turn out to be incorrect, refactoring is usually available to correct them.

It is impossible for us to say much about architecture—each organization has its own approach and either its own way of documenting the architecture or, sadly, completely inadequate documentation. Our advice is that before diving too deeply into your own solution design, you talk to whomever (hopefully somebody) in your organization is responsible for architecture.

Architecture, both enterprise architecture and systems architecture, is beyond the scope of this book. However, knowledgeable colleagues have recommended some books that we have included in the bibliography.

66 *Always design a thing by considering it in its next larger context—a chair in a room, a room in a house, a house in an environment, an environment in a city plan* 99

—Eero Saarinen

Good Design

Most people working on projects do not claim to be great designers. Fair enough. But instead of wringing our hands about our lack of design expertise, we can make use of the *principles of good design* to influence our thinking when we are designing our solutions.

In no particular order, the principles say that a design is good if it has some—hopefully all—of the following characteristics:

Obvious—People can use the design without excessive (or any) coaching or instruction. If you need to attach labels and signs to things, it indicates that those things could be redesigned.

Spare—Spare solutions are free of unnecessary functionality or decoration and are always easy to use.

Differentiated—There is a clear and beneficial distinction between your solution and what came before. For example, the jet engine versus the propeller; the smartphone versus the one plugged into the wall; streaming music versus buying discs. All of these solutions show a distinguishable advancement.

Enduring—There is a difference between fashion and endurance. Levis 501 jeans is an enduring (since about 1890) design. No other jeans design has lasted more than a few years. Unix was first developed in the 1970s. Roman typefaces started with, er, the Romans. If you incorporate the rest of these principles in your design, you'll get one that endures.

These are qualities you strive for. If your solution has most of them, it is far more likely to be accepted and used—probably also enjoyed.

What Are You Designing?

You, in conjunction with the product owner and other product people, business stakeholders, and always, where possible, customers, are designing a *business solution* to the problem. A business solution is more than a software product. It takes into account the people and the devices, the activities and the information, needed to make the solution work in its intended environment. It also must take into account the world immediately outside the solution. Consider the three elements shown in Figure 5.4.

Figure 5.4

There are three elements to consider: the internal user, the automated product and its attached databases, and the immediate outside world that is usually, but not always, your external customers.

Each of these elements can connect to any of the others. Sometimes there might be a three-way connection. This means that your solution design is about the *interaction* between the elements—automated product, user, outside world—and the *information* needed for that interaction. Indeed, it's impossible to separate the interaction from the information; each drives the other. To make the best of that, the designer must understand the task being done, the information being used to do that task, and the interaction that will bring about the satisfactory and convenient completion of the task. This is illustrated in Figure 5.5.

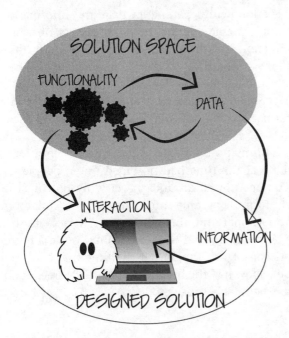

Figure 5.5

The solution space contains the essential functionality and its data. These components are used to design the business solution.

❝ *Design everything on the assumption that people are not heartless or stupid but marvelously capable, given the chance.* ❞

—John Chris Jones

Of course, you do not exactly design the involved humans, but you do design the interactions they participate in. Your design comes in the form of a script or operating instructions, or a product that is so obvious to the outside customers that they unhesitatingly interact with the product.

Designing the Information

There is an important difference between data and information. Data is the raw material—the numbers, the facts—and is generally not usable by humans. Information is what we humans process and use.

All the flights from all the airlines from all the airports on all the days of the week is *data*. The small number of flights that depart from an airport convenient to you, that will arrive at a time of your choosing, that offer a fare that you are willing to pay, and that have availability, is *information*.

Information is for human consumption, and because it is reasonable to expect that your users are human, you must design the information such that it is fit for human consumption. Designing the information is selecting which data is to be used and when and how it is turned into useful information. To put that another way, designing the information is deciding which stages of the interaction need which information, and in some cases, rearranging the interaction to make a better presentation of the information.

Consider the following example of data and information: in 1854, there was a cholera epidemic in the Soho district of central London. As happens in cholera outbreaks, many people died; in this case, it was 50,000 Londoners. The data on deaths was available—the authorities had records of the people who had died and their address at the time of death. John Snow, a physician who happened to live in Soho, constructed information from this data and presented it in the map shown in Figure 5.6.

Snow made his map from the data about deaths, locations, and water pumps. London at the time had no piped water; people fetched their water from pumps dotted around the city. By putting the data into topographical form, it became information. Snow's map now revealed that a disproportionate number of deaths—in fact, most of those in Soho—were clustered around the water pump in Broad Street. Despite official skepticism (it was thought at the time that cholera was an airborne disease), Snow had the handle of the Broad Street pump removed, and the outbreak quickly subsided.

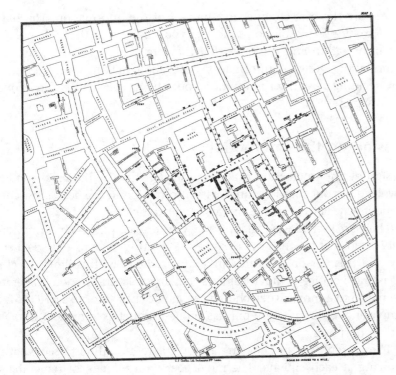

Figure 5.6

John Snow's map, sometimes called "the map that changed to world," plotted the cholera death locations and the 13 water pumps in the district. He used the topographical information displayed by the map to demonstrate that the source of the cholera was one water pump in Broad Street. Source: Published by C.F. Cheffins, Lith, Southhampton Buildings, London, England, 1854.

Did John Snow design the information? Yes, he suspected that the cholera deaths were linked to water, and by exposing the geographical relationship between water pumps and deaths, he was in effect designing the information. His design formed the data into information that enabled him to do his task—in this case, saving lives. Snow's actions were noted in the United States, with the result that authorities began working on improving sanitation and the water supply. Cholera outbreaks that were part of the first half of the 19th century, particularly in small towns, began to disappear. As a business analyst, you are not usually involved in cholera outbreaks and saving lives, but you are involved in designing information that enables your stakeholders to do their work in the most effective manner.

A footnote to the John Snow cholera story: At the time, there was a brewery in Broad Street quite close to the lethal water pump. Snow interviewed the owner, a Mr. Higgins, who told him that the workers had an allowance of beer each day, and as far as he knew, none of the workers drank water, preferring instead to drink the beer. None of the brewery workers were infected. This might be useful information in the event of a cholera outbreak in your neighborhood.

You are the best designer for the user of the information. You have been studying the solution space, so you understand the audience for the information and the tasks that they are doing when they use the information. Design of information is not about making pretty graphics, but deciding how the information could be most usefully and conveniently presented.

Designing the Interaction

Designing the interaction is about ensuring that the humans who are involved in your solution can use its information in the best, most convenient way. Let's illustrate that with an example.

There are several ways that people want to access movie information, but let's look at the instance of someone wanting to go to a movie. Let's say that this person is located in a fair-sized city with a choice of cinemas and a choice of movies at these cinemas. Naturally enough, before people go to a movie, they choose the movie they want to see. This is a simple enough transaction but has enough subtleties to make it suitable for our purposes.

The current way of choosing a movie is to go online to see what is showing at each cinema. The moviegoer writes down, or remembers, each potential movie, its start time, and its cinema before going on to look at the next cinema's offerings. When all available cinemas have been inspected, the moviegoer reviews the information to find the optimal movie. Optimal in this case is a movie that the moviegoer wants to see and is starting (or ending) at a convenient time and showing in a convenient cinema. (Humans love convenience.)

If you were to come up with a scenario of the current situation, it would look something like the following:

1. The moviegoer looks up and writes down (or remembers) movies based on personal preferences (genre, actor, director, or other attributes that the moviegoer considers important).

2. The moviegoer filters the movies based on preferred time of screening and location of cinema.

3. If necessary, the moviegoer looks up reviews of the filtered movies. The movie's poster is often a good indicator of the mood of the movie, and this can be found if wanted.

4. The moviegoer looks up availability of parking, driving time, or public transport options.

5. The moviegoer selects a movie.

There are some problems with this—mainly the need to keep lists and juggle the information. We spoke earlier about the essence of the problem, and in this case the essence is that the moviegoer selects the optimal (movie preferences, times, location) movie.

From this essence, and the previous scenario, you can see that there are about a dozen items of information that the moviegoer needs if she is to select the best option:

Screening time—Start time, end time

Location—Distance, travel time, travel mode (personal or public transport), parking availability if needed

Movie—Genre, director, actors, reviews, poster, mood, or style

Interaction design is deciding how to prioritize and present the information in the most meaningful and usable way so that the moviegoer can decide, quickly and conveniently, without the need for temporary notes.

The future scenario would be something like this:

1. The moviegoer provides personal preferences or retrieves previously recorded preferences.

2. The moviegoer provides the preferred start time.

3. The moviegoer provides her current location. (This might be available from the moviegoer's technology.)

4. The solution provides the most likely candidates in preferential order.

5. The moviegoer selects a movie from this short list.

6. If required, the moviegoer buys tickets using the solution.

The above interaction results in the information shown in Figure 5.7. This is getting close to the domain of the UX design. (We'll talk about that next.)

Looking at Figure 5.7, start in the middle. The house icon represents home, or wherever the moviegoer happens to be at the time. The lines radiating out from home indicate the travel distance; and the curvature of the line indicates the difficulty of the travel. The car or bus symbol indicates the mode of transport. The size of the parking sign indicates the availability and convenience of parking. The clock is larger or smaller depending on its nearness to the previously stated preference for start time. Finally, the size of the poster is a prediction of how much the moviegoer would enjoy the movie based on her preferences and movie attendance history.

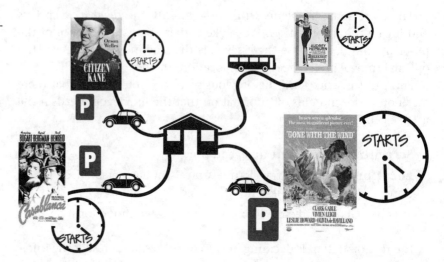

In this case, the information is saying that the moviegoer should see *Gone with the Wind*. *Casablanca* appears as the second choice, but it starts half an hour earlier, which might not fit as well with the planned attendance time.

It is significant that only these four movies are shown; others failed to make the short list because they fell outside the moviegoer's preferences or the parameters set for this occasion. Although you must not overwhelm the user with unnecessary information, you might add an option to see other movies that did not make in onto the short list. You would do this in case there is an outlier that, although not as convenient, tickles the curiosity of the moviegoer.

The point is not to design the graphics, but to design the information—what information is needed, what is not needed, and how and when the information is shown to the user. All this allows your user to make quick, convenient decisions.

UX Design

The task of the UX designer is to design an experience such that the user finds it useful, convenient, and pleasurable. The UX designer seeks to improve the user satisfaction with the product by providing an interaction tailored to the user's perceptions. UX designers are skilled at understanding how people respond. Therefore, they form their solutions so that users can respond efficiently and effectively. UX designers sometimes have a knowledge of ethnography, or at least an understanding of how people react and behave.

Graphic design should be part of the UX designer's arsenal. Being able to craft pleasing, informative, and intuitive graphics is an important contributor to the overall experience of the user. A knowledge of language—which words are appropriate, and which should not be used—helps the product to be more comprehensible to its users.

The UX designer wants to design the best possible interaction between the product and its users. If you are a business analyst (or other team member), this is also your goal. The difference between the BA and the UX roles is their approach to the task.

The UX designer is approaching the task from the solution side, and the business analyst is coming from the problem side. The business analyst has been studying the functional and informational needs and has studied and interviewed the people who are to interact with the solution. The UX designer forms this knowledge into an accurate and responsive user experience.

We can say that the UX designer comes armed with skills, and the business analyst comes armed with knowledge. Figure 5.8 shows the two disciplines meeting somewhere in the middle. This is slightly idealized; the exact meeting point varies from project to project.

Not all organizations employ a specialist UX designer or a usability expert. Sometimes UX and usability are done by short-term contractors, and sometimes it falls to the business analyst and others in the team who have the required aptitude or interest. UX and usability are outside the scope of this book, but if you are interested, we urge you to explore some of the UX resources available online.

> ❝ Y'all talk about UX like it's just another feature. For a user, it literally is the product. Full stop. Everything else is inside the baseball. ❞
>
> —Startup L. Jackson (Twitter)

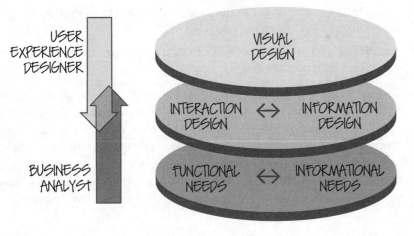

WITH ACKNOWLEDGEMENT TO JESSE JAMES GARRETT

Figure 5.8

Through his investigation, the business analyst learns the functional and informational requirements. The second level of the diagram shows how these needs are designed into the solution. This overlaps with the UX designer, who provides the visual design for the solution.

If you're about to launch a major website upon which the success of your business depends, you will invest heavily in skilled UX and usability designers. On the other hand, if your project is a routine, in-house, noncritical one, the business analyst and the team collaborate to do most—and possibly all—the UX design.

The solution you provide will not be the first one your users have seen. Expectations are high. Your users have undoubtedly used smartphones and tablets that have very usable interfaces. Similarly, your users will have been browsing thousands of websites, used dozens of apps, and have seen how good UX design can be. Don't disappoint them.

Designing Convenience

When you design to provide the right interaction with the right information, you design to provide *convenience*. Humans love convenience, and given a choice in which price does not come into it, a human always selects the most convenient option available:

- We subscribe to daily newspapers on our tablets because we can read them in bed or over breakfast.

- We love smartphones because it is more convenient to have a camera, diary, and text messages on the same device.

- We use laptop computers because it is more convenient to carry our work around with us.

- Many people prefer tablets to laptops because they are lighter and thus more convenient to carry around.

Humans love convenience and always opt for the most convenient of the available options.

- Online shopping is usually more convenient than visiting several stores to find the item you need.

- Debit and credit cards and direct transfers are more convenient than cash and checks.

We are willing to pay for convenience whenever we can afford it. We buy microwave ovens and dishwashers; we buy Kindles and iPads; we pay for GPS navigation systems because they are more convenient than paper maps; we pay subscriptions for streamed music services. If you look at some of the most impressive commercial success stories in the past decade or so—Google, Netflix, Amazon, Uber, Federal Express, First Direct bank in the UK—all provide convenience as the major part of their offering.

It is more convenient if you can save someone's time. Consider the business process that you are designing. Can you make it quicker by reorganizing it? Can you eliminate any steps from the process?

Can you provide some extra information or extra functionality (or perhaps less functionality) that would make the user's or customer's task easier and more convenient? Can you do the homework for the customer?

Is there some technology that would make any task more convenient? Your authors are particularly enamored with how Touch ID and facial recognition on their smartphones and computers allows them to avoid usernames and passwords when logging onto their bank. Bank passwords, of necessity, are long, complex, hard to remember, and difficult to type accurately on a phone. Would your customers find it more convenient to use an access technology that is different from what you currently offer?

Which of the following would you rather hear?

"Welcome to Buzzard Airlines. Your call is important to us. Your call may be recorded for quality and training purposes. Please select from the following options: to make a booking press 1; to cancel or change a booking press 2; for all other options, press 3 (and we'll then give you another menu)."

or:

"Peregrine Airlines. Please say what you want, and while we are putting you through to the appropriate person, we'll tell you that your call may be recorded for quality and training purposes."

We would like to drop the last part, but there is a legal requirement to inform someone that they are being recorded.

Our colleague Shane Hastie tells us that his preferred airline, Air New Zealand (Shane's a Kiwi), can connect his frequent flyer number and status to his phone number. When he calls, he is automatically recognized, and his frequent flyer number is retrieved along with the next reservation. There are options to change to other frequent flyer numbers or booking, but most of the time Shane is calling from his own phone about his own bookings, so naturally he calls Air New Zealand in preference to other available airlines. Convenience wins again.

Is there anything—anything at all—that your user is doing that you can do for him? Can you remember something for your users, such as their preferences, clothing sizes, or previous transactions? Can you provide background information (the "what is this" links you see on the web, for example) that helps your user make decisions?

Always, when you are designing, put yourself behind the eyes of the person who will be using your solution or doing the work that you design. What is most convenient to you? What is it that you can change to make the task easier or make the work flow more smoothly?

Incremental, Iterative, and Evolutionary Design

Throughout the rest of this book, we have talked about an iterative approach to business analysis and developing your solution. Design is no different. Backtracking and fast-forwarding should be considered normal.

Some of your designing is done early. We mentioned that the significant architectural decisions are made early in the project. Some designing is done once the customer's problem is correctly understood, and you need to form your solution such that stories and requirements can be written. Other designing is done during the development cycle. This is shown in Figure 5.9.

Before designing anything, ask if you should do it now or if it can be responsibly delayed until needed. Leaving things, where possible, is usually preferable; by the time you get to it, you know more about the problem.

Design is iterative; it is never a straight-line trajectory from the beginning to the final product. You must allow for this and welcome it. However, it is not endless. You should always, albeit reluctantly, set up either

> 66 I believe that architecture, as anything else in life, is evolutionary. Ideas evolve; they don't come from outer space and crash into the drawing board. 99
>
> —Bjarke Ingels, architect

Figure 5.9

Design is not an isolated activity. It co-exists with other activities that are discovering more about the solution to be designed. The design activity is itself discovering things that need to be investigated by the other activities.

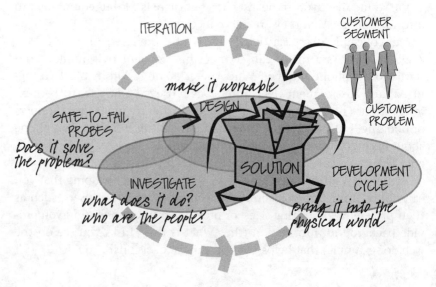

a time box for it or define exit criteria so that you have an agreed end-point. But while you are designing, at various times—perhaps these can be pegged to your development cycle—it pays to step back and review:

- Does the component I am designing fit comfortably into the over-all business solution?
- Is the design evolving into the best possible solution for my customer segment?
- Do I have, or can I get, customer feedback?
- Can my customers help me improve the design?
- Can I find an even better way to design this component?
- Am I still solving the right problem? Or is my design becoming irrelevant? (Don't laugh; this happens.)

Sometimes when you step back, you see a problem that requires you to rework the design. This is no bad thing provided you are still within your time box. When you are forced to rework, you will almost always find your subsequent design to be better than it was. Such is the effect of iteration.

Change happens. Part of stepping back is looking over your shoulder to see if there are changes in your organization or in the outside world that impact your design; there will be at some stage. These changes make design an iterative activity. Changes do not always come from outside your project. Your design activity overlaps your discovery activity, and the possibility of discovering some new facet to the problem is always there. As you design, you raise more questions, the answers to which might cause a change to the design. So be it.

Enabling Technology

Something that might influence your design is the presence of *enabling technology*. This is a device, machine, or some piece of technology that you can use to implement your design.

For example, you might make use of a virtual personal assistant (VPA). At the time of writing, VPAs such as Siri, Google Now, Echo, and the like are restricted to retrieval of information—usually prompted by voice commands—and can initiate straightforward functionality such as play-ing music, turning on the lights, and heating. However, by the time you read this, VPAs will have incorporated artificial intelligence (AI) and moved further forward into the realm of anticipating their users' needs and performing the appropriate processing and informational tasks. You can treat the VPA as a piece of technology that enables some of the essential tasks you have identified for your solution.

Virtual reality (VR) and artificial intelligence (AI) engines are also available and can be incorporated in your design for some of your essence. AI can also be built into other devices to enhance their appeal and applicability to your design.

For example, in an earlier chapter, we discussed a beer distribution business and how one of the problems they needed to solve for their customers was how to ensure that the customer (bar, restaurant or liquor store) had sufficient stock on hand to meet all demand, but not so much that the beer would become stale or exceed the customer's inventory budget. Using AI as part of the solution would most likely result in a better situation. Having RFID tags attached to the cases of beer would allow automated scanning of the customer's stock room to fine-tune the predictions. Then using driverless vehicles (AI and VR) to deliver the beer would allow for more frequent, smaller deliveries. This scenario is shown in Figure 5.10.

Figure 5.10

The technology enables this design of the future work.

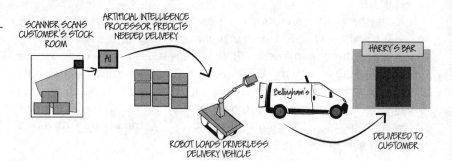

Please keep in mind that technology moves forward in a relentless progression. Most of that which we have mentioned earlier might have become commonplace or even outdated by the time you read this.

The point is not to rush into a technological solution simply because the technology exists, but to use enabling technology to design better solutions to solve your customers' problems.

Recording Your Design

Probably the easiest way to pass along your design to others is a combination of scenarios, storyboards, and sketches. The storyboard shows each step of the interaction and the information presented by that step. See the example in Figure 5.11.

Sometimes the narrative of your business solution is a little longer. See the example in Figure 5.12.

A sketch, often called a *wireframe*, is usually sufficient to show the information that the user sees. It should not be a complete screen design—that's for the UX designer. It should be just enough for you to be able to present the design to others. See the example in Figure 5.13.

BRAD AND JANET TAKE THE FAMILY AWAY FOR THE WEEKEND.

SOLUTION SENSES THE CAR LEAVING, LOCKS THE DOORS, AND TURNS ON THE BURGLAR ALARM.
SOLUTION ACTIVATES THE RANDOM LIGHTS PROGRAM AND TURNS DOWN THE HEATING.

BEFORE THEY RETURN... JANET PHONES THE SOLUTION TO CHECK THE FOOD SUPPLIES AT HOME. SHE ASKS THE SOLUTION TO THAW A FROZEN CHICKEN.

THE SOLUTION DETECTS THE CAR AND ITS OCCUPANTS, OPENS THE GARAGE DOOR, AND UNSETS THE BURGLAR ALARM. SOLUTION PLAYS THEIR FAVORITE HOMECOMING MUSIC AND STARTS COOKING THE CHICKEN.

Figure 5.11

An example of a storyboard for a home management solution.

ELENA HAS WRITTEN A BOOK.

NAME:
PASSWORD:
SHE LOGS ON TO NETAUTHORS.COM AND OPENS AN ACCOUNT

ROMANCE SCI-FI TRAVEL
SHE SELECTS THE GENRE OF THE BOOK SHE HAS WRITTEN.

Figure 5.12

A storyboard for a business solution that enables budding authors to write and publish their own books. The solution provides writing assistance to the author.

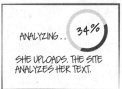

UPLOAD
SHE IS GIVEN A CHOICE OF UPLOADING HER TEXT OR WRITING ONLINE.

ANALYZING .. 34%
SHE UPLOADS. THE SITE ANALYZES HER TEXT.

THE SITE ADVISES ..

YOUR STYLE OF WRITING IS NOT QUITE SUITABLE FOR SCIENCE-FICTION. WE SUGGEST YOU SHORTEN YOUR SENTENCES AS THIS APPEALS TO MOST SCI-FI FANS. WE SUGGEST THAT YOUR USE OF TECHNOLOGICAL TERMS COULD BE MADE MORE EVERYDAY — STORIES APPEAL MORE WHEN THE AUDIENCE CAN RELATE STRONGLY TO THE TECHNOLOGY.

IF YOU WOULD SELECT A CHAPTER FROM YOUR BOOK AS TYPICAL OF YOUR STORY, WE CAN AUTO-EDIT IT AND LET YOU SEE WHAT IT WOULD BE LIKE IF IT USED OUR SUGGESTIONS.

THE SITE OFFERS AUTO-EDITING

● ● ●

PUBLISH!

Figure 5.13

A quick sketch or wireframe. The sketch has enough information to indicate the functionality, but not enough to make anyone think that it is the finished product.

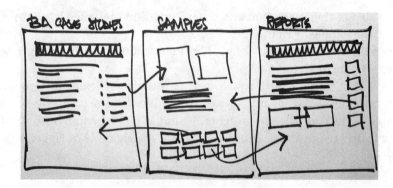

The rationale for your design—why you chose one option over another—is as important as the design itself.

Feel free to use whatever medium you like. You might also use a rich picture such as is shown in Figure 5.10. Keep in mind that great art is not needed—nobody expects you to be Michelangelo. If you are not happy with your drawing skills, there are plenty of apps that can draw it for you.

You might have a quick look at some of the people who write about and coach graphical thinking and sketching. Dan Roam and Penny Pullan are two of our favorites.

There are other options available to you for presenting your design: role playing, process models, stories, quick and dirty software simulations, and so on. Use whichever combination you feel appropriate for your solution and your team.

Regardless of how you do it, the objective is to be able to present your ideas for the design and solicit further ideas.

Along with the design, you must pass on the *rationale* for your design. The reasoning that went into your design—why you selected one option instead of another—is important for your developers and your maintainers. Anything you do is likely to last a few years, more likely a few decades. The people in the future who have to modify and update your solution need to know why things are as they are. They can see *what* the solution is doing, but they need to know *why* it is doing it if they are to make changes and not inadvertently corrupt the original intention. It is not hard to attach a rationale to your design; it will result in the developers doing a better job and producing a solution that is faithful to your intentions.

And that brings us to the end of this section on design. Design is necessary if you want your users to find your solution both useful and usable, and ultimately used. Design is not about making beautiful interfaces—although that is encouraged—but about making the functionality and information work in the best possible manner.

Writing the Right Stories

6

• Writing stories • Story maps • Enhancing your stories
• Kanban • Prioritizing the stories • Quality needs
• Minimum viable product • Development cycles

Stories are used by most agile teams, and if you use them, it is best that they are written so that they deliver the maximum value to the customer and the sponsor.

Let's start by not calling them "user stories." By assuming a user, you are narrowing your thinking to someone sitting in front of a computer or holding a device. The best stories come not from thinking about computers, but from thinking about the business problem you are solving.

Stories have several uses. One is to indicate the need for some functionality or qualities that solve a problem for the customer segment. But stories are not the whole story. Stories are not the detailed requirements, but *placeholders for requirements*. This means that the story is discussed and the detailed requirements for the product are fleshed out. These requirements must, of course, ensure that the product solves the right problem.

Given its use as a placeholder for requirements, it is crucial that the story holds the right place and solves the right problem. If the story is the wrong story, it misleads the development team, which is then unlikely to reach the right solution.

The story is also *a unit of development*. That is, each development iteration undertakes to develop a story—and most of the time, several stories.

Stories are often written on cards, and this informal approach sits well with the role of the story—something that is discussed, moved around, prioritized, stuck on a wall as part of a story map (more on that later), and can be worked on and changed as you discover more about the real need. There are software tools available to record your stories. These are

> *The best stories come not from thinking about solutions, but from thinking about the business problem you are solving.*

useful for large or distributed teams, but wherever possible, we urge you to consider using cards for their flexibility. For the rest of this chapter, we will talk about stories as if they are written on cards.

Besides being a placeholder for requirements, stories, when developed, deliver value to both the customer and the business. Let's briefly revisit the value proposition that we talked about in Chapter 2, "Do You Know What Your Customers Value?" There we discussed how the proposition sets down what the customer (or user for in-house development) values.

As an example, let's look at a small business called *Chicchi* (Italian for "beans," as in coffee beans). Chicchi is a business that trains people to become baristas so that they can find employment making top-quality coffee for customers in coffee shops, bars, and restaurants. Consider this value proposition for one of the customer segments:

```
As a trainee barista, I receive value when I become
a skilled, qualified barista.
```

This value proposition shows the value to the barista. The value to the business owner comes when trainees complete their courses and pay for them. This means, naturally enough, that any stories you write contribute to the goal of training baristas. Let's talk about how you arrive at these stories.

Business Events

A business event represents the functionality that is the business solution's response to some significant external or time-triggered happening.

A business event represents the functionality that is the business solution's response to some significant external or time-triggered happening. (We discussed these fully in Chapter 4, "Investigate the Solution Space"). The business event is a high-level story, and some people call it an *epic*. However, there is no satisfactory definition of *epic* apart from "large story that may contain other stories or epics," which is not exactly helpful.

So instead of using this vague and overused term, we use *business event*. We know exactly what a business event is, what triggers it, where it starts, where it ends, and exactly how much functionality makes up the response to the business event. The business event gives us a story that is a bounded, traceable descriptor of the solution's response to the business event. The response is triggered the moment an external entity initiates a request and ends when the request is completely fulfilled. The response to an event is a unique collection of activities. The set of business events describes the complete functionality of the business solution. In other words, the solution does nothing but respond to business events.

You write a business event story to look like this:

```
As a [customer segment]

I can have [functionality that responds to my
business event]

So that I receive [business value].
```

Note the intention of the business event story. It is not about the product but is looking outward at the customer. This is because it is the customer, or some other external entity, that triggers the business to respond to the business event. Moreover, the business event invites you to step back and look not only at the customer, but also at the response from the business. In other words, business events are about the business, and not, for the moment, about the product you intend to build.

The business event is usually too big a story to be implemented in one iteration, so it must be broken down, or sliced, to stories small enough to implement. However, we can put that aside for the moment and concentrate on the solution needs at the higher—business event—level.

Let's go back to Chicchi; its context model is shown in Figure 6.1. Apart from scoping the solution space, the context model shows the flows of data entering and leaving that space. Each of these flows is connected to a business event. Look at the list of business events that follow, and you can trace each of them back to one or more flows on the context model.

Business events are about the business, and not, for the moment, about the product you intend to build.

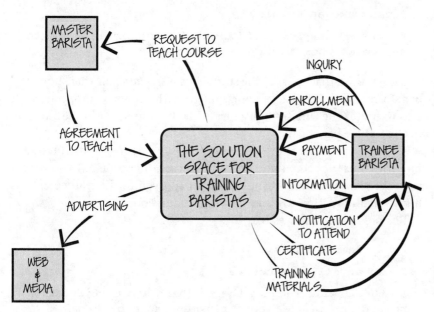

Figure 6.1

The context model for the Chicchi solution space. This model shows the data that flows in and out of the solution space. Each of these data flows indicates the presence of a business event.

The context model shows the *raison d'être* for the business solution. The data flows, and their business events provide services. These services are the result of the bargains struck between the solution and its ecosystem. "I'll give you this data, and you give me that information."

In no particular order, the list of business events (or touchpoints) looks like this:

1. The trainee barista makes an inquiry.
2. The trainee barista enrolls in a course.
3. It's time to notify the trainee barista to attend the course.
4. The trainee barista pays for the course.
5. It's time to issue a certificate to the graduating trainee.
6. It's time to advertise the courses.
7. It's time to request the master barista to teach a course.
8. The master barista agrees to teach the course.
9. It's time to hold a class.

There would be a few more, but they would be housekeeping things like cancelling a course, changing dates, and so on. This list will suffice for the moment.

For each of the business events, you can write a story. For example, from business event #1, we get:

```
As a trainee barista

I can make an inquiry

so that I receive sufficient information for me to
decide whether to take a course.
```

Note the "so that" part of the story. This is the *rationale* that shows the benefit received. It must, of course, align with the value proposition. It also indicates the functionality needed if the response is to be valuable to the trainee barista.

The inquiry in this story could be almost anything, and all relevant inquiries must be accommodated. In this case, the value to the business (and the trainee) comes if the information given to the trainee entices him, and allows him, to make a favorable decision.

Business event #2 gives this:

```
As a trainee barista

I can enroll in a course

so that I will receive the training and certification
needed for me to find employment as a barista.
```

The enrollment business event is necessary because training is not a single-session affair that can be conducted on a walk-in basis. There are multiple lessons over multiple days in the course, and a master barista is booked to teach them. This makes it necessary for trainees to enroll (and of course, pay). The value to the customer segment (trainee baristas) is that they are moving toward their qualification. This business event does not guarantee that they will complete the training, but they must enroll before they go any further.

Business event #3 would give this story:

```
As the training organization

I can notify all trainees to attend courses

So that they will attend on time and I can charge
them for their training.
```

We suggest that you take a few moments to write the stories for the rest of the business events. For each of them, ensure that you are writing about the functionality (not the automated product) the solution needs to deliver the required business value.

By the way, you don't have to write business event stories in the format, "As a, I can." You might consider just naming them for the functionality they deliver. For the preceding three stories, their cards could simply read like this:

```
Answer an inquiry

Enroll a trainee

Notify trainee to attend
```

And if you want another option, just write the card with the name of the business event. This would give you the following:

```
The trainee barista makes an inquiry

The trainee barista enrolls in a course

It's time to notify the trainee barista to attend the
course
```

However, these abbreviated formats do not have a rationale and are not as useful. We have more to say on rationale in a moment.

Write your business event cards in whatever way you find most effective for you and your team, and please ensure that the whole team is using the same approach. You might also consider differentiating the business event stories from others by writing them on different colored cards.

Writing Stories

Let's look at some of the issues that you encounter when you are writing stories regardless of whether they are business event stories or lower level stories.

"As a ..."

The first part to the story indicates the person (or system) receiving the benefit from it. Be as descriptive as you can here, and try not to write "As a user." This is close to meaningless and does not help the conversation about functionality. On the other hand, "As a patient checking into a hospital" and "As a professional photographer" are the beginning of useful stories that are more likely to bring about the right solution.

Try Not to Write "I Want"

Why not? Consider this story:

```
As a teacher

I want to search for a book using the title

So that I can check the price and availability.
```

This is the kind of story that gives stories a bad name. First, it is written as the assumed solution and almost completely disregards the needs of the customer even though it appears to be the customer writing it.

When a story uses the words "I want, what follows *is almost always a solution*—in this case, "search for a book using the title." The solution as stated is what the teacher thought he needed to do to solve his problem.

Consider the "so that" that follows the assumed solution:

```
So that I can check the price and availability.
```

Here's the problem—by having an assumed solution after *I want*, the next line of the story describes what the assumed solution will do for the role, but it does not indicate its value. You still don't know why he wants to check price and availability.

Let's rework the story by first discarding the assumed solution and replacing it with the original story's justification:

```
As a teacher

I can check the price and availability

So that ?
```

Ask "why?" again and again

Let's talk to our teacher and ask why he wants to check price and availability. Keep asking "why?" until you are satisfied that you have discovered the underlying reason for the functionality. Let's say he tells you that he is putting together a reading list for his students, and he does not want to recommend books that are either too expensive or simply not available.

By asking "why?," you are looking for the rationale. The rationale justifies the story and also demonstrates its value. We urge you to always include a rationale because it is the most important component of the story. Consider this:

- The rationale displays the value received by the customer segment.
- The value must be sufficient to warrant developing the story.
- The rationale indicates the effort that the developers and testers should expend on the story.
- The rationale is needed to prioritize your stories.

Once you have found the rationale for this story, you could rewrite it as this:

```
As a teacher

I can produce a reading list for my students

So that they receive a reading list of my preferred
books, which are available and do not exceed the
school's budget for such lists.
```

Ask "why?" until you uncover the real need. Then write that need into your story.

Sure, you could say, "As a teacher I *want* to give my students a reading list," and it would do the job, but by thinking "can" (or "am able to" or "need to"), you are more likely to elicit what it is the customer needs to do instead of how he wants to do it.

Your authors are assuming the teacher wants the solution to alter his list if some of the preferred books are not available in sufficient quantities. He would also want the list to be adjusted by the solution should any of the books break the budget. The teacher would supply a list of alternative books should any of the preferred list be problematic.

This story is valuable to the customer segment, the teacher. Yes, it might be more difficult to develop than the original *assumed solution*, but instead of providing a half-baked solution in which the teacher searches for prices and availability at multiple sources, the solution now finds the best prices and automatically adds the source to the list.

Moreover, the clerical task of modeling the list so that the maximum number of first-preference books are on it can be done by the solution, leaving the teacher to get on with being more creative and inspiring with his teaching materials.

Now that we have told you to use "I can" and not "I want," we feel obliged to add that the actual words are less important than asking "why?" and getting to the real need of the story.

The Two-Line Story

You might consider writing your stories using only two lines. Our colleague Peter Hruschka suggests that if you switch your attention away from a solution, you think about benefits. Every story must have a *beneficiary*, along with the *benefit* to be received. The beneficiary is straightforward; it's the customer segment or the sponsor. The benefit is the *outcome* that the beneficiary desires. So, let's skip over the functionality and write the story describing only the beneficiary and the benefit. It would look like this:

```
As a teacher (beneficiary)

I can give my students a reading list of my pre-
ferred books that are available and do not exceed the
school's budget for such lists. (benefit)
```

This story has the advantage of not attempting to describe a solution to the problem, just the desired outcome and who desires it. You will see more examples of this two-line format in this chapter.

Story Maps

Story maps are attributed to Jeff Patton. He introduced them in his book *User Story Mapping*. Here we are using the story map in a slightly different way; we are using it as a repository, as a common ground for the discovery and delivery activities we discussed in Chapter 1. The story map is the village green notice board, a community blog, the refrigerator door, and the epicenter of your project such as we show in Figure 6.2. Both discovery and delivery contribute to the map.

Instead of being a flat backlog, the story map provides an understandable overview of the solution to be implemented—understandable to the business stakeholders as well as the development team. It is the result of everybody—yes, we really mean everybody—collaborating on the project.

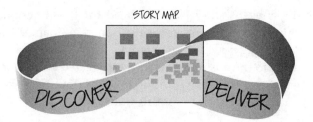

STORY MAP

DISCOVER   DELIVER

Figure 6.2

The continuous Möbius strip of discover and deliver. The story map acts as a common repository to record the discoveries and plan the deliveries.

We should point out that your story map is probably going to be very large—much larger than any example we can show on a book page. If you are using cards to write your stories (and we hope you are), you will need a wall, a collection of pin boards, or some other significant space to hold your map. You can put it on the floor if you like but beware the overnight janitors with powerful vacuum cleaners. Prudence suggests that you frequently photograph your story map in case of tsunamis, hurricanes, or human-instigated misadventures.

Before we go too far, have a quick look at the blank map in Figure 6.3. It shows the components of the map. We will fill in the blanks as we go along; it helps if you have an idea of what this thing looks like.

The top row of the story map contains the *business events* arranged horizontally. This row gives you and your stakeholders an overview of the complete solution to be built. Probably each business event has some automation to be developed for it, but in some cases, there might be business events that are completely manual. Include them in your map for the sake of completeness and orientation, but annotate them accordingly.

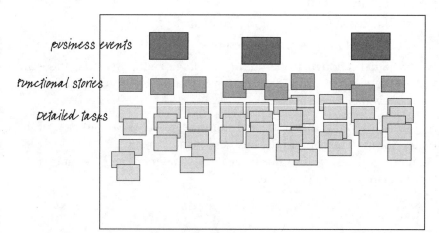

business events

functional stories

detailed tasks

Figure 6.3

A blank story map. The annotations show the terms we are using to describe the map's components. Keep in mind that your map will be wider—that is, you will have more business events than we can show here.

The business event story is a masthead for the functionality that responds to the business event. As we mentioned in Chapter 4, a business event is a happening in which an external entity—such as a customer—makes a request to the business or is a time-triggered event. For example, let's take the case of someone wanting to make travel reservations. The (two-line) business event story for this would be:

```
As a traveler
I can travel on the airlines and flights of my choice.
```

The business event is, "A traveler requests to make a journey." The responding functionality results in our traveler finding and booking her optimal flights. These would depend on her preferences of departure and arrival times, cost, airlines, class of travel, number of changes and stops, departure and arrival airports (there are sometimes several in a city), frequent flyer points, and so on. She also must make a reservation with the airline and pay for the flights. From all that you would reasonably conclude that the functionality for this business event is too large to be implemented in one development cycle. Naturally enough, you would break it into smaller stories.

Functional Stories

The first breakdown of the business event gives what we shall call *functional stories*. The functional stories are a collective for the functionality that responds to the business event. Functional stories are all these:

- Recognizable steps of the functionality needed to respond to the business event
- Identifiable chunks of functionality
- Standalone pieces of the response
- Small enough to be useful, but large enough so that there are between two and five functional stories breaking down a business event story

Suffice it to say, the functional stories represent the broad view of the steps taken to respond to the business event.

Let's go back to the traveler making a reservation. The embryonic story map is shown in Figure 6.4.

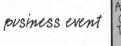

Figure 6.4

Given the intentions of the business event, the team has broken the business event into four functional stories. This group of stories gives an overview of the functionality of the intended product.

You can simply indicate the required functionality as we have in Figure 6.4, or you can write it in the normal story format. If there is no need to break it down, and you think it is suitable for one development cycle, use the story form. Otherwise, a simple verb-object statement is probably sufficient for the moment.

Given-When-Then

If you prefer to express things as *given-when-then*, you can readily apply it to functional stories. If you are not familiar with this concept, "given" describes an existing state, "when" is some action taken, and "then" is the outcome of the functional story. For example:

```
Given that the traveler has an account

When the traveler supplies an origin and a destination

Then the traveler is presented with the optimal
flights for her preferences.
```

The given-when-then statement can be used as part of the explanation of the functional story, as well as the basis for testing it.

The row of functional stories under the business event gives you (and your stakeholders) an overview of what the business does in response to a traveler wanting to travel—that is, to find the optimal flights, book seats, and pay.

Breaking Down the Functional Stories

This is often referred to as *slicing*, but whatever you wish to call it, we are referring to the breaking down of the functional stories into their component tasks. The aim is to produce a map of the components of the intended product that provides the deliverers with an explanation of what they are to deliver, the discoverers with a chart of what has been discovered, and the intended customers with what it is that they will have delivered to them. Consider Figure 6.5.

What we see here are the components that make up the bicycle. If you are the manufacturer, you make all these individual pieces and fit them together. This is not far off what you do when building software. However, unlike the bicycle manufacturer, you probably do not want to deal with the atomic components, but groups of components. And if you want to explain the bicycle to someone, you might talk about groups of groups. The pedal assembly would be a group, as would the rear-wheel gear assembly. You could put these two groups together, add in the chain, and call the resulting group "transmission." You can make it much easier to talk to prospective customers by grouping the atomic components in meaningful ways.

That's the way it is with the story map. You can look at the atomic tasks, but it is usually more useful to look at groups of tasks or whatever grouping or view that will advance your understanding of the product. The story map—you might like to think of it as a product map—is your guide to what is to be constructed.

The slicing depends on who wields the knife (or scalpel if we are talking fine-grained dissection of the functional story). In Figure 6.6, we illustrate the likely source of slices.

Figure 6.5

An exploded view of a 1977 Raleigh bicycle: Raleigh Record 26 DL129. (*Credit: Used with the kind permission of Raleigh UK*)

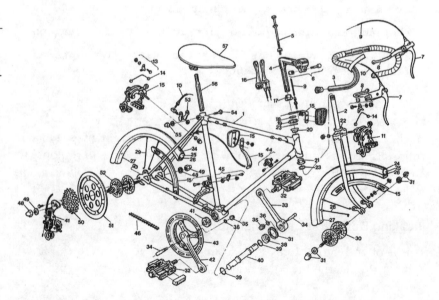

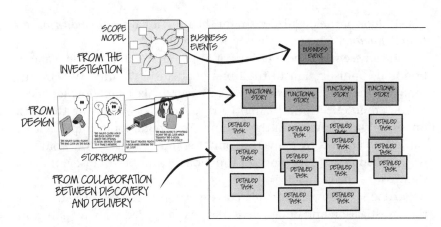

Figure 6.6

This illustrates how the slices come about. This is for one business event only.

Here you see that business events come from the investigation and scoping of the business solution. Business events represent some fundamental activity that usually originates from an outside source. Business events give us the customer view of the solution.

As we have pointed out, anything worthwhile is designed, and the functional stories come from the design. As a very rough rule of thumb, each panel of a storyboard drawn during design would translate to one *functional story*.

The further breakdown into *detailed tasks* is done by the whole team. These tasks are partially derived from how the stakeholders see the product, partially from how the developers see it, and partly from how the UX designer sees it, overlaid with breakdowns as to how the product owner decides the product should be developed.

Detailed Tasks

The detailed tasks are the basic units of functionality. Their purpose is to show the things to be done, or the actions, that complete the work of the functional story. You might think of them as the components of the functional story.

You might also think that each of the tasks is an implementable story. Although this is possible, we prefer to look at these detailed tasks as the way to ensure that the needed functionality is delivered by the product. This is most visible if you arrange the tasks in a column under their functional story.

The tasks belonging to a functional story are probably done in the same continuous piece of time. If you were using the product that carries out these tasks, you would probably not stop before completing them. If there is a need to stop, it might indicate the need for a new functional story.

Let's look at the detailed tasks for the functional story *Find flights to/ from destination*. These are shown in Figure 6.7.

You can see from these tasks that as you descend, they add elaboration and sophistication to the functional story. The first two are the fundamental ones; the last three are there to make a better experience.

You are in effect prioritizing the detailed tasks by putting the most important tasks highest in the column. You could, for example, release a minimal product by delivering only the top two tasks. You would do this to demonstrate its range of functionality, rather than depth, as a showcase of the complete solution yet to come.

No doubt, some of the detailed tasks will have been discovered during the investigation and design activities that preceded story mapping. As long as they fit the intentions of the functional story, they can be added to the map at any time.

You continue adding the detailed tasks by breaking each functional story into its basic components. Figure 6.8 shows the result (in an abstracted form) of breaking one business event into its functional stories and then into the detailed tasks.

Figure 6.7

The detailed tasks are arranged in a column under the functional story. They show the basic actions needed by the functional story.

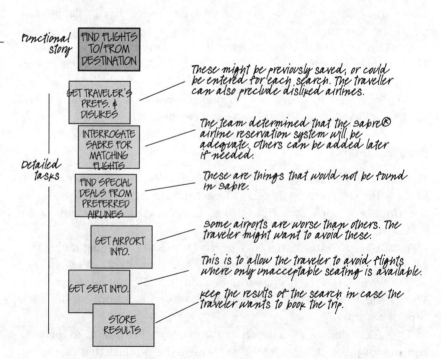

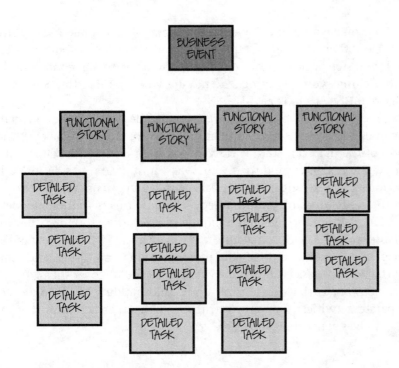

Figure 6.8

A partial story map. This shows only the tasks related to one business event.

Developing the Map

Now that you have done this for one business event, you would do it for the rest of them, but probably not immediately. You are constantly prioritizing the business events, so you are always working on the highest priority ones. Additionally, because the detailed tasks that are lower in the column are the more sophisticated and refined tasks, you might choose to leave these until later and add them as tasks when you reach that point in your delivery.

A more complete map is illustrated in Figure 6.9. This figure shows four business events. You would have more than four events—usually many more.

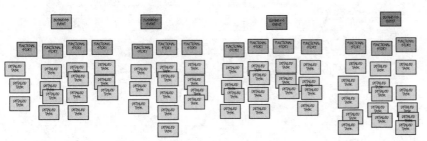

Figure 6.9

A more complete story map. The cluster of stories under each business event provides the functionality needed for that piece of the business. Your maps will be much wider (and possibly deeper) than this illustration.

Your map would only look like this close to the completion of delivery. Until then, it would be built on demand according to your priorities.

If you step back a little and consider the story map in context of the other things you are doing, the picture will look like that shown in Figure 6.10. Let's look at that.

Note that the discovery activities overlap. They are iterative and incremental, and you are constantly jumping between them. The construction of the map can start as early as you like—perhaps as soon as you know the customers and their values. As you start to find solutions and perform your investigation, you learn things and can use the map as one of the repositories of your knowledge. Some artifacts—process models, data models, and so on—might not be suitable for a story map. But the map is an ideal place to record the business events (the top row of the map) and to add wireframes and personas. Functional stories and some of the detailed tasks can be added as soon as you discover them.

The point is that writing the stories and building the map are not separate activities; they are concurrent with other activities that are themselves concurrent activities.

Figure 6.10

The activities that were discussed in the preceding chapters are concurrent and contribute, one way or another, to the story map.

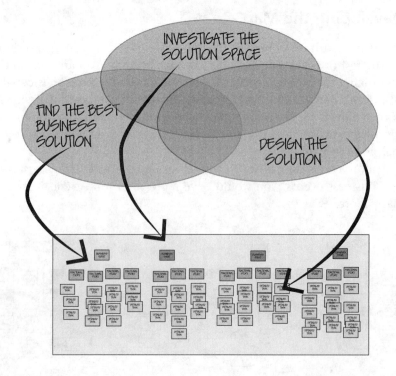

Enhancing Your Stories

The business event story (in fact, any story) contributes to the goal of the project, and thereby contributes something of value to the sponsor. The "so that" portion of the story indicates the value to the customer segment.

```
As a trainee barista

I can receive notification to attend courses

So that I attend on time and receive the full benefit
from my training.
```

The value to the sponsor comes when all enrolled trainees have enough information, and incentive, to be at the training venue at the appointed time. This can be tested easily enough—all the students are there at the beginning of the first lesson. But that means live testing, and if things don't work as planned (now, there's a surprise), it's a little late to make corrections.

Acceptance Criteria

You should begin to think of what the solution must do to ensure that every trainee is in possession of the correct attendance instructions. You might request an acknowledgement that the instructions have been received. You might consider using a communication medium that cannot send the joining message to a spam folder. Both of these can be achieved by simply telephoning the trainee. But let's not become involved in implementation details. Instead, let's add *acceptance criteria* to the story. They look like this:

```
It is certain that the trainee is in possession of
the joining instructions.

The trainee has all the information needed to find
the training venue.

The trainee has enough information to arrive on time.

The trainee is aware of what she should bring with
her.

The trainee is aware of the suggested dress code and
restrictions.
```

You can, if you choose, add test cases to the story, but don't feel the need to do this. We find that most business analysts are not great testers, but they're great at writing acceptance criteria.

You have to check that the implemented story meets all the criteria and that it delivers the value set down in the story. This was, as you recall:

`So that I attend on time and receive the full benefit`
`from my training.`

Or to put that another way, the acceptance criteria should be an elaboration of the "so that" line of the story.

The People Involved

You should know, or have good indications of, the eventual users or beneficiaries of your story—in the preceding case, the trainee baristas. This information comes from your investigation of the solution space and from your original determination of the customer segments. You can annotate the story with expectations about the users to help the designers and developers make this story more usable and convenient. This is shown in Figure 6.11.

The baristas are mainly in their twenties. They want joining instructions on their phones or mobile devices (or whatever technology twenty

Figure 6.11

The business event is triggered by the back office when it is time, and the beneficiary is the trainee barista. The profiles of these users (or their personas) are added to the map. This guides the team members as they identify the detailed tasks and the quality needs.

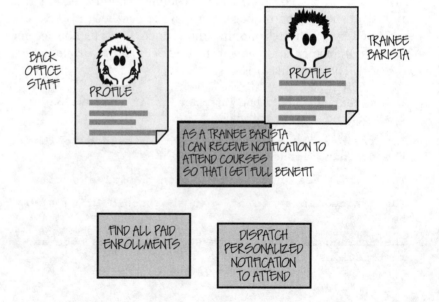

somethings are using when you read this). They want to be addressed in an informal, friendly way. They want the training organization to sound authoritative but not authoritarian. They want the notification to link to their future career as a barista.

All these factors are cultural, or anthropological if you prefer, and you would have uncovered them during your investigation of the solution space. If not, now's the time to find out about them and not just guess. The better you understand your customers, the better the solution you deliver.

Wireframes

You might consider enhancing either the business event or the functional stories with a wireframe sketch of the interface or panels from the design storyboard. Figure 6.12 shows such a sketch. The intention is not so much to design an interface, but to guide the designers.

A sketch at this stage is just that—a sketch. It is not intended to be the final design. Neither is it a detailed specification of the intended interface nor something that anyone should treat as complete and unalterable.

A wireframe is accessible to the stakeholders. Some of them have trouble saying what they envisage, but a sketch done with the stakeholder in the room can elicit her needs. This is intended to be a communication device, a spark for a conversation, and a guide for the team.

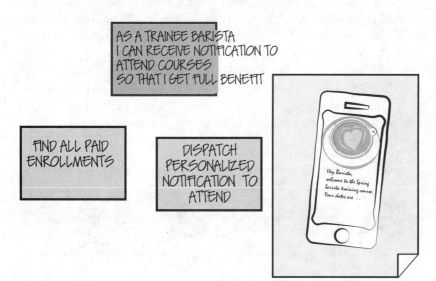

Figure 6.12

A wireframe sketch of the output from the functional story is added to the map as a guide for the developers and designers.

You must remember that, to a user, the interface *is* the product; by sketching an interface, you are sketching the user's perception of the product.

This paper and pencil approach is quick, and most importantly, gives no indication that the wireframe is anything but a sketch. The sketch invites stakeholders to discuss it and make improvements.

Prioritizing the Map

There are multiple ways to prioritize, and no one way is best. But the best way to start is by prioritizing the business events. From your investigation, you know the business events (or most of them) when you start your map, so the first action—and one that will be repeated many times—is to prioritize the top row. This gives you a map with the business events lined up left to right in priority order, as shown in Figure 6.13.

Your most usual prioritization criterion is value. Value means value to the customer segment (which might also be the user of your product). Value might equate to frequency of use, it might be revenue gained or cost saved, it can be convenience, or it can be the take-up of the product. Value to the client is usually in the order of legal compliance (it's valuable to stay out of jail), contractual obligations (don't get sued), and then supplying the client's products or services.

Although value is the most common criterion for assigning priority, you must consider others. You might think about proof of concept, time needed to develop, risk (do the riskiest ones first), politics, or almost anything else. Whatever your priorities are, they change often. It pays to revisit prioritization frequently.

When we prioritize, we automatically think of the glamorous, high-visibility items. But there's value to you at the other end of the scale. Assigning a low priority to something optimizes your project time; the low-priority items do not have to be built right away, and perhaps they will never be built.

Figure 6.13

These business events have been prioritized and moved into a left-to right sequence. The numbers on the events are their original IDs, which is probably their order of discovery.

The arrangement of business events shown in Figure 6.13 suggests that you move the business event cards to show priority, but doing so might break the narrative flow. If you prefer, don't move the cards, but annotate them with their priority. Prioritizing the business events might suggest that you deliver the product one business event at a time. Each delivery increment would include all, or most of, the functionality that sits below each business event. The advantage of this is that your customers see a partial product with each delivery, with the functionality of the delivered product being more or less complete.

But you might choose to do it differently; consider the alternative shown in Figure 6.14.

In this prioritization scheme, the business events and (any attached tasks) have been arranged so that the releases are staged to include several business events. You and your product owner would determine the makeup of each release.

Alternatively, you could use the delivery strategy shown in Figure 6.15.

Figure 6.14

Here the business events have been prioritized into releases. The releases are largely determined by the product owner and reflect the importance of having parts of final product available to meet tactical needs.

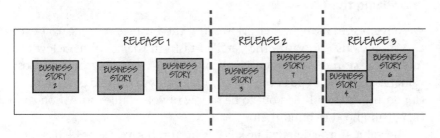

Figure 6.15

This shows the product being released in horizontal slices.

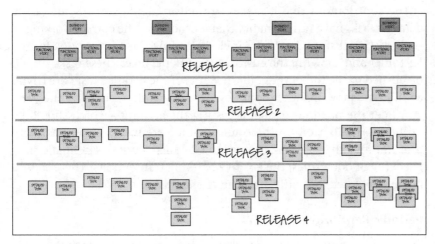

Now we have sliced the map horizontally. The early releases would contain a broad but shallow version of the product. You might choose to do this if you need to demonstrate all the capabilities of the product, albeit in skeleton form. Subsequent releases add functionality to the skeleton, one layer of flesh at a time.

Dependencies Among Business Events

When prioritizing, make allowances for *dependencies* among business events or tasks. Ideally, there would be no dependencies, and you would be free to deliver in whichever order you and your stakeholders choose. However, sometimes there are tasks that must be developed before you can develop others. The obvious example is when one task (or story, or business event) creates data to be used by another. Developing these out of sequence would result in a malfunctioning release. Sometimes you can fake this dependent data for the sake of a release, but usually it is best to understand the dependencies and annotate your tasks and stories accordingly.

Prioritizing the Tasks

We have been talking about prioritizing the business events. You can, and should, also prioritize the detailed tasks in the columns below the functional stories. The intention is always to work only on the most valuable stuff and to push the low-priority items to the end of the queue. Hopefully, they will turn out to be so low in your value estimation that there is no need to build them.

The value of the detailed task is important, but you should also look at the contribution that it makes to the functional story. Some of the detailed tasks have functionality that is crucial for the correct working of the functional story. Examples include finding the correct book for the customer and showing the customer's bank balance. These tasks should be pushed to the top of the column. Some of the detailed tasks are trivial additions—showing other books by the same author; showing the bank customer the previous date of accessing the account—which should be pushed to the bottom of the column. Some are pieces of functionality that improve the sophistication of the detailed stories—automatic spell checking of book titles; the last five banking transactions. These should be implemented, but only after the crucial tasks.

Periodic Reprioritization

You have prioritized the map and are delivering increments to the product in what you have decided is the most valuable sequence. However, a release might trigger the stakeholders to realize that the prioritization is not optimal. For example, they might decide that completing the release of one business event is preferable to proceeding with a partial release of another business event. Changes to the stakeholders' business or environment can also cause you to revisit your priorities. As a result, you reprioritize—frequently—your map and your releases.

There is no right and wrong way to prioritize, and there are no hard rules. Your strategy will most likely be a combination of those shown above as you react to the needs of your stakeholders and your project.

Kanban

A Kanban board shows the work in progress and the work that has been delivered.

Some teams prefer to use a *Kanban* board instead of a story map or to use a Kanban board in conjunction with a story map. Kanban was first developed by Taiichi Ohno of Toyota to improve manufacturing efficiency. Now teams use it to control the work of their project.

The main difference is that a story map shows the functionality of the product being delivered; a Kanban board shows work in progress and work that has been delivered. The story map approaches the subject from the product perspective, and Kanban from the project perspective.

You might find Kanban useful, so this is a quick introduction. Let's start with the simplified Kanban board shown in Figure 6.16.

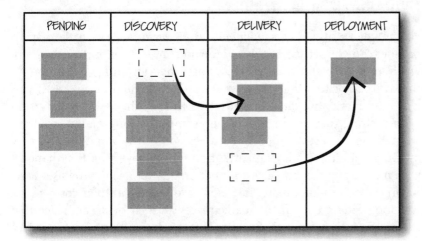

Figure 6.16

A Kanban board showing the flow of work being done. Each of the cards represents a project, a feature, a story or any set of tasks to be done together. The cards are moved between columns to indicate their work status.

The Kanban board shows work in progress and work that has been completed. The work is divided into Pending, Discovery, Delivery, and Deployment columns. Let's ignore for the moment that we consider discovery and delivery part of the same continuum; we'll divide the work this way for the purpose of illustration. Each card on the board represents an amount of work to be done. This could be anything from a story to a project; let's just call it a card.

The board shows that one of the five cards has been completed by the discovery team and has been passed to delivery. Let's say that the delivery team has the capacity for only four cards. This creates a bottleneck; one of the advantages of the Kanban board is visually showing such work impediments.

The Kanban board shows the status of the card. You see that delivery has finished one of its cards and moved it to deployment status, thus freeing up capacity to take on the next of the finished cards from the Discovery column.

The board shown in Figure 6.16 is simple. Some are simpler and show To Do—In Progress—Done only. Most are more complex, with the columns showing a finer division of the work. Some boards split each work column into In Progress and Done. There is no Kanban board ready-made to fit your circumstances: you have to fine-tune yours as you go.

Many teams have great success using the Kanban approach. If this is your preference, please read what we have to say about prioritization. The refinement of your Kanban board is done according to your priorities.

Minimum Viable Product

You might think about a *minimum viable product*—how little of your product can you release to the wider world? Advocates of the minimum viable product claim that having something—anything—out there so that you can be first in the marketplace is beneficial. In some cases, this is a valid tactic: humans tend to place their faith in the first version of something they see or hear. One example (among many) is Buffer, a social media posting app. An early version of the app didn't do very much, but it attracted enough attention for the developer to enhance it with more complete (and useful) functionality for its growing user base.

On the other hand, many start-ups have found—to their cost—that a skeleton product fails in the marketplace, spurned by an audience that rejects the lack of enough functionality to do anything useful. Advocates of lean start-up say that getting something out there quickly is all that matters, but look at the most successful products—Microsoft Office, Adobe Photoshop, Amazon, iPhone. None of these was the first to market.

(Ask your parents if they remember WordStar, Display, Book Stacks Unlimited, or Simon Personal Communicator.) Successful products are successful because they are best of their class—they solve a real problem that the customer wants solved, and do it in the best possible way.

You have to make your own call about a minimum valuable product (MVP). Don't be led by the dogma or the slogans; release a MVP only if it suits your purposes. And keep in mind that most MVPs are a guess—you usually find out if it is viable only after you have released it.

You might think about a "vanilla" product—one with just enough functionality to demonstrate your product, and nothing more. This will be built upon as subsequent releases take place.

Keep in mind that the existing system is, to your client, the MVP. If you are changing or enhancing an existing system (most of the time you are), your first releases must do something more than was done before.

MVPs can be misused. The point of business analysis is to ensure that you are solving a real problem that people need—and want—a solution to. Your safe-to-fail probes and investigations tell you—clearly—whether you are solving the right problem. If you are using MVPs to discover the problem, you are doing it the hard way.

To your client, any existing solution is the minimum viable product.

Quality Needs

A short aside: this is where our industry's lack of established terminology leads us into deep and murky waters. Doctors the world over can agree that your shin bone is called the Tibia (there's also the Fibula down there), but we cannot agree on what to call qualities. You might know them as nonfunctional requirements, constraints, qualitative requirements, quality of service requirements, quality goals, properties, or some variation on these.

Some people say that security is a quality; some say it is a functional need. Some people separate nonfunctional requirements from qualities; others see these things as constraints. We cannot satisfy every reader's terminology, so we shall bundle up all these things and call them *qualities*. Regardless of what you call them, they are important and cannot be ignored. We will try to explain them so that they are meaningful to you.

Why do we need qualities? Well, it is one thing for your product to do something. However, it is the way in which it does it that determines success or failure of the product. Would you buy a mobile phone that is hard to use and ugly? Would you download an app that runs on only one version of one browser? Would you buy online from a site with a track record of security breaches? Of course not. Yet each year products are rolled out in which the quality needs for the product have been

It is the way in which your product does whatever it does that determines its success or failure.

ignored. It's impossible to give you examples of these products because they disappear so quickly from the marketplace, or in the case of apps, from their users' devices.

In short, provided the functionality is met, it is the qualities that determine the acceptance or rejection of your product.

When you investigated the solution space for your proposed business solution, you were partly appraising the solution for its suitability within its environment, and partly learning about the people in and around the solution space. It is these people that you must satisfy, and it is the qualities—the usability, the security, the look & feel, the performance, and so on—that determine whether they accept or reject your product.

We do not mean to imply that these qualities are something that can be left until last and then bolted on to a story map. You should have discovered most of the required qualities during your investigation of the solution space as you were discovering the required functionality.

If you come from a business analysis background, you probably know these things as nonfunctional requirements. If you are writing a traditional specification, these qualities are written as individual requirements. It is then up to the developers to apply them to the functionality as appropriate. If you are using a story map, we suggest that the quality needs are appended to the appropriate stories and tasks on the map. This is shown in Figure 6.17.

Figure 6.17

This shows a single business event and one of the subordinate columns. The quality needs are attached to the stories and detailed tasks. The qualities are not stories, but needs or constraints that apply to the stories. You might consider using different colored cards for these.

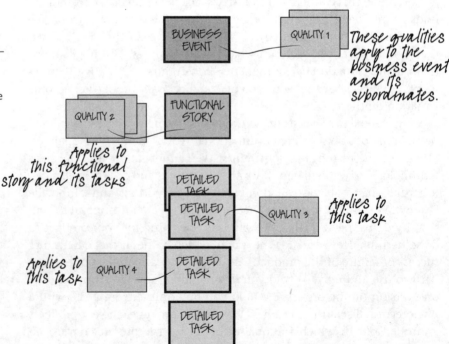

Quality 1 and any other qualities attached to the business event apply to anything below it. All the functional stories and detailed tasks that belong to this business event must comply with this quality.

One of the business event level qualities might be say, *usability*. This quality specifies the needed degree of usability for the intended users of that event. For example, are they first-time users, rocket scientists, people in a hurry, people who don't speak the native language, or people with some other special circumstance?

Another quality at the business event level is *security*. The security needs are suitable to protect this kind of user or customer, as well as protect the client organization from the user or customer.

Note the qualities shown in Figure 6.17 that are attached to the functional story apply to its subordinates. One of these might be about the performance needs—all the subordinate detailed tasks must be executed within a given time or allow for certain throughput volumes. A quality attached to a detailed task is aimed only at that task and would probably not be appropriate for other tasks.

The effect of this hierarchical arrangement of the quality needs is that they act as constraints on whatever is below. Thus, for any release of the product, you must be able to demonstrate that it possesses the required qualities. That, in turn, means that you incorporate these qualities when writing stories and planning development iterations. Moreover, they become part of your *definition of done*.

Qualities: What Do They Look Like?

A little earlier, you saw the example of a business event in which a traveler wanted to find the flight that was optimal for her destination and travel preferences. This is shown in Figure 6.18, with the appropriate qualities attached.

Let's look at these qualities and how you might express them.

Security—Here you would cite the security standards that apply to your company or industry or the product under development.

```
Advance Passenger Information (API) and Passenger
Name Records (PNR) must comply with IATA security
standards.
```

Figure 6.18

Some of the stories and tasks in the column have their quality needs attached. Keep in mind that the qualities for the business event and functional stories apply to the detailed tasks below them.

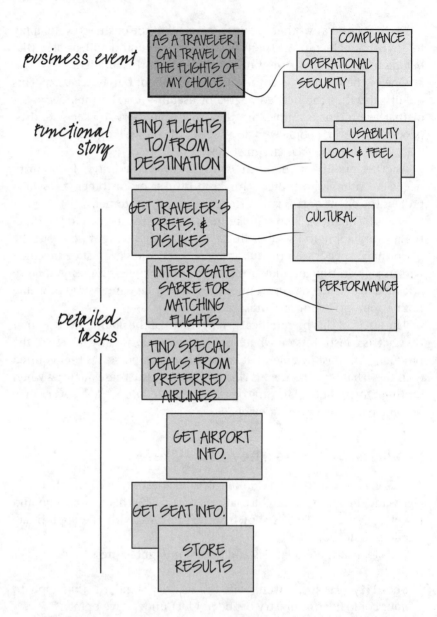

Operational—These quality needs are about the technological environment your users/customers are expected to use. For example, if your product is aimed at a web audience, it is appropriate to specify the browsers and devices you expect your audience to use. This product interacts with the Sabre system, so Sabre becomes part of your environmental constraints.

Compliance—This deals with the laws and industry standards applicable to your product. GDPR, the European data protection laws, would be appropriate here even if you are in the United States, as would national consumer protection and privacy laws. No doubt, your company lawyers will find other applicable legislation.

```
API and PNR must comply with the data protection laws
of departure and arrival countries.
```

Moving down to the functional story, we see this:

Usability—Here your concern is that customers find it easy and intuitive to use your product. You might write this as a story:

```
As a traveler

I can successfully use the product on my first attempt

So that I find my flight in a time that I consider
commensurate with the complexity of my journey.
```

Or you could express this as a target condition:

```
First-time users must find their right flight within a
time commensurate with the complexity of the journey
and number of options.
```

What is "commensurate"? Someone flying to, say, Paducah, Kentucky, who has a limited number of airlines and flights would expect to find the appropriate flight in less than one minute. On the other hand, someone flying to London has a bewildering choice of flights, airlines, times, and special deals. But because this product is intended to whittle these down to a small number of options, let us say that a first-time user needs no more than three minutes to find the most suitable flight. These target times must, of course, be confirmed with your UX designer and product management.

So we work down the column.

Look & Feel

```
Use an appearance that appears easy to use so that
customers hesitate no more than three seconds before
using it on first sight.

Conforms to FindYourFlight.com branding standards.
```

If the product is a mission-critical one, it is worth spending the time and resources to ensure it is attractive enough.

Cultural

```
Use terminology that is applicable to the customer's
log-on country. Observe addressing and telephone con-
ventions, as well as language differences. Examples
include "round trip" versus "return trip" and "out-
ward and inward" legs.
```

Performance

```
The data from Sabre must be displayed for the
customer in no more than 2 seconds.
```

We will look at more of the qualities in a moment.

Qualities at the Product Level

We have been talking about qualities as they would be attached to lower-level stories and tasks, but some qualities apply to the entire product. You can, and should, think about these as acceptance criteria for each release of the product and, obviously, the final release of your completed (as much as anything is complete) solution.

For example, usability needs most likely apply to the whole product:

```
The product is to be used by bank customers without
training. There are no expectations of proficiency
with computers or other devices.
```

Also, at the product level would be this look & feel quality for a hospital medical device:

```
The product should conform to the AlphaMedical
appearance standards, and all controls conform to
established conventions.
```

These qualities at the product level guide most of the tasks for the product and become acceptance criteria for them. This quality also guides the designers and developers.

By the way, if these qualities seem vague or indeterminate, they're not. Please keep reading.

Fit Criteria for Quality Needs

Some of the quality needs might seem a little fuzzy at first look. But that does not mean they are not fit for purpose; it means that they are not yet finished.

The quality needs at some stage become part of your acceptance criteria. This means that you must be able to measure them if acceptance testing is to have any meaning. While a look & feel quality can legitimately be "stylish and attractive," it must have a measurement if it is to be tested.

We refer to this measurement as a *fit criterion*. The term comes from the writings of Christopher Alexander, when he speaks of being able to determine whether a product fits its requirements. We wrote about this extensively in *Mastering the Requirements Process*. Thousands of teams around the world use fit criteria to make their quality attributes testable.

It comes down to understanding the need for the quality. Suppose for a moment that you wrote the "stylish and attractive" quality in a normal story format:

```
As a traveler looking for flights

I want a stylish and attractive product

So that I feel good about using the product and am
likely to use it again.
```

Picking up on the justification, we find that the reason for having an attractive product is to entice people to use it repeatedly. You can easily measure repeat use. Suppose that you talk to the business people and they tell you that while, on average, Americans take 1.5 flights per year, your site is aimed at people who fly more frequently. You could reasonably expect them to make up to five flights per year.

So you can measure whether the product meets its quality needs with a fit criterion:

```
60% of customers return to the site within 3 months.
```

If this is achieved, the product is considered to be "stylish and attractive."

Naturally enough, you cannot wait three months to see if this works, so you would test this quality with simulations. The value to the sponsor of repeat business tells us that it is worthwhile investing in simulations.

You can append a fit criterion to a quality need, or you can rewrite the quality to include the fit criterion:

    The product is stylish and attractive enough to ensure
    that 60% of customers return within 3 months.

You also have the option of writing the quality into your stories or tasks.

If you are using *test-driven development* or a variation of it, what we have said about writing a fit criterion into the quality should make writing your tests easier.

By digging deeply enough into the need for this quality (by repeatedly asking "why?"), the quality becomes in effect an acceptance criterion—it means that the quality is now testable. And that, after all, is the point.

The Volere Template

There are other qualities; you might consider the following ones derived from our Volere Template, which you can find at www.volere.org.

Look & Feel

This is about the appearance of the product—its mood and its style. Your client may have special needs for the product, such as corporate branding, appeal to an audience, and so on. This does not mean that you design the appearance of the interface, but describe its needs.

For example, the Chicchi barista training course site—that is the customer-facing part of your solution—might have a look & feel quality like this:

    Potential barista trainees are attracted to the site
    by its coffee-related appearance, and on average
    start using it within 3 seconds of encountering it.

The Chicchi business does not want to lose customers because the site is not sufficiently inviting and connected to coffee. This story can be tested by presenting prototypes and measuring a test panel's reactions, hesitations, and responses. You can measure how long trainee baristas hesitate before starting to use the product. You can measure whether they recognize it as a barista training site, and so on.

Usability

Naturally, your product should be easy to use. And naturally, you expect your designers and developers to make it as easy and convenient as possible. However, you should point out any exceptional usability needs.

> This product is a self-operated machine that airline passengers use to check their bags. Many will be encountering the product for the first time, and many will have little understanding of English. 85% of passengers must be able to successfully check a bag within 2 minutes on their first attempt.

Performance

Performance quality needs are often taken for granted, which is always a mistake. Performance covers how fast, how many, how big, how scalable. It also covers endurance where appropriate.

> The organization has half a million customers, and this number is projected to double within 10 years. Each customer has a half-megabyte record which is able to be retrieved in less than 1.5 seconds.

Operational and Environmental

This quality need is also interesting in that there is the probability that the operator will be wearing gloves for the cold. If a gloved operator cannot use the product, the product will be considered a failure.

> The product is used by truck drivers, often while outside the truck. It must survive a fall from the cab of a truck to the roadway and be readable at night. Temperatures will often be below freezing.

Maintainability and Support

Consider whether support will be provided by a help desk or some other external entity or whether the product should be entirely self-supporting. You must consider whether your users are capable of using self-support to solve their problems or whether they are the kind of people who need a certain amount of hand-holding.

Security

Consider your users or customers, their environment, the possibility of attack by hackers or viruses, the protection of private information, and lots more. The cost to your organization of a security failure is such that a security expert should be included in the conversations for any aspect of the product that has a possibility of unwanted interference.

Cultural

We take ourselves, our culture, and our values for granted, but it is folly to assume that everyone sees things the same way we do. It is worth considering whether your product will be used by people significantly different from the development team. Although you do not have to be overly politically correct, it will do you good not to offend your customers.

> **Images used on the web product must be ethnically diverse.**
>
> **Users may use any of the five most widely spoken languages.**

Also, consider imposing restrictions on religious or political symbols, images that might be misunderstood, or animals or other things that might be offensive. You might get away with annoying Raëlians (people who believe that an extraterrestrial species is responsible for the genesis of humans), but you might find it poor value if you antagonize 1.3 billion Catholics.

Compliance

These days, laws multiply faster than rabbits. Sometimes the penalties for not complying with the laws are draconian, which makes it imperative for your product to comply with all applicable and relevant laws. Additionally, you must construct your product so that, as far as possible, it cannot be used fraudulently.

You need to check with your company lawyers to find the laws that apply to your product. There are too many of them (we mean laws, but it could also apply to lawyers), and they are too subtle (the laws, not the lawyers) for you to know them all.

Exceptions and Alternatives

So far, we have been talking about tasks and stories as if nothing ever goes wrong. This is a good thing to do initially, but we know that in real life things do go wrong. Frequently.

We suggest that you always start with the "happy case" and then go back over the tasks and stories and determine the exceptions and alternatives.

Exceptions are unwanted but inevitable happenings—a customer enters an incorrect credit card number; a passenger name does not match the name on the passport; the driver cannot find the delivery address; someone tries to do something that violates a business rule. Each of these exceptions must be catered for, either with new tasks or stories or with additional requirements for your existing stories.

Alternatives happen when you deliberately give your customer a choice—gold card holders receive free choice of seats and don't pay for checked baggage; a customer can designate different billing and delivery addresses; customers can either open an account or check out as guests.

The most effective way to find the exceptions and alternatives is to go through your happy case stories and tasks and ask two simple questions:

"What can go wrong with this?"

"Do we want to provide an alternative to this?"

Let's look at the column of tasks as shown in Figure 6.19. This is one of the business events for a site that streams high-class, high-quality music.

These exceptions and alternatives can be verbally communicated to the development team, appended to your story map, or noted on the card. They are likely to be part of the same development cycle, so they should be kept close to the original task. Keep in mind that the exceptions and alternatives are part of the acceptance criteria for a release.

In some cases, an alternative might require an additional set of tasks or an additional functional story. Add these to your story map and note the departure point from the original set of tasks.

By working through the tasks, you discover the exceptions and the alternatives. It is far better to do this after the happy case is settled because then you can do it methodically and be certain that you have uncovered all the relevant unhappy cases.

> *Exceptions are unwanted but inevitable; alternatives are choices you give to your customers.*

Figure 6.19

The exceptions and alternatives have been noted alongside the tasks in the column under the functional story.

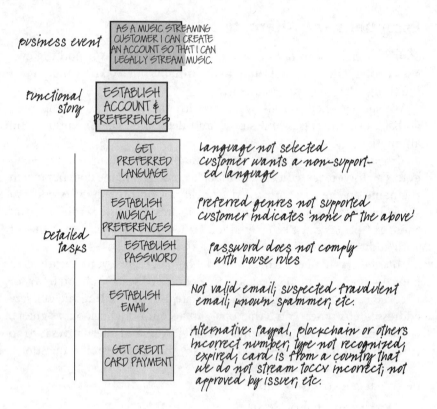

business event — AS A MUSIC STREAMING CUSTOMER I CAN CREATE AN ACCOUNT SO THAT I CAN LEGALLY STREAM MUSIC.

functional story — ESTABLISH ACCOUNT & PREFERENCES

Detailed tasks

GET PREFERRED LANGUAGE — *language not selected* *customer wants a non-support-ed language*

ESTABLISH MUSICAL PREFERENCES — *preferred genres not supported* *customer indicates 'none of the above'*

ESTABLISH PASSWORD — *password does not comply with house rules*

ESTABLISH EMAIL — *Not valid email; suspected fraudulent email; known spammer; etc.*

GET CREDIT CARD PAYMENT — *Alternative: paypal, blockchain or others incorrect number; type not recognized; expired; card is from a country that we do not stream to; ccv incorrect; not approved by issuer; etc.*

Stories and Development Cycles

A story can be a unit of development. That is, a development cycle produces working software (or any other product) from one or more stories. The story should carry enough information to enable a conversation about the precise details of what is to be built by the end of the current cycle.

So far in this chapter, we have been talking about functional stories, detailed tasks, quality needs, constraints, and a few other things. These are the things that are added to the story map by the discovery activities. They are usually added as they are discovered; more to record the discoveries than plan their development. This suggests that the artifacts on the story map are of random size, of differing importance, and therefore not a suitable basis for planning release cycles. This is as it should be because the discoverers should not be constrained by development cycles. To say that a story can only be written if it can be developed in one cycle is nonsense. That ignores the fundamental task of the story: to record the existence of a need.

The solution to this mismatch of size is easy. It's called *backlog grooming, backlog management, backlog refinement, story time*, and probably several other names. Whatever you want to call it (we shall use the term refinement) it is where the product people and the team decide the prioritization and thereby which parts of the product are the next to be developed.

Whether you refine the story map or transplant its stories to a separate backlog for refinement does not matter for our purposes here. We shall talk as if you are using the story map.

The story map shows business events, functional stories, and detailed tasks. As part of your refinement, you decide how much of that functionality you want for a story. You either write a new story to include all the detailed tasks you have just selected, or you bundle up the appropriate cards and put a rubber band around them. Giving the bundle a name will make it more convenient for discussion.

Have a quick look back at Figure 6.7, which shows a functional story and six detailed tasks in the column below it. Ask yourself how much of this would fit into your development cycle. Different teams in different organizations have different cycle times, so you would have a different answer to this question than the next person. Your cycle time might accommodate one detailed task, all the detailed tasks related to one functional story, or something in between. We refer you to Figure 6.20 as an example.

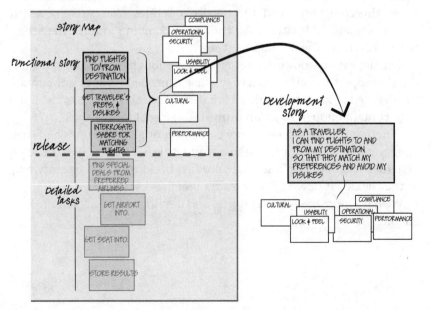

Figure 6.20

The dotted line on the story map indicates the planned release. The functional story and some of the detailed tasks are ideal candidates for a development story.

Let's say that you have decided that the top two detailed tasks—Get traveler's preferences & dislikes, and Interrogate Sabre for matching flights—are what you want to achieve from your cycle for your next release. This gives you a story that, if you write it in the conventional format, would be as follows:

```
As a traveler

I can find flights to and from my destination

So that they match my preferences and avoid my dislikes
```

This story delivers value to the customer, to the organization, and to the ongoing development of the product. The traveler finds the flights she likes the most and is likely to come back for more; the organization gets value from the traveler's repeated visits.

You should also know the qualities needed for this story. The qualities attached to the relevant part of the map as shown in Figure 6.18 apply to your story. They should either be written into the story, or more conveniently, be bundled with the story.

We also mentioned exceptions and alternatives. You would refer to your story map for the relevant ones.

Any other constraints, along with any wireframes, are added as notes to the story.

This now gives you a solid story that guides your development cycle. You know the functionality and why that functionality is needed. You know the constraints and the needed qualities. You also know any exceptions and alternatives. All the above combine to form the acceptance criteria for the development story.

The story is now powerful because it has enough information to guide the developers to deliver precisely what is needed. It does not contain the detailed requirements; those are fleshed out during the cycle. But it does contain enough to set an unmistakable goal for the cycle.

Whether you write a new story card, or bundle up the tasks and their quality needs, exceptions, and so on, and call that a story is your choice. Whether you maintain a separate product backlog or use the story map as the backlog is down to your team's preferences.

We have more to say about stories and development cycles in the next chapter.

Summary

Although the title of this chapter is concerned with writing stories, it is really about using stories to accumulate information from the discovery activities and using the story map to plan delivery activities.

The discovery of the business problem and the business needs is centered on business events. Business events are the fundamental building blocks, and you can base your stories, your map, and much of the development cycles on business events. We discussed how the business event story is broken down with functional stories and detailed tasks. These are useful when the functionality needed to respond to the business is significant enough to require partitioning to a lower level. In some cases, of course, the business event story is suitable for development without the need for any breakdown.

The story map holds a picture of the solution to be developed, how much of it has been discovered, and how much has been delivered. It is a suitable device for prioritizing the parts of the solution so that your discovery and delivery activities are always aimed where they are the most valuable.

And that brings us to the end of the techniques part of this book. We have looked at the activities to be done to ensure that the product you deliver is the right product, that it solves the right problem, and that it delivers the right value.

In the next chapter, we see how all these fit together. See you there.

Jack Be Nimble, Jack Be Quick

7

> • *Agile thinking* • *Wicked problems and Gordian knots*
> • *Jumping over the silos* • *Working with iterative development cycles*
> • *Lean thinking* • *Traditional business analysis*

Jack Be Nimble

You have no doubt gathered by now that we are using the word *agile* to mean adaptable, nimble, open-minded, and responsive. We know that when a team is behaving in an open-minded manner, the team members are able to change their approach, admit that an idea might not be the best one, and bring about a far better outcome. And while we think the expressions, "think in an agile way," "have an agile mind-set," and so on are admirable, they are not much use to us unless we have some practical guidelines on how we might think this way.

So let's talk about how we might think and act in an agile, nimble, open-minded way. The preceding chapters in this book looked at agile things to do; now we would like to talk a little about how you might do them.

Why should we want to do these things? Because experience has taught us—agile analysts, product owners, and team members—that what people ask for is not always what they need; neither is it always what they want. Experience has also taught us that the first solutions that are proposed—quite often these are merely *assumed* solutions—are not necessarily the right ones. We have learned the value of challenging assumptions and conventional wisdom. Importantly, we have learned that discovering the right problem, and deriving the optimal solution for it, is the fastest way to produce the right outcome. Getting it right does not mean it takes a long time.

Jack be nimble
Jack be quick
Jack jump over the candlestick

(Credit: Lebrecht Music & Arts/ Alamy Stock Photo)

So let's look at some of the things that can help you to become more agile, or nimble, in your thinking.

Wicked Problems and Gordian Knots

Sometimes the problem is more than a routine one with a routine solution. Sometimes the problem is complicated (consisting of many interrelated parts), and sometimes it is beyond complicated and we must think of it as a complex, chaotic, or wicked problem. Road traffic is a wicked problem. There are many variables and random variations—a truck breaks down, a building close to the road catches fire, and traffic accidents occur. You might also know these problems by other names. Here we are touching on systems theory, chaos theory, complexity science, and several other ideas and naming conventions about chaotic systems and messy problems.

Let us explain the heading by means of this allegorical story.

A legend from centuries ago has it that an oracle at Telmessos decreed that the next man who drove into the city in an oxcart would become the king of the Phrygians. (You'll have to look this up.) As it happened, the next man through the gate driving an oxcart was Gordias, and he was duly declared to be the king. (This way of choosing a leader might seem a little bizarre, but given the state of today's world, we might have better luck if we used this approach to choose our political leaders.) Before striding off to take up his kingly duties, Gordias tied his oxcart to a post using an elaborate knot, which brings us to the point of the story: the knot proved impossible for anyone to untangle, despite another decree that whoever could unravel the Gordian knot was destined to become the ruler of all Asia.

Skip forward a few centuries, and onto the scene comes Alexander the Great. Alex is magnificently ambitious; he wants to rule over the vastness of Asia, so he sets about untangling the Gordian knot. Realizing after a while that he was getting nowhere with the knot, Big Al unsheathed his sword and sliced the knot in half with a single stroke.

Did he solve the problem of the Gordian knot?

No and yes.

He didn't solve the problem in the way he was supposed to; that is, he didn't unravel the knot. But he came up with a solution.

The Gordian knot here is a metaphor for a unique, complex, wicked problem—a problem that is so difficult that it is impossible (or close to it) to say what the requirements are and to say whether any proposed solution is right or wrong. All we can say is that a solution might be better or worse, but given the complexity of the problem, it might be impossible to determine which of several proposed solutions is the best one.

We solve Gordian problems by experimentation. For example, Alexander might have experimented with other solutions, such as releasing insects into the knot to see if they would chew it apart. He might have set fire to it. He might have subjected it to intense infrared light causing the rope to rot. (This would have been quite a feat in the fourth century BC.) He might have lifted the linchpin out of the post to release the knot.

There are no completely right solutions to Gordian problems, just better or worse ones.

There is nothing to say that any of these solutions is better than the other. All we can say is that Alexander found a solution.

Let's leave Alexander to go off and conquer Asia and come back to Jack (and Jacqueline, our nimble analysts and their friends on the team). Let us consider what would happen if, instead of looking at each problem as routine with a routine solution having an "as is" and a "to be," Jack sees all business problems as wicked, or Gordian, problems. Instead of grinding out a routine solution that delivers mediocre value, he places himself in a situation in which he is forced to find a progressive solution and to perhaps go beyond the original problem to find solutions that bring greater benefits to his clients.

Instead of saying, "This is as it is now, and this is what we want it to be" (the routine, assumed solution), Jack, Jacqueline and the team say, "How might we solve this problem? What other solutions can we find for this problem? What better value might we deliver to our customers?"

Instead of delivering the routine billing system, can you find a more convenient way for your customers to pay for their energy consumption (or anything else)? Instead of your customers ordering their office consumables online, can you find a predictive, preemptive, effortless way of supplying them?

Although this seems to be going beyond the original brief and might seem to be spending unnecessary time, you must keep in mind that the real objective of your project is not to deliver a mediocre system in the minimum amount of time but to deliver the maximum possible value. (Keep in mind that delivering value and delivering a product are not necessarily the same thing.)

You must make your client aware of the potential value rather than the assumed value.

We are not for a moment suggesting that you have unlimited time on your hands. After many years of project work, we understand that projects should last not a minute longer than absolutely necessary. However, experience has shown us the immense amount of time wasted by projects delivering poor results. Instead of wasting time, let's time-box the work of generating and experimenting with solutions. Let's not close in on the first assumed solution but allow a little time for further discovery to find new value to deliver. You must make your client aware of the potential value rather than the assumed value.

You should also take into account the continuing—dare we say eternal?—nature of solution development. Whatever you deliver will, sooner or later, need to be modified or redeveloped. The world continues to change, and our solutions must be kept alive by keeping them current. This means that the Möbius strip illustrated in Figure 7.1 is not only a metaphor for a solution development project, but also for the lifetime of the solution. The best way known to slow down the redevelopment of solutions is to deliver the best possible solution—one that is so closely matched to the essential needs that its customers do not want it to change.

How might you do this? How might you discover and deliver better, more long-lasting solutions?

The Next Right Answer

Jack and Jacqueline are always thinking about, and looking for, *the next right answer*. Consider this scenario: you are presented with an assumed solution—the product—and asked to build it. You faithfully build it, and once built it turns out that no, that's not quite what is needed. "We'll have to do it again, but we'll get it right this time."

Instead of the above scenario, consider not building what is asked for. Instead, ask if there is a better solution—one that better matches the problem, one that delivers better value in a better way. *And there will always be a better solution*; it's the next one you think of. And the next one after that.

Very few of the notable consumer products come to market in the same form as they were first proposed; they go through rethinks and iterations and many, many prototypes before they make it to the production line. The best buildings are designed and redesigned before the

Figure 7.1

Agile business analysis discovery and delivery is a continuous activity, shown here as a Möbius strip. The Möbius strip has no beginning or end, signifying that discovery and delivery are not joined by a straight line from "as is" to "to be." The strip also reminds us of the ongoing maintenance and redevelopment of our solutions.

construction crews move in. The best software is never the first thing proposed. Rather, it is rethought—sometimes many times—before being constructed.

There are reasons these changes of mind happen. Sometimes the team members realize that they have misunderstood the problem and need to rethink their solution. Sometimes, though less often, they realize they have implemented the wrong solution to the problem. Sometimes the ecosystem changes mid project, and this results in the team rethinking its solution. And sometimes, partway through the implementation, the team simply has a better idea. None of these scenarios should be considered failures. They all contribute to a better end product.

This is not to say that the project is delayed indefinitely while endless redesigns are presented. But it is to say that you should be open-minded and inquisitive. Agile analysts don't meekly accept the first proposal. They challenge it and usually find a better one.

The next right answer is sure to be better than the one you have now.

Agile analysts don't meekly accept the first proposal. They challenge it and usually find a better one.

Looking Outwards

You cannot be expected to always be a magical source of great ideas. Nobody can. However, when we don't have our own great ideas, it's a great idea to look at someone else's ideas. Much of the time, great ideas can be found outside your own team, department, organization, or industry. Industrial designers are constantly borrowing ideas; architects, artists, and musicians are inspired by others. This does not mean plagiarizing other people's inventions, but abstracting from ideas, adapting them, and being inspired by them to find better solutions for yourself.

Making abstractions about one piece of work often leads to solutions that apply to your piece of work. Henry Ford came up with the idea of his Model T assembly line after seeing how a meat processing plant worked. The tricuspid valve from the human heart was adapted to make one-way valves for water and shampoo bottles. Velcro was invented when Swiss engineer Georges de Mestra noticed how burrs from the burdock plant stuck to his trousers and his dog after a walk in the mountains.

There are an infinite number of wonderful ideas out there just waiting for you to make an abstraction, make an adaption, and make an innovative solution for your customer's problem.

Continuous Improvement

We know that "continuous improvement" is a tired cliché. But before you skip this section, please give us seven seconds. We know you're exposed to thousands of self-help books, videos, advice, inspirational messages, and other miscellaneous well-meaning but not helpful drivel. Most of that stuff won't help you be a more nimble team member. Perhaps some of the rest of this section won't either. But it might. Thanks for your seven seconds. You are now free to read or skip as you wish.

There are two things that you can make better: yourself and your clients' business processes. They are interrelated—the better you are, the better they will be. The converse is also true.

There is an old saying:

"If it ain't broke, don't fix it."

You hear this all the time—usually from people trying to avoid their responsibilities and avoid doing any useful work. But look what happens when you reverse the sentiment of the quote:

If it ain't broke, fix it.

Was your Nokia phone broken when Apple announced the iPhone? Could you still make calls and do the things you bought the Nokia (or whatever phone you owned) for? Of course, you could. Yet you and two billion other people bought an iPhone, an Android, or a Google phone. Why? To get something that worked better for you—better than the working product you already had.

You read books; they work. You can turn the pages and absorb the words, receive entertainment or knowledge, enjoy the experience. Reading a book works. Yet millions of people now do some—sometimes all—of their reading on a Kindle reader or some tablet device. Reading books wasn't a broken activity; we just found a way to make it more convenient. Or consider the current upsurge in millennials listening to audiobooks. Books weren't broken, young people wanted a different, more expedient way to have their books.

Do you think that Samsung waits for customer complaints before improving its phones? Nope, it just goes ahead and makes a better phone. Do you think Amazon waits for customer feedback before finding new ways to make its shopping experience better and slicker? What about your bank? Are its systems as good as they can be? Are the systems continuously upgrading and improving? If your bank is not impressing you with its best services and customer experience, it is time to change your bank (or your insurance provider, or your energy company, or your phone company, or your shops, or anything else that you deal with).

Necessity is no longer the mother of invention. Improvement is.

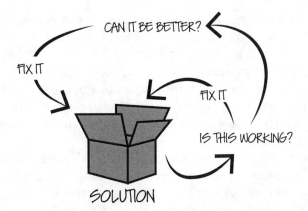

Figure 7.2

If it ain't broke, fix it.

The best fixes, the best improvements, usually come not from dysfunctional products and systems, but from healthy ones in which the custodians are interested in continuous improvement. Necessity is no longer the mother of invention. Improvement is. This is illustrated in Figure 7.2.

Why Are They Complaining?

You're at home. There's a pair of dirty socks on the floor, and it irritates you. You complain to the other (or others) that live with you. Let us for the sake of illustration say that your complaint is erudite, well-reasoned, crafted in elegant and meaningful language, includes some ingenious disparagements, and is worthy of the great orators. Your audience is naturally stunned into submissive silence. Now take a moment to stop your flow of words and ask yourself, "What am I really complaining about?"

Is it simply that someone left socks on the floor? Or is this a complaint about habitual untidiness? Or that the washing machine is broken, and you know laundry is piling up? Or there is nowhere suitable for depositing dirty laundry? Or the owner of the socks doesn't have enough socks and a dirty pair gives him one less, and if he could just stir himself to do his laundry occasionally, he (and you) wouldn't have this problem? Or could it be that your dwelling is too small and you need to share a room, which you don't want to do, particularly with someone who leaves dirty socks lying around? We'll stop these questions; you've got the point.

There are lots of reasons to complain, and all too often people complain about the wrong thing. Or to put that a better way, the subject of their complaint and the reason for their complaint are not the same thing. You were talking about socks; the underlying problem was sharing a room.

Continuous improvement can only happen when you address the root cause of the problem.

Let's leave the socks where they are and go to work. Your client is complaining about something, and it is safe to say that the complaint is not about dirty socks. But what is it really? If you accept what is said at face value and metaphorically pick up the socks, you merely respond to the first complaint. But is that the actual cause of the complaint? Until you find the root cause, anything you do is no more than putting a Band-Aid over the apparent wound and failing to identify and eliminate the actual problem.

Does your complainer understand the root cause? Or is he complaining about the symptoms of it? Is this person complaining about something because he lacks the authority or knowledge to complain about his real issue? Is he in denial about his contribution to the problem?

This is not easy, but you need to keep swimming upstream, questioning every effect and its cause until there can be nothing left to question. Only then will you arrive at what you need to fix. Continuous improvement only happens when you address the root cause of the problem.

Enlightened Anarchy

Every organization has a procedures manual. This manual sets out how the organization's business processes should be carried out, gives the rules for the processes, and usually has a few pages of inspirational words to say about what a wonderful thing it is that the corporation has put together this procedure manual. People in the organization believe their processes and their systems run in close alignment with the procedures manual.

But it's not all true. That woman in accounting, whom everybody seems to like, is busy and enjoying her work. If you can ever get her to tell you the secret, it would sound something like this:

> "We're supposed to use guaranteed bank loans for our Asian suppliers, but some of the Hong Kong banks are very slow to come through with these. I get around that by using irrevocable letters of credit. I can get these very quickly, and my friend Bobby in the foreign department puts them through his system to make it look like guaranteed bank loans. The result of this is that we pay the suppliers more quickly, and Alex, our procurement manager, has an informal agreement with most of the suppliers, which results in us getting a 2% discount for prompt payment. They love it, we love it, and our bank has assured us that it is the best thing to do; just please don't tell the operations director because she's a real stickler for procedures. If we did it her way it would be slower and require a couple of extra people, and we would pay more for our supplies."

This is a *shadow system*. Shadow systems exist in practically every organization, and they are put there by the shadow people. These are the people who see ways that they can improve their systems and have neither the interest nor the time for the tedious negotiations needed to change the procedures manual.

The nimble analyst often works in the shadows. If there is a better, simpler way to do something, and providing it does not transgress any meaningful business rule, then Jacqueline goes ahead, builds an effective shadow system, and does not mention it to anyone who is not immediately affected. She gradually brings the best of the shadow systems into the mainstream.

We are by no means advocating complete lawlessness here, but we have seen benefits from people operating in the shadows. You must approach this thoughtfully and leave behind enough documentation to allow others to follow. You must, of course, create a superior system. Providing your results are useful to others and do no harm, we see little wrong with a measured amount of enlightened anarchy.

Jack Be Quick

How long does good analysis take? Isn't analysis all about doing things that some projects skip over? Yes, it is. And we do it because we know that doing the right things and solving the right problems is the fastest way to deliver the right solutions. Until you solve the customer's real problem, you haven't provided any value, and you certainly haven't completed your project.

Simply because they are the right things to do does not mean that they take a long time.

Let's go back to Bernie's Books. You know this business from Chapter 1, "Agile Business Analysis," so we can use it to talk about how much time is needed for the analysis activities.

Let's make this simple and say that you have access and cooperation from the business stakeholders and that any questions you ask will get an immediate answer. Also assume that you have ready access to any other information you need.

Hour 1: Customer Segments

You interview Bernie and find the customer segments. You will recall that we spoke about three segments: the loyal customers, the twenty-somethings, and the book cover bandits. We shall also include the store sales clerks as a customer segment even though they don't buy anything. A few minutes more with Bernie and his assistants reveals a few more

segments. You discover the gift-giver segment, but because it is a long way to Christmas, you put that one aside. The rest of the segments are so small that you decide there is no value pursuing them at this stage.

In your own projects, you will usually have many more than four segments, so you must perform triage on them. There are some segments that are crucial to your business—the ones that provide a significant share of revenue, or segments that your organization cannot do without. You probably do not have enough resources to deal with all the segments at the same time, so pick the mission-critical segments and deal with them first.

Bernie tells you that the twentysomethings segment is the most valuable to him. They don't spend as much as the loyal customers, but to give the business a future, it is vital that he cultivate them and turn them into loyal customers. The loyal customers will, he assumes, remain loyal for some time, so you and Bernie decide to make them second priority. The store clerks are considered a high priority because probably anything you do involves them.

Within the first hour, you have identified the customer segments that are the target for your early solutions.

As we mentioned, when you do this for your own projects, you will find more than four customer segments. However many there are, it will rarely be more than you can discover in the first hour.

Hour 2: Value Propositions

Keep Bernie close to you, as you need to determine value propositions for the highest priority customer segments. You have four of them, so this shouldn't take long. At your work, you would do everything to include as many of the real customers as resources allow. You could also consult people from the marketing department, along with other people who have an interest in the customers. Product owners and managers, or other people with decision rights, should automatically be part of this activity. Bernie doesn't have a separate marketing department, but he can answer any marketing questions.

Back in Chapter 1 you read this:

```
As a twentysomething,

I receive value when I discover that buying books
from Bernie's is a better experience than buying from
wherever I bought them before.
```

Let's question Bernie and the customers a little more about this. You must ensure that this proposition is correct; you are basing a lot on it. Let's say that after some discussion, you, Bernie and other interested parties agree that this is the appropriate value proposition for this segment. The actual customers from the segment agree that this is indeed valuable to them.

You also have the store clerks segment, and after a little consultation, you arrive at this value proposition:

> ```
> As a store clerk selling books
> ```
>
> ```
> I receive value when I can do my selling work so
> quickly that I can spend more time interacting
> with the customers
> ```

The store clerks need to be able to process their tasks quickly because they want all the time they can get to talk to the customers. They feel that their greatest contribution comes from being helpful and knowledgeable and encouraging the customers. Bernie tells you that he runs a successful store because customers enjoy buying their books from him, and the clerks contribute a lot to the experience.

At the end of hour two, you have a set of agreed-upon value propositions.

Hour 3: Solving the Right Problem

The value proposition for the twentysomethings segment is about making an enjoyable experience in the bookstore and about persuading them that Bernie's is the place where they should buy their books. You ask Bernie why he wants to do this. What problem is he trying to solve? He tells you that he wants to increase the number of twentysomethings who buy from him. You negotiate with Bernie for a little while and agree that the problem to solve is this one:

> ```
> How do we attract 200 new twentysomethings each year,
> each of whom buy five books from Bernie during the
> year?
> ```

The numbers in the problem statement come from Bernie. He has looked at his customer lists and has calculated that if he can attract 200 new young customers a year, it will replenish and grow his customer base. We know the customer segment receives value if they enjoy the experience of buying from Bernie, so any solutions you come up with must have an element of enjoyment in them.

Now that we know the problem we are trying to solve, we must find solutions to both entice twentysomethings to the store and to make the book buying experience enjoyable.

In Chapter 1, we looked at a solution whereby the e-book version of a purchased book could be passed to a twentysomething by a parent or a friend.

It was a good solution, but it alone won't solve the problem. You need more.

You and your team ask the question, "How might we solve this problem?" You set about generating as many candidate solutions as you can. Don't worry too much for the moment whether your candidates are possible, feasible, or affordable; we'll deal with that in the next hour. Just keep on for a little while exploring the possibilities.

Suppose that after an hour, you have a list of candidates something like the following.

- Geo-targeted smartphone information on books and things of interest in Bernie's
- Social media posts about selected books and events
- In-store talks and event by authors or other people of interest to the twentysomethings
- Aggregate social media to find topics of books of interest and send targeted offers to twentysomethings
- Research and stock the books that are attractive to twentysomethings
- In-store coffee shop with music favored by twentysomethings
- Discount vouchers given with purchases in selected nearby stores
- AI applications to make better predictions about twentysomething's reading habits and other behavior
- An effort to make Bernie's a place where one is likely to meet other interesting twentysomethings
- A BernieReader app designed around the twentysomething segment

There are probably more, but that will suffice for now.

Hour 4: Safe-to-Fail Probes

This might take a little longer. It's now noon, so you have lunch sent in for this session. You want to keep going and not lose the momentum of the morning.

You run a series of safe-to-fail probes on your candidate solutions. Each probe determines the feasibility of the solution to ensure that, if developed, it will solve the problem and deliver the required value.

You can run these probes any way you like. We spoke about probes in Chapter 3, "Are You Solving the Right Problem?," so please revisit if you want more detail.

Probably the easiest and most visual way to probe is to use sketches and storyboards. Do these quickly on whiteboards or flipcharts; there is no need for great art. The point is to be able to display the candidate solution in such a way that everyone sees it, understands it, and can evaluate it.

The sketch should show enough of the solution's functionality to enable the team to evaluate it. You are probing to see if it works, if it is feasible, and if it is the best way to solve the customer's problem:

- Does it solve the problem and deliver the required value?
- Does it produce the desired outcome?
- Does it solve the problem in a compelling manner?
- Is it a good solution? Can it be better?
- Will its users be able to use it?
- Will its users want to use it?
- Can it be upgraded to deliver extra value?
- Can the solution be developed?
- What will it cost (approximately) in time and/or money?
- What cost does Bernie allow to attract a customer, and can this solution be built within that cost?
- Does it require resources that you do not have?
- Would it work within the existing operational infrastructure?
- Do you need extra permissions from elsewhere, either inside or outside the organization?
- Is the development cost reasonable given the delivered value?

And so on. You might find that the unique circumstances of your project raise other probing questions.

Two hours have elapsed since you started probing. The pizzas are now a fading memory (except for the people standing around the guy who had the sardine pizza with extra peppers, garlic, and onions).

Some of your candidates are by now crumpled flipchart pages lying discarded in the recycling bins. More join them. Some candidate solutions are by themselves unsuitable, but when combined with others, or parts of others, make excellent solutions.

Is this solving the problem, and is this the right problem to solve?

Each time you find a workable, feasible solution, you confirm with Bernie and the customers: is this solution solving the right problem, and is this in fact the right problem to solve?

You also confer with Bernie about business policy. Being a small business, Bernie can answer policy questions quickly. In your own work, the time needed to get policy decisions might slow you down a little. These decisions are typically made several organizational levels above the project team. For our purposes here, let us say that with Bernie on board, there is no delay in getting an answer to policy questions.

At some point, the winning candidate emerges. This is the solution that sparkles. Everyone agrees that it is the best of all possibilities and loves it. Bernie has a surprised but pleased look on his face.

This solution solves the problem, delivers the value, and has a beneficial outcome. This is the solution you want to build.

The Rest of the Day and Some of Tomorrow: Design the Solution

Whatever you build will be used by somebody. Think about that somebody. Think of them as a person with intelligence and responses and instincts pretty much like your own. Think of them as a human. Your purpose in designing their solution is not to awe them with beautiful interfaces and clever animations, but to give them a solution that they will use, find pleasant to use, and want to use.

Design isn't crafting a beautiful textured button with breath-taking animation. It's figuring out if there's a way to get rid of the button altogether.

—Edward Tufte

Let's turn to forming your solution so that it interacts in the most favorable way with its audience and wider environment. Think about your customer segment and how the people in that segment think. What are they doing when they use your solution? What information do they need, and at what stage of a process do they need it? What functionality is convenient for them? What is inconvenient? You should see the solution through their eyes and form the required functionality into something that makes them better at whatever they are doing.

This might take a little time. It requires thinking and experimenting and trying ideas.

You spend a few hours sketching and trying out ideas. This is not an endless activity, but you have to give it adequate time. Other stakeholders are part of the action; there is lots of sketching and graphics, lots of whiteboard and flipchart sketches, lots of discussion about wireframes and prototypes, lots of ideas that lead to lots of better ideas.

As you work with your team, your solution emerges. It's like watching the butterfly emerge from the chrysalis. It starts as an unattractive colorless blob hanging from a branch, and through struggle and convolutions,

(Credit: MediaGroup_BestForYou/Shutterstock)

transforms itself to the glorious insect that brings delight to everyone who sees it.

Emerging from this design activity is a description of the product to be built. This description can be in any form—use whatever you find convenient and communicable. You might consider using a story map to record your design—this was described in the previous chapter. You might also consider writing stories. However, at this stage stories might be too fragmented a description, and it is better to stick with broader, higher-level formats, such as sketches and process diagrams, until your design is formed enough to start thinking about construction details.

Jumpin' Jack Flash

Was Jack quick? We think so.

First, Jack prioritized. Once the customer segments were identified, Jack and Bernie selected the one that would yield the greatest value. Jack worked on this segment and, for the moment, ignored the others. Although Jack, Jacqueline, and the team generated lots of potential solutions, they quickly narrowed it down to the one that would give them the best results. This prioritization means that they will iterate and go back to pick up the pieces they have left behind. However, by proceeding to develop the piece they have just designed, they deliver a quick, tangible result—the most valuable piece of the complete solution.

This is not necessarily the minimum viable product, but it is a minimal product that will deliver value to Bernie as quickly as possible.

We have talked about the activities separately for the sake of discussion, but when you do them, they overlap. They are iterative, they are repeating, they are discovery and learning activities. They are not a procession, but activities that flow together. You are jumping from one activity to another so that they produce together, and their results emerge together.

Let's look at some other aspect of business analysis agility.

Jack and Jacqueline Jump over the Candlestick

We would like to think that all business analysts are agile and nimble, and all projects are agile and nimble. But we know better. We also know that opportunities for being agile are not always there.

So, let us think about your situation and where you fit on the scale shown in Figure 7.3.

So how do you move further toward the left end of the scale? By jumping.

Jumping the Silos

Many—probably most—organizations are arranged in silos. By *silo*, we mean a unit within an organization that does not share information, either deliberately or otherwise, with the rest of the organization. Projects, departments, divisions, or even people sitting at nearby desks don't share their knowledge. Why? Isn't everybody on the same team? Aren't we all working toward the same organizational end goal?

Sort of.

Figure 7.3

Pure agile business analysis is at one end of the scale. At the other is the more traditional way of doing things. Both are good, but it's more practical to avoid the extremes. That said, we would like to be somewhere on the left side of this scale.

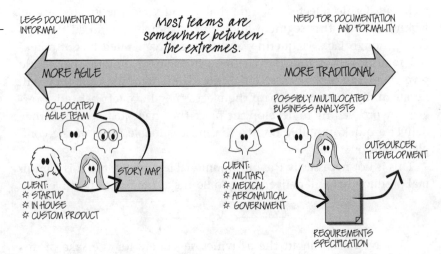

Silos start out as reasonable organizational units to take advantage of human specializations, but later they become entrenched because of interdepartmental or interproject jealousy or rivalry. Or because people are unwilling to give away knowledge that might have taken weeks to acquire. Sometimes people are simply unaware that others might benefit from their knowledge.

A common problem with silos is that teams often feel constrained to deliver a solution contained within their own silo. They feel that they do not have permission to venture beyond their silo; they feel that the inhabitants of another silo will not welcome them or not cooperate with them—that the development team in the other silo will be unresponsive to them or that the chain of command is too difficult to navigate.

A common problem with silos is that teams often feel constrained to deliver a solution contained within their own silo.

This runs contrary to our business problems. Most of the time, a business process is a chain of activities that weaves its way through several silos. Additionally, you would like your customers to be unaware that you have an internal structure. Please don't inflict your silo structure on them.

Getting the right result might mean having teams from several silos cooperating. Chris Matts, an agile coach, talks of a "scrum of scrums" where the teams come together to coalesce their ideas.

Perhaps the best approach to jumping silos comes from an adaptation of the work practices at Spotify. Using the Spotify terminology, you form a *tribe*, which is made up of the development teams in each of the silos that have a connection to the complete business process. The tribe is a matrix whereby the people in it have three allegiances. One allegiance is to the project or business process being developed or changed. There might be a project manager or similar person overseeing the complete business process. Another allegiance is to the team members' manager within the silo (department, division, whatever). The third allegiance is to the team member's area of competency. For example, a team member who is the main person for testing would get together with the testers from the other teams in the tribe to share knowledge and discuss problems. Similarly, the business analysts collaborate closely to ensure all aspects of the business process are covered. However, the team is still responsible for the part of the process within its silo. This approach is illustrated in Figure 7.4.

Figure 7.4

The silos are the vertical columns. These are departments or divisions within the organization; the management structure is shown. The business process crosses these four silos. The teams are formed into a tribe for the purpose of building/modifying the business process. The thin line connects people with the same competency in different teams.

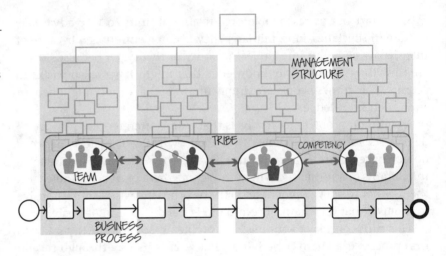

Another way of informally jumping the silos is to use the white space. Look at any organizational chart, and you see a hierarchy with the boxes representing people or roles in neat towers pyramiding down the page. The connecting lines are vertical. There is nothing to stop you from penciling in an informal line between the box that represents you and the person or role whose cooperation you need. We do not know too many managers who actively discourage cooperation when the outcome will be demonstrably beneficial. Our colleagues Tom de Marco and Tim Lister wrote about "The White Space" in their influential book *Peopleware—Productive Projects and Teams*.

Moreover, we are seeing more and more business analysts who are not attached to a silo and can do more to spread ideas between the silos. The enterprise architect is a valuable ally here. The architect's role must be involved with the whole of the organization and not just its separate component silos.

Avoiding Sign-Offs

Many organizations require documents to be signed. The signature is intended to indicate that the organization has reached a stage of development that necessitates documents being treated differently or handed off to another team. There are reasons for signing documents, but often quality control is not one of them. Sometimes—unfortunately often—the real objective of sign-off is to become disengaged from the document and the activities it represents.

We have observed that there are usually three stages associated with a formal sign-off:

1. Prepare the document for signing. This usually means there is a temptation to include more documentation than less. The resultant bulky document is passed along with a "read this and sign it if you agree" request.

2. Wait for the document to be signed. The waiting time has little to do with the complexity of the document and much to do with the abilities of the signatories and their willingness to commit.

3. Stage 3 is wondering if the signatories read the document, whether they understood it, and whether having it signed makes any difference to what comes next.

The biggest problem here is that the sign-off comes at the *end* of the document's production, not at its beginning. But is it at the *beginning* of a document's life—or any other work product—that the most attention and commitment is needed. Whatever you are producing, you need people to engage in the process, not wash their hands of it.

To be quick and adaptive, you must give your stakeholders work products—documents, maps, stories, models, specifications, prototypes, whatever—that they can both understand and engage with. Ask for a progressive *sign-on*, not sign-off.

Ask for sign-on, not sign-off.

The Blue Zone

The following is extracted from a book of essays we wrote with our Atlantic Systems Guild partners. The book is *Adrenaline Junkies and Template Zombies*, published by Dorset House, now owned by Pearson. We acknowledge their kind permission to reproduce this essay because it is an appropriate example of jumping over the candlestick.

(Credit: First flight, 120 feet in 12 seconds, 10:35 a.m.; Kitty Hawk, North Carolina, Library of Congress Prints and Photographs Division [LC-DIG-ppprs-00626])

❝ *Orville Wright didn't have a pilot's license.* ❞

—Richard Tait, Cranium

Meet Winston. Winston typifies a certain personality that you encounter from time to time on development projects. He's not quite an anarchist, but he seems to report only to himself. He appears to do pretty much what he sees as best for the project, regardless of his marching orders. And yet, he never really goes too far. He just stretches his authority—and sometimes his manager's patience—near to the breaking point. Winston operates in the blue zone.

When a manager hands out assignments, among other things he sets boundaries. He sets boundaries to give the recipient enough latitude to achieve the objectives of the assignment, while taking into account the team member's abilities. The manager also tries to prevent different assignments from overlapping or colliding.

Thoughtful task definition establishes a wide lane within which the assigned team member may operate freely. However, it is almost impossible to specify exactly everything that needs to be done as part of the assignment. We think of project assignments as creating three zones of authorization;The green zone consists of the things that are explicitly a part of the assignment: the core of the work to be done.The red zone includes anything that is explicitly excluded from the scope of the assignment.The blue zone is everything else: activities that are neither required nor prohibited by the assignment. In other words, this lies between the green and red zones.

Our colleague Winston believes that he can do anything that he has not been explicitly told not to do. Not only will he carry out the assignment as stated (his green zone), but he feels he should do anything in the blue zone he thinks needs to be done to achieve the best outcome. His only criterion for acting is that whatever he does must be beneficial to his project. He doesn't wait for permission; he doesn't ask for it. He just does whatever he thinks needs to be done.

There is more to Winston. We sometimes see him attempting to persuade the team leader to let him operate in the red zone. Permission to do what he has been told explicitly not to do is the only permission he seeks.

Having a Winston on your team is a real benefit. Although life with him can be hair-raising, he gets things done. And his adventurous nature means he often comes up with better and more innovative solutions than were envisioned by his manager.

Agile Business Analysis and Iterative Development Cycles

In the previous chapter, we spoke about the story map. You might prefer to use a flat backlog, or a Kanban board, or something else—but for the sake of simplicity, we shall assume you and your team use a story map.

The story map is a significant artifact, as it acts as the central repository for project knowledge. The map is loaded by the discovery activity, refined by the product people, and unloaded by the delivery activity. This is summarized in Figure 7.5.

The Product Owner Coordinates

In the diagram, we referred to "product people." For many of you using Scrum, this would be a product owner and/or a product manager. For some, it might be a project leader. Whatever you call it (we shall talk about the product owner), this role is responsible for the refinement of the story map/backlog and its prioritization.

By setting the priority of the stories, the product owner is directing both the discovery and the delivery. Let us say that the discoverers—probably business analysts—have discovered all or most of the business events. The business events would be revealed fairly early in the discovery activity. Once they are known, a rudimentary story is written for each business event, and these are added to, and form the top row of the map.

Once there, the product owner, in conjunction with the stakeholders and the rest of the team, prioritizes the event stories. This prioritization establishes the work sequence for the discoverers and deliverers.

The Discovery Activity Responds to Priorities

Discovery in the beginning can be rudimentary and would not delve too deeply until the need for detail has been established. However, once the priority for each business event has been established, the discoverers—presumably Jack and Jacqueline acting as business analysts—can focus their attention where it is needed.

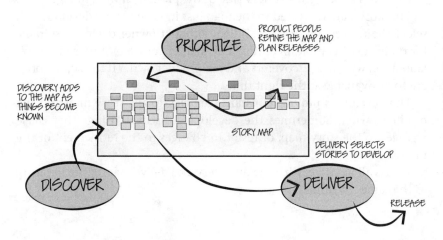

Figure 7.5

The story map is the hub of the project. Each activity is contributing to, and feeding from, the map.

Figure 7.6 shows the discovery process adding detail to the story map.

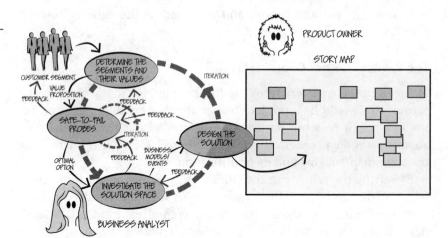

Once most of the business events have been discovered, it is possible to conduct the discovery activity in such a way as to concentrate on what is considered to be important by the product owner, and to ignore the low-priority events.

The story map enables the business analysts to see the gaps in the high-priority events, and to focus their discovery such that they are constantly feeding the delivery activity. Naturally enough, the discovery has to be quick enough to feed the map so as not to delay the delivery. However, we stress that the stories the discoverers add to the map must be the right stories (that's what this book is about); otherwise, delays occur when the wrong product is delivered (and rejected) or the deliverers have to spend time figuring out what the story should be.

Now let's look at the delivery side of the process, shown in Figure 7.7.

The stories are delivered to the map just in time for the developers to select the functionality they and the product owner decide is suitable for their next iteration, or sprint. This will of course require a close collaboration with the discoverers and the product owner if the right stories are to be available at the right time.

The developers provide constant feedback to the story map and the product owner. Sometimes the developers discover things that cause changes to the story map, or result in changes to the refinement of the map.

This is all iterative, with the discovery and delivery activities iterating to the same rhythm.

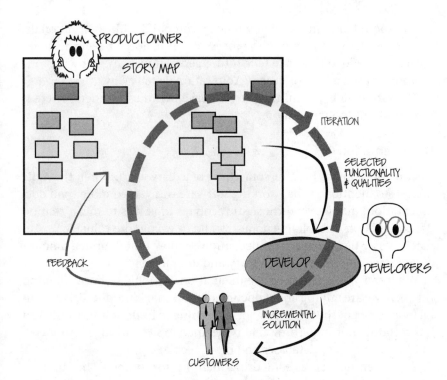

Figure 7.7

The delivery activity is also responding to the priorities assigned to the business events. Stories are developed iteratively resulting in partial releases to the customers. Note the feedback from the development process— this helps the product owner to fine tune the map.

And Jill Came Tumbling After

There is always someone coming after you; the product you build today could well last several decades. If you don't believe that, ask your IT manager how old some of the company's still-operating software is. Don't be surprised if you find systems older than you. Change is happening constantly, which means we must constantly maintain our systems, sometimes for several decades, to keep them relevant.

Suppose for a moment that it is your job to modify a system that was built, say, 15 years ago.

What documentation would you find helpful? What the system does? Nope, you can get that from reading its code or observing its output. The thing you can't get from the code or output is *why* it does it. And almost always, when you know *why* something is happening, it becomes much easier to know *what* you must do to change it.

It is the *rationale* for your decisions and the product's functionality that you must leave behind for others. We suggest—very strongly—that your design decisions, your explanations as to why a process works the way it does, the reasons you give as to why particular data are kept should be recorded in some form and guarded.

It is the rationale for your decisions and the product's functionality that you must leave behind for others.

You should also annotate any models you build with their rationale. Why is an activity part of the process when it doesn't seem to make sense? Your added rationale tells future generations why. Why was one solution chosen ahead of others? Your rationale tells why.

The rationale is the minimum you leave behind for others. There is more, but not too much more.

Documentation

Documentation has become something of a dirty word. When the Agile Manifesto mentioned that working software was valued more than documentation, many overenthusiastic acolytes took this to mean that no documentation—absolutely none—would be even more valuable. Fortunately, wiser heads have prevailed, and we know that a limited amount of documentation is both necessary and desirable.

The best documentation is produced as a natural by-product of doing work.

Whatever your attitude to documentation, it should be borne in mind that here we are talking about documentation that is produced as a natural by-product of the work; it is not something to be done afterward. And it is certainly not something that is destined to sit, unread and unloved, in filing cabinets or databases and never seen again.

You need to leave something behind for others—the trail of breadcrumbs—(we'll stop this nursery rhyme stuff soon) for the next person to follow in your footsteps, and hopefully Jill also leaves her own trail for others. Think of this as communication with your grandchildren. How much documentation do you need to leave behind for them?

Knowledge Artifacts

The following has been adapted from a project that your authors are involved in called *Nucleus—The Minimum Viable Knowledge*. As its name suggests, the intention is to specify the absolute minimal amount of documentation that enables the project to succeed. We are equating documentation with knowledge on the basis that as you learn things during business analysis, you record them. This is the knowledge that must be gained and recorded for the duration of the project and longer.

What follows is the bare-bones minimum. We are certain that you will want to add to this. We doubt you want to subtract.

Project Goals

Start at the top where you find the *organization's goal*. In most cases, the goal of the organization is to make a profit. That much is obvious, but the interesting thing is what it does to make a profit. Even if yours is a not-for-profit organization, it does the same as a profit organization, it performs business activities. These can be supplying services, producing products, or almost anything else. These services are supplied to the organization's customers. For the purposes of business analysis, it is expedient to divide these into *customer segments* depending on what they need.

The customers keep buying from the organization only if it provides some value to them. This means that we can derive a *value proposition* for each customer segment.

These three artifacts—the organization's goals, the customer segments, and their value propositions—can be bundled together and called the *project goals*. In short, the goal of the project is to deliver the value proposition to each of the customer segments and thereby deliver value to the sponsor. You can see these artifacts in Figure 7.8.

You must ensure that everybody on the team is well and truly aware of the project goals. Sometimes in the heat of battle they are forgotten, corrupted, or ignored. The project wanders off course, rudderless, and

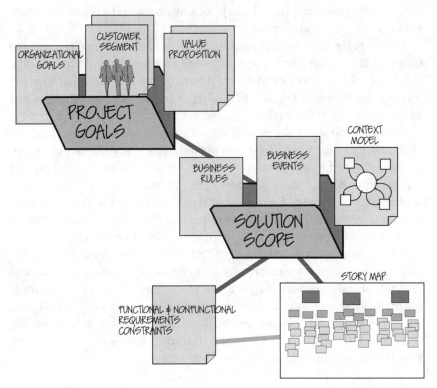

Figure 7.8

The minimal, viable set of knowledge artifacts.

the final result is of little use to the customer segment. It fails to solve the right problem and does not deliver value.

Certainly, you will probably discover along the way that your goals are changing as the organization's ecosystem changes, or that a new and better goal/segment/value emerges. It happens all the time. Reconvene with your sponsor and your team, discuss, argue, and re-establish the project goals collection. It is, after all, the supreme navigational artifact for your project.

To provide the value to the customers, the sponsoring organization usually requires some solutions—automated systems, machines, services, and so on. And that brings us to our next bundle of artifacts.

Solution Scope

The *solution scope* is a collective that links the information you gather about the business processes that makes up your chosen solution.

You might have discarded the notes, models, and sketches used in your safe-to-fail probes, or you might have kept them. They are probably interesting, but not all of them are necessary keepsakes. However, because you are making your decisions based on your safe-to-fail probes, we urge you to transfer the rationale for any decisions to the documentation arising from your probes.

The solution scope collective should show the reason that scope was chosen.

For example, you should annotate your *context model* with the reasons that you chose that particular scope over another. That alone will save you hours of rediscovery and debate down the road. This applies to other models and sketches. Leaving behind your reasons for something is just as important as the something you're leaving.

There are *business rules* associated with any business scope. These are the rules that you would have discovered earlier in your investigation. These rules should be recorded so that anybody attached to the project has access to them. Your organization might have a central repository of business rules, so there is no need to repeat them. In the central repository, you might find it convenient to tag any rules that are applicable to your project to save the time of people who need to refer to them.

The solution scope collective also contains a list of *business events*. Business events are a natural way to partition the solution space and lead to natural solutions. We urge you to use them. The reason business events work so well is that they originate from the outside. In this way, they partition your solution in the same way that your customers see your solution. They are not arbitrary internal choices dictated by your politics or your internal management structures.

Story Maps

The *story map* shown earlier in Figure 7.5 is derived from the business events. We described in the previous chapter how the top row of the map is a set of cards—one for each business event. The cards shown in the columns below each of the business events illustrate the way you have chosen to implement them.

The advantage of a story map is that it gives you an overview of the solution and how you intend to develop it. The story map as we described it in the previous chapter is primarily a breakdown of the functionality; it shows the tasks needed for each of the business events. Along with the tasks, the story map should show the quality needs or nonfunctional requirements. These indicate how well the product carries out its functionality. You might also attach any wireframes or sketches that you have developed. Finally, make sure that, where necessary, you attach the rationale to your story map artifacts.

Leaving behind your reasons for doing something is as important as what you did.

One reason for using a story map, or any other form of backlog, is that stories are an outstanding way of tracking the progress of the project. A simple count of the number of stories is far better than guesswork. This count can be augmented by adding story points to the cards.

So if stories are useful, why don't we start with stories and forget this other documentation stuff? The reason is that stories are almost always about a solution. If you start the project writing about the product you intend to build, you are thinking about a solution, not the problem. This means you have assumed the solution. Without correctly understanding the problem, any solution is possibly the wrong one. Stories are often spoken of as an invitation to a conversation about the problem, but they are still stories about an assumed solution. That is far too narrow a view to help you discover the real problem.

That brings us to the end of documentation, or to use more acceptable words, the artifacts from your analysis that the developers use to deliver, and what you are leaving behind for future generations of maintainers. Do this carefully; it is probably the most significant determinant of the future cost of maintaining the product that you are so lovingly building today.

Jack Sprat Could Eat No Fat

Lean thinking—lean development, lean IT principles, and so on—is a good thing. Its origins can usually be traced, one way or another, to

Toyota's Production System, and that in turn came from earlier work. The intention here is not to chant, "think lean" and "eliminate waste," but to make something useful from the underpinning ideas.

Naturally, we would all like to be lean and eliminate as much waste as possible. However, that's about the same as saying "eat a healthy diet." We all know that's admirable, but what is a "healthy diet," and how do we ensure that we are eating one? Our intention here is to see what you can do to enhance your lean thinking while going about your daily discovery and delivery tasks.

We shall use the Japanese words that are normally employed when talking about waste and its elimination.

Muda is waste. And in a moment, we'll look at the types of waste. But knowing these types is not necessarily useful unless we know what causes them and what we can do to stop causing them.

Let's start with *Muda* and its contributors. You will find variations on these names if you look through the literature, but nothing so fundamental as to divert our cause here. We'll use the list that reveals the cute initial letter acronym DOWNTIME.

Defects—The time taken to remove defects is waste. This indicates that we should try to produce things that do not contain defects.

Overproduction—Producing things that are not needed by the customer or the product and add no value. For our purposes, this means that there must be a relentless focus on rationale, justification, and prioritization. If the justification for anything is weak or its priority is low, it usually indicates that it's not needed.

Waiting—This is the delay while waiting for some upstream process to finish or to deliver a needed artifact. This could be because discovery is taking too long, delivery has started too soon, or your planning lacks the correct understanding of what must be done.

Nonused talent—It is obviously wasteful to have capable people sitting idly by or not being used where their talents indicate they should be. This is either a team problem in which the self-organizing team fails to recognize its own talents, or management is treating people as interchangeable components.

Transport—At Toyota, this means moving car components unnecessarily from one place to another. In your case, it is hand-offs, or having to move discovery and delivery artifacts between groups.

Colocated teams usually eliminate this kind of waste by collaborating on the artifacts. For example, the story map contains artifacts from a number of sources and reduces the need to move them.

Inventory—This one has more to do with factory production, but having discovery or delivery artifacts completed long before they are needed counts as inventory. This kind of waste is usually overcome with better planning and prioritization.

Motion—This is unnecessary movement of team members and stakeholders. This should also be taken to mean the wasted motion that comes from too much fragmentation of people's tasks or having people participating in too many concurrent projects.

Excess processing—This kind of waste comes from doing things the hard way, the long way, or doing too many things upfront that are not needed. We do not need to elaborate on overelaborate development processes. You have almost finished reading a book on how to make your own process as lean, nimble, and effective as possible.

It ought to be that we can easily spot most of the things on the list and eliminate them. But it's not quite that simple. There are two other factors that contribute to a lack of leanness.

Mura is unevenness and how it disrupts production.

Muri is overburden or unreasonable demands made on production.

Consider the cause-and-effect diagram shown in Figure 7.9. Here we see the three components of waste—*Muda, Mura* and *Muri*—and the effect they have on each other.

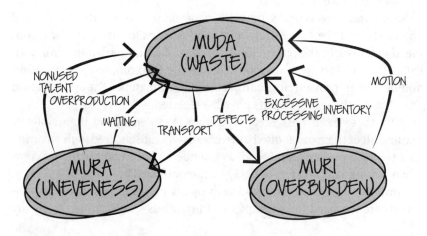

Figure 7.9

The three parts of waste should be seen together if you are to use the lean ideas to improve your own processes.

Getting rid of too much *Muda* (waste) does not necessarily work; instead, it probably causes *Muri* (overburden), which reciprocates by causing *Muda* (waste). *Mura* (unevenness) causes *Muda*, and *Muda* can in turn cause *Mura*.

Mura (unevenness) usually comes about because of inadequate planning and organization. The result is nonused talent, overproduction, and waiting. On the other hand, unnecessary transport (moving things around) is waste, and in turn it causes unevenness.

Muri (overburden) happens when unreasonable workloads are imposed, or where the team makes poor choices regarding its desired rate of production or sprint duration. Excessive processing, excessive inventory, and excessive motion are symptoms of overburden, and they naturally cause waste. Defects are waste because they overburden the team with the need for extra work to correct them.

Eliminating waste is an ongoing, self-improvement process. The way to eliminate waste is to improve your process; in turn, your improved process eliminates waste. This is simply a natural part of constant self-improvement and is part of being an agile, flexible, nimble analyst.

Traditional Business Analysis

Traditional, or sequential, business analysis refers to writing a requirements document to serve as the foundation for the system development effort. The requirements document is usually completed, or mostly completed, before construction begins. At least, that's what's normally meant by *traditional process*. This is often known as *waterfall*—which is misleading—and far too many people spend far too much time telling you how evil, wasteful, calamitous the waterfall process is.

It doesn't have to be.

Some amazing systems have been developed using the traditional approach, and there are often very good reasons for using it. For example, if you work in the pharmaceutical or medical arenas, or in aeronautical or the military, you are required to write the complete specification and be able to prove that the implementation matches the specification and that all the requirements have been tested.

Why these industries? Because human lives depend on their systems. Because all of them are audited by overseers who are charged with ensuring that the systems work, and work as intended. That's comforting to know when you are at 39,000 feet or having a tumor treated by a linear accelerator.

Similarly, for most outsourcing projects or some government projects, there is a need for a complete and rigorous specification. There are also organizations that, for one reason or another, want to produce a specification.

Of course, there are many instances of noncritical development efforts that produced far too much documentation, but that does not mean that *no* documentation is the answer. Naturally, there have been specifications that were badly written and produced the wrong result. But blaming the specification because of the person who wrote it is wrong.

So what should you do if you are working in the traditional way?

Most of what we have written in this book also applies to the traditional business analyst. Let's look at a traditional project.

Before reading further, please expunge from your mind the thought of a team of business analysts working for month after month producing a requirements document that is so thick it can only be moved using a forklift. And, once produced, the document is barely touched by the developers, who know that they will not be able to find what they need from it, and in any event, even if they deliver the wrong product, nobody will know because nobody can read the huge specification and prove them wrong. So who cares?

Those days are gone. Long gone. Nobody does it like that anymore. They haven't for years.

Traditional Process

The traditional process produces a complete specification before starting construction, but what you should do to produce that specification is more or less the same as if you were using an agile approach.

You identify the customer segments and their problems You solve the right problem. You design a business solution that attracts its audience and slots neatly into its environment. You ensure the right product is developed.

The differences lie in the approach you take to these tasks. Consider the process shown in Figure 7.10: the discovery side of an agile process. You have seen this diagram in previous chapters, and we have written about the details in previous chapters, so there is no need to describe these activities again here.

Note in this figure the feedback and iteration arrows. These are the things that make the difference for traditional projects. Your aim is to produce the requirements document at the end, but you do not necessarily produce it all at once. The way you do it depends on the kind of problem you are solving.

Let's start by dividing problems into routine, complicated, and complex.

Figure 7.10

The discovery activities. These are also appropriate for traditional projects.

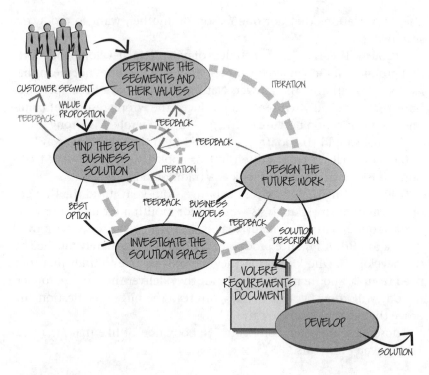

Routine Problems

Routine problems exist in a well-understood domain and are the kind of problems that you and your organization have solved numerous times. You work for a logistics company; you have another logistics problem. You work for a movie distributor; this is another movie distribution problem. Moreover, you probably have only a few customer segments for routine problems.

How big is this problem? If you consider this to be a small to moderate problem, it's possible to collect all the customer segments and their individual problems. You can then proceed with all of them at the same time, finding business solutions that solve the problem, moving through investigation and designing the solution. Design means designing the total package for all your segments, which you then specify in your requirements document.

If your routine problem is large, you would probably divide the customer segments at the time of identification and work through the activities producing the requirements document for a subset of segments. You might make use of business events to prioritize and partition further. The large iteration arrow shown in Figure 7.10 indicates that you iterate

Routine problems exist in a well-understood domain and are the kind of problems that you and your organization have solved numerous times.

back and pick up the next segment, do the same again, and repeat until the solution for all the segments has been specified.

Complicated Problems

Let's say that your problem is beyond routine. Complicated problems have lots of components interacting with each other. It's a difficult problem in that it might be partly or wholly unknown to you, but you are still able to determine if it is working correctly. For example, a commercial airplane is complicated, as are some websites. Amazon's site springs to mind as an example of a complicated problem—there are lots of components, and they need to work correctly together for you to pay and have your stuff delivered tomorrow.

Complicated problems have lots of components interacting with each other.

Let's start with a medium-size complicated problem. As usual, you determine the customer segments and then select a few of the higher priority ones. Work through finding the best solutions, and investigate them as usual. Instead of designing the work for them, iterate. Go back and pick up the next set of segments and repeat the process. When you have finished investigating all the segments, you design the whole solution at the same time. It is necessary to do it this way because you must ensure that all the components of the complicated solution work together.

This is a large task. You can, of course, subdivide the design now that you know the whole of it, using pieces of the solution that have similar characteristics as your partitioning theme.

If your complicated problem is very large—say, something as big as air traffic control—then slicing and iterating is quite intricate. The difficulty lies in coordinating the various sections of the solution so that they work in harmony when you've finished.

Complex Problems

Complex or wicked problems are those with too many unknowns, or too many unpredictable effects, to be able to determine absolutely if any solution is working correctly. For example, the economy and mapping the seabed are complex problems. There are too many unpredictable causes and effects.

By way of illustration, suppose you are charged with building a solution to predict crime. Consider the number of variables that contribute to crime: criminals, their attitudes and upbringing, opportunities, financial situation, weather, locality, presence of police or security guards, and so on. Each of the variables has an effect on one or more

Complex problems are those with too many unknowns, or too many unpredictable effects, to be able to determine absolutely if any solution is working correctly.

others. This results in a level of complexity that makes it difficult, if not impossible, to determine if the results are accurate. The predictive policing systems in operation at the time of writing are good, but nobody can really say if the results are as accurate as they could be.

For complex problems, the first step is to identify the known, or routine, parts of the problem. These are most likely the automated parts, which are more predictable than the human parts. Depending on the size of the problem, you would select a subset of the known problems and work the discovery activities up to and including design. Although you probably produce a requirements document for the design, it is important not to commit to developing it yet.

Iterate for the rest of the routine parts of the problem until they have all been designed.

Now it becomes both tricky and fascinating. You have to model the effects of the routine parts of the solution as they interact with the unpredictable elements of the problem. You are using something like the safe-to-fail probes we spoke of earlier to determine the feasibility of your complete solution.

Once you are satisfied that you have designed the optimal components, produce your requirements document and proceed to development. It might be that you have already developed some of the components of your complex system; you needed them to make your testing more realistic. This is often necessary, but it is also necessary to keep in mind that your developed components are, until proven, an experiment.

The Requirements Document

There is no law that demands that requirements documents are heavy handed and unwieldy. They can be lean and useful.

The *requirements document*, sometimes known a *requirement specification*, is a document that has caused heated discussion within our industry. It has been blamed for practically every problem with solution delivery that does not involve natural disasters. And it is true that there have been many examples of appalling requirements documents that were badly written, too big, too late, or overflowing with extraneous and irrelevant information.

We have written a book, *Mastering the Requirements Process*, that covers in detail how you produce this document. It needs more space to describe than remains here, so we will confine ourselves to giving you a brief outline of the contents of a good requirements specification.

The first thing about writing requirements documents is that they must be kept as minimal as possible. There is always a temptation to write more than is needed in the hope that doing so makes the document more authoritative. It doesn't.

The requirements document must be structured so that your readers can find whatever they are looking for as conveniently as possible. Your requirements need to be traceable, so they should be identified in a way that allows you to trace the requirement through development and testing. When making changes to requirements, it is necessary to be able to identify the impact of that change throughout the rest of the specification. Consistent naming makes this possible, and considerably easier.

Consider the partitioning that you have been using throughout your analysis. Have you, for example, been doing your analysis one or two customer segments for each iteration? If so, does it make sense to present your requirements grouped by customer segment? If you have used business events to partition things, you might consider writing the requirements document event by event.

There are various ways of writing a requirements document, and you can find examples and samples on the web and in textbooks. We'll briefly touch on our own *Volere Requirements Specification Template*, which is a guide to writing a requirements document. It works and has been downloaded thousands of times by organizations and business analysts around the world.

The *Volere* specification begins with the *constraints* imposed on the solution. Constraints here are the factors that restrict the way in which the solution can be designed, and the scope of the solution. These constraints can be environmental constraints, design constraints, and so on.

Then come the *functional requirements*. The functional requirements specify the part of the solution that does something—calculating, manipulating, forecasting, and so on. These are described with requirements that begin, "The product shall ..." and then a verb indicating the required action.

Functionality is only useful if it is done in a way that fits with its audience and its environment. The next section of the template presents the *nonfunctional requirements*. We have also referred to these as *quality needs* in earlier parts of this book.

We wrote about these nonfunctional requirements in the previous chapter, so we won't do more here than repeat the list of types:

- **Look & Feel Requirements**—Appearance, style, and so on.
- **Usability**—Ease of use, personalization, internationalization, learning, understandability, politeness, accessibility, convenience.
- **Performance**—Speed and latency, safety, precision and accuracy, reliability and availability, robustness, fault-tolerance, capacity, scalability or extensibility, longevity.

- **Operational and Environmental**—Expected physical environment, wider environment, requirements for interfacing with other systems, release, backward compatibility.

- **Maintainability and Support**—Maintenance, supportability, adaptability.

- **Security**—Access, integrity, privacy, audit, immunity.

- **Cultural**—Aspects relating to human reactions.

- **Compliance**—Legal standards.

The nonfunctional requirements are written as a series of statements starting "The product shall" and then the appropriate adjective. This statement sometimes can be a little vague, so you follow it with a rationale that states the reason for the need. Then comes the *fit criterion*, which measures the requirement and makes it testable.

- **Description**—The product shall be attractive and attention-getting.

- **Rationale**—The product is used as a demonstration product at trade fairs. If visitors do not make some use of the product, the exhibitor forgoes potential customers.

- **Fit criterion**—70% of visitors begin using the product within 4 seconds of first seeing and having access to it.

You can see more of the Volere Requirements Specification Template at www.volere.org.

Keep in mind that requirements specifications are almost never written wholesale. Business analysts write them iteratively, adding to the document as information becomes known.

And, before we leave it, most analysts find it convenient to include a project lexicon so that all readers of the document are aware of the terms being used and their meaning.

They Have Licked the Platter Clean

And so, dear reader, we have come to the end.

But we hope that this is not the end, but a beginning for you. We hope that this is where you begin to see your task of business analysis differently; that you look at your client's problem in a different, more open way and discover new insights into it; that you use your agility and nimbleness to discover better problems to solve and find better, more imaginative solutions for them.

We hope that within these pages, you have discovered for yourself insights and ideas that will make your business analysis work better and more fulfilling, and through that, you make your client's work better and more fulfilling.

We wish you well.

—James Robertson and Suzanne Robertson

Glossary

What follows is a list of terms and concepts used in *Business Analysis Agility*.

Agile   When we use this word in this book, it means small "a" agile. Big "A" Agile means one of the Agile methods. We are agnostic as to which Agile development method you are using (if any) and employ *agile* to discuss the ability of the business analyst to respond to changing circumstances and unexpected discoveries and to deliver real customer value.

Business Analysis   Business analysis is the discipline of identifying business needs, determining solutions to business problems, and identifying business opportunities. Solutions often include software systems but may also consist of process improvement, organizational change or strategic planning, and policy development.

Business Analyst (or Business Analysis Practitioner)   This term should be interpreted to mean anyone doing business analysis regardless of their job title. Our experience has been that business analysis is not the sole province of business analysts but is undertaken to various degrees by product owners, business stakeholders, agile team members, sometimes developers, and almost anyone in the organization who is studying the work with a view to improving it.

Business Event   A business event is an external or time-triggered happening that causes your solution space to respond according to its business rules. Examples of business events are these: customer pays an invoice, traveler checks in for a flight, and time to send out electricity bills.

Business Goal   The business goal involves achieving an improvement to the business. This usually involves a project(s) to develop solutions to deliver the improvement. This improvement brings business value to the organization.

Business Rules Business rules set down the conditions under which people and automated solutions must operate in the organization. They are, in effect, the internal laws of the business.

Business Value The benefit that your organization wants to receive as a result of providing a solution to the problem. This must be measurable and will be used as a guide for choosing between alternative solutions.

Constraint A constraint is a restriction placed upon the way you solve a problem. Your solution is unacceptable unless it meets the constraints.

Customer Properties The characteristics, attitudes, and abilities of the customers. Properties also refer to the customer's possessions, such as his smartphone, credit card, and coffee cup.

Customer Segment A group of people who have a set of common characteristics or needs that make them unique. For our purposes here, *customer segment* should also be taken to mean *user segment*. We prefer to call them *customers* because focusing on pleasing a customer with specific characteristics expands thinking more than pleasing a generalized user.

Data Data is the raw material—the numbers, the facts—and is generally not usable by humans until it is transformed into relevant information.

Design Design is the shaping of ideas and requirements into solutions for the intended audience. It is about finding the best solution to the essential problem; about finding the best way to present the needed information; about using the process and data models from the investigation activity in an imaginative way; and about devising the solution that fits most comfortably with the users' mental models and cultural assumptions.

Design Thinking This is about synthesizing a design or putting together the elements that make for the best human experience with your product. If your solution interfaces with other automated solutions, you will also be designing the "best automated experience" for your solution.

Detailed Tasks Basic units of functionality that describe the things to be done, or the actions that will complete the work of the functional stories.

Double Loop Double loop learning means that instead of repeatedly trying to find solutions to the problem, you loop further back, question the original problem, and see if by questioning it, you find a more valuable problem to solve.

Ecosystem   The environment surrounding the business or the solution. The ecosystem is the part of the real world that interacts with and/or influences the business/solution.

Essence   The essence of a piece of work is *what* it does—its underlying policy and the rules it follows regardless of how the work is carried out.

Fit Criterion   A measurement of a requirement that allows a solution to a requirement to be classified as either the solution fits the requirement, or the solution does not fit the requirement. This is used to arrive at an unambiguous and testable understanding of the meaning of a requirement. Fit criteria are sometimes referred to as acceptance criteria.

Gordian Knot   We use the Gordian knot—a knot impossible to untangle—as a metaphor for a unique, complex, wicked problem. It's a problem that is so difficult it appears impossible to say whether any proposed solution is right or wrong.

Information   Information is what we humans process and use to do work and make decisions.

Innovation   Innovation is fresh thinking. We use innovation to find new and better ways to solve problems.

Lean   Lean software development is a translation of lean manufacturing principles and practices to the software development domain. Lean is adapted from the Toyota Production System.

Muda, Mura, Muri   Japanese words meaning *waste, unevenness, overburden*. Inspired by lean development, we use these words to explore what we can do to avoid all the different types of waste that occur during the daily discovery and delivery tasks.

Opportunity   You can think of opportunities as the converse of problems—there is nothing to fix, but there is the chance to make something better. These opportunities arise during normal business analysis activities.

Persona   A virtual person constructed with a knowledge of the characteristics of the people who inhabit a specific customer segment. The persona represents the segment during discovery and delivery.

Problem, or Customer Problem   The problem is what we find a solution for that will achieve the value proposition, given the customer's needs, constraints, and properties.

We are using the word *problem* to mean any of these:

- A change to your customer's business that necessitates changes to one or more automated or human systems
- An opportunity or a new idea that you can take advantage of
- A problem that necessitates some development actions to rectify

Product   Your product is whatever you plan to build. It will form part of your solution. Your product could be software, hardware, a service, or a consumer product.

Requirement   A requirement is a capability or quality that the delivered solution must have in order to fulfill the customer's needs and solve the customer's problem.

We can categorize requirements into the following:

- **Functional**—These are things that the solution does, or facilities that it supplies.
- **Qualities or nonfunctional**—These are qualities that make the functionality work in a way that the customer will find pleasing and appropriate. Examples include usability, security, and operational.
- **Constraints**—These are mandated restrictions and can be treated as requirements.

Safe-to-Fail Probe   Small-scale experiment to test the hypothesis that a proposed solution solves the customer's problem and provides the required value.

Sequential Development   *See* Traditional Development.

Service Thinking   Service thinking is looking beyond the product to the service that the product supports. This necessitates taking the end-to-end view of the problem rather than being limited to just the automated or changed part of the solution.

Shadow System   When the official business procedures do not work, people invent alternative ways of working to get the job done. These alternative ways are referred to as shadow systems because they do not directly map to the official business procedures.

Silo   A unit within an organization that does not share information, either deliberately or otherwise, with the rest of the organization. Silos usually start out as reasonable organizational units to take advantage of human specializations, but later they become entrenched because of interdepartmental or interproject jealousy or rivalry.

Sketch, Wireframe, Prototype A sketch is a rapidly executed drawing that is not intended as a finished work. Sketches are used to communicate ideas and questions, and they encourage feedback from people who recognize and change the sketch. The terms *sketch, wireframe,* and *prototype* are used interchangeably in this book.

Solution The solution is what you deliver. Your solution solves the customer's problem. The best solution is the optimal compromise between the value proposition, the customers' needs, and the sponsor's business goals. Note that the solution can include manual and organizational processes along with automated product.

Solution Space This is the extent of the business area, or the work area, needed to contain the business solution. The product you build is part of the solution space. The rest of the space is occupied by the people and interfacing automated systems.

Sponsor The person paying for your project and who receives value from your solution. This might be an external customer, an internal manager, or a product or program manager.

Stakeholder This term should be taken to mean a person with an interest in the solution. Certainly, it includes users and customers, but it also includes people with specialized knowledge—subject matter experts, security consultants, lawyers, user experience (UX) designers, technology specialists, and so on. Stakeholders provide input to your analysis, but they do not necessarily have veto power.

Story A story describes a need and the reason for the need from the viewpoint of a specified role. Stories are often used as placeholders for detailed requirements.

We can usefully categorize stories:

- **Business Event Stories**—Traceable back to a business event
- **Functional Stories**—Standalone chunks of functionality that respond to a business event
- **Development Stories**—The collection of detailed tasks that the team has decided to package together and deliver with a development cycle

Story Map   The story map provides a pictorial overview of the solution to be implemented. The stories are arranged with the business event stories in a row across the top of the map, and the functionality needed to respond to the business event is arranged in meaningful columns under the event story.

Systems Thinking   Systems thinking, also known as systemic thinking, is concerned with the system as a whole. This takes into account all the components—both technological and sociological—regardless of whether they are contained within or outside the organization. This discipline is concerned with looking widely enough to understand how all the components affect each other and uncovering conflicts, assumptions, and missing links.

Traditional Development   This means that you are assembling a requirements specification before constructing the product. There is nothing wrong with doing that, and in many cases, there is a real need to do so—outsourcing, government, medical, and military projects come to mind. We assume that about half the readers of this book work on traditional projects—also referred to as sequential development. Almost everything in this book also applies to traditional projects.

Value Proposition   A statement of what the customer segment values, and by inference, the problem to be solved.

Wireframe   *See* Sketch, Wireframe, Prototype.

Work   You can think of *work* as the solution space—the space that you intend to improve as a result of your business analysis activities. Additionally, work is work regardless of whether it is done by a human or a computer or any other machine or piece of technology.

Bibliography

We have included books in this list if they are particularly focused toward business analysis, help to understand agile, are classic texts on some aspect of solution development, or provide insights from another field that would be of use to business analysts.

Ackoff, Russell, and Herbert Addison. *Systems Thinking for Curious Managers: With 40 New Management f-Laws.* Charmouth, Dorset, UK: Triarchy Press, 2010.

Ambler, Scott W., and Mark Lines. *Disciplined Agile Delivery: A Practitioner's Guide to Agile Software Delivery in the Enterprise.* Indianapolis: IBM Press, 2012.

Brooks, Frederick. *The Mythical Man-Month: Essays on Software Engineering, 20th Anniversary Edition.* New York: Addison-Wesley, 1995.

Cadle, James, Debra Paul, and Paul Turner. *Business Analysis Techniques.* London: BCS, 2010.

Case, Amber. *Calm Technology: Principles and Patterns for Non-Intrusive Design.* Sebastopol, CA: O'Reilly Media, 2015.

Cockburn, Alistair. *Agile Software Development.* New York: Addison-Wesley, 2001.

Cohn, Mike. *Succeeding with Agile: Software Development Using Scrum.* New York: Addison-Wesley Professional, 2009.

Cohn, Mike. *User Stories Applied: For Agile Software Development.* New York: Addison-Wesley, 2004.

DeMarco, Tom, Peter Hruschka, Tim Lister, Steve McMenamin, James Robertson, and Suzanne Robertson. *Adrenaline Junkies and Template Zombies: Patterns of Project Behaviour.* New York: Dorset House, 2009.

DeMarco, Tom, and Tim Lister. *Peopleware*. 3rd ed. New York: Dorset House, 2013.

Evans, Eric. *Domain-Driven Design: Tackling Complexity in the Heart of Software*. New York: Addison Wesley, 2003.

Fowler, Martin. *Patterns of Enterprise Application Architecture*. New York: Addison Wesley, 2002.

Gause, Donald, and Jerry Weinberg. *Are Your Lights On? How to Figure Out What the Problem Really Is*. New York: Dorset House, 1990.

Gottesdiener, Ellen, and Mary Gorman. *Discover to Deliver: Agile Product Planning and Analysis*. Acton, MA: EBG Consulting, Inc. 2012.

Hofmeister, Christine, Robert Nord, and Dilip Soni. *Applied Software Architecture*. New York: Addison Wesley, 1999.

Holtzblatt, Karen, Jessamyn Burns Wendell, and Shelley Wood. *Rapid Contextual Design: A How-To Guide to Key Techniques for User-Centered Design*. Burlington, MA: Morgan Kaufmann, 2004.

International Institute of Business Analysts. *The Business Analysis Body of Knowledge BABOK Version 3*. Oakville, Canada: IIBA, 2014.

Kalbach, James. *Mapping Experiences: A Complete Guide to Creating Value Through Journeys, Blueprints, and Diagrams*. Sebastopol, CA: O'Reilly Media, 2016.

Krug, Steve. *Don't Make Me Think: A Common Sense Approach to Web and Mobile Usability*. 3rd ed. San Francisco: New Riders, 2014.

Laplante, Phillip. *Requirements Engineering for Software and Systems* (Applied Software Engineering Series). Boca Raton, FL: Auerbach Publications, 2009.

Leffingwell, Dean, Alex Yakyma, Richard Knaster, Drew Jemilo, and Inbar Oren. *SAFe Reference Guide 4.0*. New York: Addison Wesley, 2017.

Levy, Jaime. *UX Strategy: How to Devise Innovative Digital Products That People Want*. Sebastopol, CA: O'Reilly Media, 2015.

Maiden, Neil, and Suzanne Robertson. *Integrating Creativity into Requirements Processes: Experiences with an Air Traffic Management System*. Washington, DC: International Conference on Software Engineering, May 2005.

Marsh, Joel. *UX for Beginners: A Crash Course in 100 Short Lessons.* Sebastopol, CA: O'Reilly Media, 2016.

McMenamin, Steve, and John Palmer. *Essential Systems Analysis.* New York: Yourdon Press, 1984.

Miller, Roxanne. *The Quest for Software Requirements.* Milwaukee, WI: Maven Mark Books, 2009.

Myer, Bertrand. *Agile! The Good, The Hype, And The Ugly.* Zurich: Springer, 2014.

Nixon, Natalie W. et al. *Strategic Design Thinking.* London: Bloomsbury, 2016.

Norman, Donald A. *The Design of Everyday Things.* New York: Basic Books, 2013.

Osterwalder, Alexander, and Yves Pigneur. *Business Model Generation: A Handbook for Visionaries, Game Changers, and Challengers.* Hoboken, NJ: John Wiley, 2010.

Patton, Jeff, and Peter Economy. *User Story Mapping: Discover the Whole Story, Build the Right Product.* Sebastopol, CA: O'Reilly Media, 2014.

Paul, Debra, and Linda Girvan. *Agile and Business Analysis: A Practical Guide for IT Professionals.* London: BCS, 2017.

Podeswa, Howard. *The Business Analyst's Handbook.* San Francisco: Course Technology, 2008.

Pullan, Penny, and James Archer. *Business Analysis & Leadership: Influencing Change.* London: Kogan Page, 2013.

Roam, Dan. *The Back of the Napkin: Solving Problems and Selling Ideas with Pictures.* London: Portfolio, 2013.

Robertson, Suzanne, and James Robertson. *Mastering the Requirements Process: Getting Requirements Right.* 3rd ed. New York: Addison-Wesley, 2012.

Robertson, Suzanne, and James Robertson. *Requirements-Led Project Management: Discovering David's Slingshot.* New York: Addison-Wesley, 2005.

Rubin, Kenneth. *Essential Scrum: A Practical Guide to the Most Popular Agile Process.* New York: Addison-Wesley, 2012.

Russell, Mike. *Wrong Until Right: How to Succeed Despite Relentless Change.* Scotts Valley, CA: CreateSpace Independent Publishing Platform, 2015.

Schwaber, Ken and Mike Beedle. *Agile Software Development with Scrum.* New York: Prentice Hall, 2002.

Snowden, Dave. *Cynefin Framework for Decision Making.* 2010. http://cognitive-edge.com.

Starke, Gernot, and Peter Hruschka. *Communicating Software Architectures with arc42.* Victoria, BC: Leanpub, 2016.

Szabo, Peter. *User Experience Mapping: Enhance UX with User Story Map, Journey Map and Diagrams.* Birmingham: Packt Publishing, 2017.

Tett, Gillian. *The Silo Effect: The Peril of Expertise and the Promise of Breaking Down Barriers.* New York: Simon & Schuster, 2016.

Wiegers, Karl. *More About Software Requirements: Thorny Issues and Practical Advice.* Redmond, WA: Microsoft Press, 2005.

Yayici, Emrah. *Business Analyst's Mentor Book: With Best Practice Business Analysis Techniques and Software Requirements Management Tips.* Kindle Edition: Emrah Yayici, 2013.

Index

REGISTER YOUR PRODUCT at informit.com/register
Access Additional Benefits and SAVE 35% on Your Next Purchase

- Download available product updates.

- Access bonus material when applicable.

- Receive exclusive offers on new editions and related products.
  (Just check the box to hear from us when setting up your account.)

- Get a coupon for 35% for your next purchase, valid for 30 days. Your code will be available in your InformIT cart. (You will also find it in the Manage Codes section of your account page.)

Registration benefits vary by product. Benefits will be listed on your account page under Registered Products.

InformIT.com–The Trusted Technology Learning Source

InformIT is the online home of information technology brands at Pearson, the world's foremost education company. At InformIT.com you can

- Shop our books, eBooks, software, and video training.
- Take advantage of our special offers and promotions (informit.com/promotions).
- Sign up for special offers and content newsletters (informit.com/newsletters).
- Read free articles and blogs by information technology experts.
- Access thousands of free chapters and video lessons.

Connect with InformIT–Visit informit.com/community

Learn about InformIT community events and programs.

the trusted technology learning source

Addison-Wesley · Cisco Press · IBM Press · Microsoft Press · Pearson IT Certification · Prentice Hall · Que · Sams · VMware Press

ALWAYS LEARNING   PEARSON